WILLIAMS-SONOMA

Soups, Salads & Starters

The Best of Williams-Sonoma Kitchen Library

Soups, Salads & Starters

GENERAL EDITOR
CHUCK WILLIAMS

RECIPE PHOTOGRAPHY
ALLAN ROSENBERG

Oxmoor
House®

Contents

Introduction

Traditionally, soups, salads, and starters have been known as supporting players on the menu. They whet the appetite and often remain in the background, allowing the featured main course its moment in the spotlight. But in today's fast-paced and health-conscious environment, these dishes have been getting more attention in their own right. When served as part of well-planned menus, or even as improvised last-minute meals, soups, salads, and starters can stand out for their ease of preparation and great flavors.

This book will help start you on your way to using your creativity and imagination to select and prepare a variety of soups, salads, and starters. You'll learn how to select fresh ingredients at the height of season and pair complementary or contrasting dishes. And you'll develop the confidence to explore recipe variations, putting your own spin on these dishes.

You'll find traditional favorites as well as innovative new ideas—quick, simple recipes in addition to many elaborate, impressive creations. Beginning and experienced cooks alike will find dishes to try and to cherish. So let's start cooking!

A WORLD OF FLAVOR

Drawn from all over the globe, the recipes in this book open up exciting new vistas of delicious tastes and delectable textures.

In Italy, meals start with an appetite stimulator, otherwise known as an antipasto. Here in *Soups, Salads & Starters*, you will find hearty, aromatic Italian antipasti such as Baby Artichokes in Prosciutto, Pizza Margherita, or Mozzarella and Tomato Crostini. In Spain, tapas—light dishes, vegetable offerings, marinated salads—are an essential way of life and are served as appetizers or snacks. Try Clams with Tomatoes and Herbs or Gazpacho to evoke the fragrant, earthy flavors of the Iberian Peninsula.

Elsewhere in the book, the strong, tangy flavors of Greece find expression in a Caviar Spread, Chicken and Lemon Soup with Orzo, and Beet Salad with Feta. India's rich, fiery cuisine is embodied by Lamb Tikka, Mulligatawny Soup, and Tandoori-Style Chicken. France inspires Provençal Fish Soup, Mini Quiches Lorraines, and Niçoise Salad. From China come Sesame Shrimp, Spareribs, and a Crab Omelet with Sweet-and-Sour Sauce. Mexico offers Tortilla Soup, Ceviche, Mushroom Quesadillas, and Stuffed Poblano Chiles.

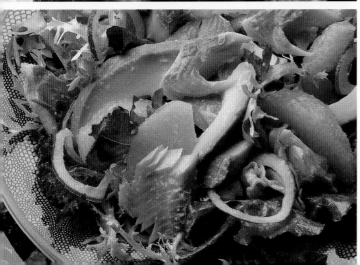

All these cuisines have developed recipes and traditions with similar principles in mind. Cooks around the world depend on ingredients that are abundant and locally grown. In that spirit of resourcefulness, many of these dishes make excellent use of leftover or seasonal ingredients. We can apply these lessons to our own cooking by looking, for example, to summer's plenitude of tomatoes for salsas, or to a winter and spring harvest of avocados to make guacamole.

These appetizers and first courses do more than simply satisfy one's hunger. Throughout the world, small dishes are used to usher in the main course and to complement other parts of the menu. Chilled Beet Borscht with Sour Cream and Vodka, for instance, works well with another Eastern European-Jewish favorite: Mini Potato Pancakes with Smoked Salmon. Greek Dolmas (stuffed grape leaves) pair beautifully with Eggplant Caviar.

Finally, soups, salads, and starters lend themselves happily to the casual and convivial atmosphere that most hosts strive for when entertaining. All over the world, cooks and hosts use food to bring people together, and the recipes in this book are perfectly suited to promoting hospitality and good cheer.

FESTIVE ENTERTAINING

What's a party without good friends, drinks, and plates of delicious finger food or canapés, refreshing salads, or heartening soups? For a successful menu, consider the presentation and the occasion: Is it a casual dinner with neighbors, a holiday brunch, or a once-in-a-life-time event? Once you set the tone and theme, you'll be free to unleash your imagination. Experiment with table settings and mix casual and elegant dishware. Take the party outside with a tequila tasting, lively mariachi music, and Mexican hors d'oeuvres. Or during cooler months, stay indoors by the fire with a hearty seafood chowder and rustic red wine.

Keep your guests' tastes in mind when deciding your menu's level of adventurousness or spiciness, and consider any dietary limitations. When selecting a menu, examine the produce at the market and choose dishes that show off the freshest seasonal ingredients. Vary the dishes in terms of temperature, spiciness, color, texture, or visual interest. Pair a chile-laden main course or starter with simple, soothing, or cooler side dishes and appetizers. Limit the number of sauces and pastries to one per meal to maintain a pleasing simplicity, and don't forget to delight the eye as well as the taste buds with edible herb or vegetable garnishes. Such careful and thoughtful menu planning will keep a cook organized and on track.

Menus can be planned according to many different themes. Couple foods from a single culture: Scallops à la Nage with a Terrine of Mediterranean Mixed Vegetables, or Tomato–Pumpkin Seed Dip with Shrimp Quesadillas and Tomatillo Salsa. Pair dishes that feature a specific ingredient such as Curried Vegetables in Filo Packets and Cheese-Filled Filo Triangles—but take care not to overdo it. Maintain a motif such as a seafood menu: Seafood Tempura and Fish Tartare. Create a sampling menu featuring one seasonal ingredient and prepare several dishes that show off, for example, the tomato and its varieties, in an array of ways.

Be creative when it comes to planning gatherings. Assemble a buffet for a cocktail party, organize a harvest supper, or throw a spring tea with heirloom silver and mix-and-match vintage tea cups. Beg, borrow, or rent appropriate dishes, flatware, glassware, and linens for a formal affair. And remember, whether you're entertaining a few friends or a large group of guests, the beauty of many soups, salads, and starters lies in the fact that the recipes can often be prepared, cooked, and assembled, fully or partially, in advance. Soups often improve when their flavors are allowed to meld for a day or so. Cold appetizers can be arranged on platters and refrigerated until guests arrive. That makes it a little easier for you, the host, to organize the event and—most importantly—to enjoy yourself.

COOKING SMARTER

When it comes to soups, salads, and starters, remember that crucial piece of advice—waste not, want not. These dishes are wonderful ways to utilize all that your kitchen has to offer. No leftover is too small to use. No exotic ingredient is too unusual to reject. These recipes are ideal for cooks who are too busy to prepare elaborate meals, yet still embrace the joys of being in the kitchen. If you're strapped for time and a traditional entrée seems too complex, rely on these starters to save time.

Soups, Salads & Starters presents a quick and easy way to experience the pleasures of food, sometimes with a minimum of effort. Make a simple and crunchy green salad with a homemade vinaigrette, put together in minutes. Simmer a large pot of soup, utilizing plainly seasoned leftovers and the odds and ends you might

find in your refrigerator, and you have a satisfying lunch or dinner starter.

Take advantage of the finest fruits and vegetables at the height of their season at your local farmers' market. Look for vivid colors and ask the growers about intriguing yet unfamiliar produce. In the winter, look for creamy avocados, broccoli, Brussels sprouts, cabbage, celery root, and Mandarin oranges. During the spring, pick out tender asparagus stalks, cucumbers, peppers, lettuce, and spinach. Summer brings a bounty, including tomatoes, corn, and green beans.

Fall abounds with cauliflower, salad greens, winter squash, and sweet potatoes.

When you settle down to plan your menus, remember that a bowl of hearty soup or a full-bodied salad can also serve as a main course, cutting your costs and increasing the versatility and value of your efforts. Spicy Seven-Bean Soup, Oyster Stew, or Hungarian Pork Goulash are all welcome on a chilly winter day. A Warm Scallop and Asparagus Salad with Orange Dressing, Shrimp Caesar Salad, or a Smoked Trout, Avocado, and Orange Salad is certain to satisfy as a light meal.

GETTING CREATIVE

Consider these recipes as a starting point for further adventures in the kitchen—and at the table. Conceived with the fundamental principles of simplicity and good flavor, they will provide a foundation for your creativity, no matter what your level of kitchen experience may be. The novice cook can expect great results by simply following the recipes, while more adventurous cooks can find variation ideas in the notes at the start of every recipe.

The addition of simple ingredients can completely transform the character of a dish. Toss noodles, rice, croutons, pieces of Parmesan rind, or freshly chopped herbs into vegetable soups. Herbs such as parsley, chervil, or dill, or strongly flavored spices such as chiles, garlic, or ginger, blend well with chicken soups. Be creative and put your own spin on stock by adding a whole head of roasted garlic, a splash of wine, dried or fresh mushrooms, or small amounts of spices such as ginger, allspice, and cloves.

Salads flourish with a little creativity. Add sliced fruit or sectioned citrus, or sprinkle fresh lettuce or greens with nuts or seeds, thinly sliced fennel, shaved Parmesan cheese, or diced roasted red pepper (capsicum). Dressings can be supplemented with small quantities of soy sauce or Worcestershire sauce. Try a touch of sweetness with a teaspoon of honey. Supply crunch with minced cucumber or cornichons. Add a kick with tiny portions of cayenne, curry powder, or prepared horseradish.

All it takes is a little imagination. Take the time to prepare and master the recipes that appeal to you, and you'll find the freedom to explore fabulous new flavors and combinations.

Fruit & Vegetable Soups

Quick Vegetable Soup

You can make this soup with any combination of fresh vegetables on hand.
Just be sure to include some potatoes or carrots. Leave the vegetables chunky
for a robust soup, or purée half of the vegetables for extra body.

2 tablespoons olive oil or
unsalted butter

1 large yellow onion, coarsely
chopped

1 baking potato, coarsely
chopped

2 carrots, coarsely chopped

1 cup (4 oz/125 g) coarsely
chopped broccoli

3 cups (24 fl oz/750 ml)
Vegetable Stock (page 316)

1 teaspoon dried oregano

1 teaspoon dried thyme

1 bay leaf

Salt and freshly ground pepper

In a large saucepan, heat the oil over medium heat. Add the onion. Sauté until it begins to soften, 3–5 minutes. Add all the vegetables, the stock, and herbs. Bring to a boil. Reduce the heat to medium-low and simmer until the vegetables are tender, 15–20 minutes.

Discard the bay leaf. Season to taste with salt and pepper. Ladle into warmed bowls and serve.

Serves 4–6

Cream of Carrot Soup

For smooth soups, purée thoroughly in a food processor or blender. If you prefer heartier soups, purée in a food mill fitted with the coarse or medium disk, or use the pulsing action of a food processor or blender.

In a saucepan over medium-low heat, melt the butter. Add the onion and garlic. Cover and reduce the heat to very low. Cook, stirring occasionally, until tender but not browned, about 10 minutes. Add the carrots and stock. Season to taste with salt and a generous sprinkling of white pepper. Raise the heat to medium. Bring to a boil. Reduce the heat to low. Cover partially and simmer until the carrots are tender, about 20 minutes.

Working in batches and using a slotted spoon, transfer the carrots and other solids to a food mill, a food processor, or a blender, depending on the desired consistency (see note). When all the carrots are puréed, stir them back into the stock remaining in the saucepan.

Place the pan over medium-low heat. Add the milk. Heat gently, stirring. Add the cilantro. Stir well. Taste and adjust the seasoning. Ladle into bowls and serve hot.

Serves 4

2 tablespoons unsalted butter

1 yellow onion, diced

1 clove garlic, finely chopped

6 carrots, 1¼ lb (625 g) total weight, peeled and diced

2 cups (16 fl oz/500 ml) Vegetable Stock (page 316)

Salt and ground white pepper

1¼ cups (10 fl oz/310 ml) whole or low-fat milk

½ cup (²/₃ oz/20 g) chopped fresh cilantro (fresh coriander)

French Onion Soup Gratinée

The secret to a good onion soup is to cook the onions slowly, so that their natural sugars can caramelize. For a more complex flavor, sauté some thinly sliced leek with the onions, and sprinkle on grated Parmesan before the Gruyère or Swiss cheese.

½ cup (4 oz/125 g) unsalted butter

4 large yellow onions, thinly sliced

Salt and freshly ground pepper

5 cups (40 fl oz/1.25 l) Vegetable Stock (page 316)

2 bay leaves

½ lb (250 g) Gruyère or Swiss cheese, shredded

4–6 slices French bread, ½ inch (12 mm) thick and toasted golden brown

In a large saucepan, melt the butter over low heat. Add the onions and season to taste with salt. Stir to coat well with the butter. Cover and cook, stirring occasionally, until very tender, 20–30 minutes.

Remove the lid. Raise the heat slightly. Cook, stirring frequently, until the onions turn a deep caramel brown, about 1 hour. Take care not to let them burn.

Add the stock and bay leaves. Raise the heat to medium. Bring to a boil. Reduce the heat to low. Cover and simmer about 30 minutes longer. Meanwhile, preheat the broiler (grill).

Discard the bay leaves. Taste the soup and adjust the seasoning with salt and pepper. Ladle the soup into heavy flameproof serving crocks or bowls placed on a baking sheet or broiler tray. Sprinkle a little of the cheese into each bowl, then place the toasted bread slices on top. Sprinkle evenly with the remaining cheese. Broil (grill) until the cheese is bubbly and golden, 2–3 minutes. Serve immediately.

Serves 4–6

Two-Mushroom Barley Soup

You can enhance this hearty soup with 1 can (1 lb/500 g) diced tomatoes and their juice, adding them with the barley. Serve with thick slices of rye or sourdough bread.

½ oz (15 g) dried porcino mushrooms

2 tablespoons vegetable oil

2 tablespoons unsalted butter

1 yellow onion, finely chopped

1 celery stalk, finely chopped

1 carrot, finely chopped

½ lb (250 g) fresh white mushrooms, thinly sliced

2½ qt (2.5 l) Vegetable Stock (page 316)

2 cups (14 oz/440 g) pearl barley, rinsed under cold running water

1 bay leaf

Salt and freshly ground pepper

¼ cup (⅓ oz/10 g) finely chopped fresh flat-leaf (Italian) parsley

Put the porcini in a small bowl. Add lukewarm water to cover. Soak until softened, about 30 minutes. Line a strainer with a double layer of cheesecloth (muslin) and set it inside a bowl. Pour the porcini and their liquid into the strainer, reserving the liquid. Finely chop the porcini and set aside.

In a large pot, warm the oil and butter over medium heat. Add the onion, celery, and carrot. Sauté until the onion is translucent, 2–3 minutes. Add the fresh mushrooms. Raise the heat to medium-high. Sauté until the mushrooms begin to soften, 2–3 minutes.

Add the stock, barley, bay leaf, and reserved porcini and soaking liquid. Bring to a boil. Reduce the heat to low. Cover partially and simmer gently, stirring occasionally, until the barley is tender and the soup is thick, 50–60 minutes.

Discard the bay leaf. Season to taste with salt and pepper. Ladle into warmed bowls and garnish with the parsley.

Serves 8–10

Leek and Potato Soup

Leave the vegetable pieces whole and cook them in water for a rustic version of this soup. For a richer, more elegant variation, purée the soup, then stir in 1 cup (8 fl oz/250 ml) light (single) cream, and rewarm gently.

In a large saucepan, melt the butter over medium heat. Add the leeks. Sauté just until they begin to soften, about 3–5 minutes. Add the stock and potatoes. Bring to a boil. Reduce the heat to low. Cover and simmer until the potatoes are very tender, about 20 minutes.

Season to taste with salt and pepper. Ladle into bowls and garnish with the chives.

Serves 8–10

¼ cup (2 oz/60 g) unsalted butter

2 lb (1 kg) leeks, white portions only, trimmed, carefully washed, and thinly sliced

6 cups (48 fl oz/1.5 l) Vegetable Stock (page 316) or water

2 lb (1 kg) baking potatoes, peeled, quartered lengthwise, and thinly sliced

Salt and ground white pepper

2 tablespoons finely chopped fresh chives

Spicy Seven-Bean Soup

This could easily be a three-, four-, five-, or six-bean soup and could include beans other than those mentioned — just use the same total volume of dried beans. Garnish it with ½ cup (¾ oz/20 g) finely chopped fresh parsley or cilantro.

Pick over the beans, discarding any misshapen beans or impurities. Put the beans in a bowl, add cold water to cover, and let soak for 4–12 hours.

In a large pot, warm the oil over medium heat. Add the garlic, bell pepper, chile, onion, carrot, celery, and red pepper flakes. Sauté until the onion is translucent, 2–3 minutes. Drain the beans and stir them into the pot along with the stock, tomatoes, tomato paste, vinegar, sugar, basil, oregano, thyme, and bay leaves. Bring to a boil. Reduce the heat to low. Cover partially and simmer until the beans are tender, 2–2½ hours.

Just before serving, discard the bay leaves. Season to taste with salt and pepper. Ladle into warmed bowls.

Serves 6–8

¼ cup (1¾ oz/55 g) *each* dried baby lima beans, black-eyed peas, chickpeas (garbanzo beans), kidney beans, small white (navy) beans, pinto beans, and red beans

¼ cup (2 fl oz/60 ml) olive oil

2 cloves garlic, finely chopped

1 red bell pepper (capsicum), seeded, deribbed, and diced

1 large fresh green Anaheim chile, finely chopped

1 *each* yellow onion, carrot, and celery stalk, finely chopped

1 teaspoon red pepper flakes

4 cups (32 fl oz/1 l) Vegetable Stock (page 316) or water

1 can (1 lb/500 g) crushed tomatoes

2 tablespoons tomato paste

1 tablespoon balsamic vinegar

1 tablespoon sugar

1 tablespoon *each* dried basil and dried oregano

½ tablespoon dried thyme

2 bay leaves

Salt and freshly ground pepper

Split Pea Soup

Split peas seem made for the soup pot, slowly cooking and softening in stock or water to produce a thick, satisfying bowl of soup. The soup is also good made with a ³/₄-lb (375-g) piece of smoked ham, added with the stock. Remove and chop before serving.

2 cups (14 oz/440 g) yellow or green split peas

¹/₄ cup (2 fl oz/60 ml) olive oil or ¹/₄ cup (2 oz/60 g) unsalted butter

2 yellow onions, finely chopped

2 carrots, finely chopped

2 celery stalks, finely chopped

2 cloves garlic, finely chopped

6–8 cups (48–64 fl oz/1.5–2 l) Vegetable Stock (page 316) or water

2 large fresh flat-leaf (Italian) parsley sprigs

2 bay leaves

1 teaspoon dried thyme

Salt and freshly ground pepper

3 tablespoons finely chopped fresh flat-leaf (Italian) parsley

Lemon wedges

Pick over the split peas, discarding any misshapen peas or impurities. Set aside.

In a large pot, warm the oil over medium heat. Add the onions, carrots, celery, and garlic. Sauté until the onions are translucent, about 5 minutes. Add 6 cups (48 fl oz/ 1.5 l) of the stock, the peas, parsley sprigs, bay leaves, and thyme. Bring to a boil. Reduce the heat to low. Cover and simmer gently, stirring occasionally, until the peas are reduced to a thick purée, about 1 ¹/₂ hours. Add more stock or water from time to time, if necessary, to keep the peas moist.

Before serving, discard the bay leaves and parsley sprigs. Season generously with salt and pepper. Ladle into warmed soup bowls. Garnish with the chopped parsley. Serve with lemon wedges.

Serves 6–8

Carrot and Watercress Soup

The appealing color, delicate sweetness, and subtle peppery flavor of watercress combine to make this soup memorable. It may be served hot or cold. You can add 1 cup (3 oz/90 g) thinly sliced green (spring) onion tops in place of the watercress.

In a large saucepan over medium-low heat, warm the oil. When the oil is hot, add the carrots, onion, celery, parsley, and thyme. Cook, stirring occasionally, until the vegetables have softened slightly and the onion has softened, about 5 minutes. Add 1/4 cup (2 fl oz/60 ml) of the stock. Cover and cook for 5 minutes longer, stirring once at the halfway point.

Add the remaining 3 3/4 cups (30 fl oz/940 ml) stock and the bread. Bring to a boil over medium-high heat. Reduce the heat to low. Cover and simmer until the carrots are very tender when pierced with the tip of a sharp knife, 20–25 minutes.

Working in batches, ladle the soup into a food processor or blender. Purée until smooth. Alternatively, pass the soup through a food mill.

If serving the soup hot, return it to the pan and stir in the watercress. Season to taste with salt and pepper. Reheat over low heat without boiling. Ladle into warmed bowls. Serve at once.

If serving the soup cold, transfer it to a bowl or another container. Stir in the watercress. Season to taste with salt and pepper. Cover and refrigerate, stirring it every hour or so, until thoroughly chilled, 4–6 hours. When ready to serve, taste and adjust the seasoning. Ladle into chilled bowls. Serve at once.

Serves 4

1 tablespoon vegetable oil

6 large carrots, 1 lb (500 g) total weight, peeled and cut into 1-inch (2.5-cm) pieces

1 yellow onion, thinly sliced

1 celery stalk, thinly sliced

3 fresh flat-leaf (Italian) parsley sprigs

1 teaspoon chopped fresh thyme or 1/4 teaspoon dried thyme

4 cups (32 fl oz/1 l) Vegetable Stock (page 316)

1 slice good-quality white sandwich bread, torn into pieces

1 1/2 cups (1 1/2 oz/45 g) chopped watercress leaves

Salt and freshly ground pepper

Cream of Mushroom Soup

For a somewhat lighter soup, substitute 3 cups (24 fl oz/750 ml) Vegetable Stock (page 316) for 2 cups (16 fl oz/500 ml) of the cream, and increase the simmering time by 5—10 minutes.

2 lb (1 kg) fresh white mushrooms

¹/₄ cup (2 fl oz/60 ml) vegetable oil

¹/₄ cup (2 oz/60 g) unsalted butter

4 large shallots, finely chopped

2 tablespoons all-purpose (plain) flour

5 cups (40 fl oz/1.25 l) heavy (double) cream

Pinch of freshly grated nutmeg

Salt and ground white pepper

2 tablespoons fresh lemon juice

1 tablespoon finely chopped fresh chives

1 tablespoon finely chopped fresh flat-leaf (Italian) parsley

Set aside 4 attractive mushrooms. Finely chop the remaining mushrooms.

In a large saucepan, warm the oil and butter over medium heat. Add the chopped mushrooms and shallots. Raise the heat to medium-high and sauté, stirring frequently, until the vegetables cook down to a thick, dark brown paste, 25–30 minutes. Partway through the cooking time, when the mushroom liquid has evaporated, sprinkle in the flour and stir it in well. Add the cream and deglaze the pan by stirring and scraping to dislodge any browned bits. Simmer, stirring occasionally, until thick, 15–20 minutes.

In small batches, purée the soup in a food mill, a food processor, or a blender. Return the purée to the pan and heat gently over low heat, stirring in the nutmeg and salt and pepper to taste.

Meanwhile, cut the reserved mushrooms into neat slices about ¹/₄ inch (6 mm) thick. In a small bowl, toss them with the lemon juice.

Ladle the soup into bowls. Garnish with the mushroom slices, chives, and parsley.

Serves 4–6

Chickpea Soup with Pita Toasts

This is a hearty soup to make on a cold winter day. Be sure to allow enough time to let the chickpeas soak for about 8 hours or overnight. Garnish with fresh thyme leaves, if desired.

If using dried chickpeas, pick over the chickpeas, discarding any misshapen peas or impurities. Rinse, drain, and place in a bowl with water to cover by 2 inches (5 cm). Let soak for 4–12 hours. Drain and place in a saucepan with fresh water to cover by 2 inches (5 cm). Bring to a boil, reduce the heat to low, cover partially, and simmer until tender, 2–2 1/2 hours. Drain and set aside. If using canned chickpeas, rinse in cold water, drain well, and set aside.

Meanwhile, to make the toasts, preheat the oven to 400°F (200°C). Prick one side of each pita bread in several places with a fork, then brush each with 1 teaspoon of the oil. Cut each round into 4 equal wedges and place on an ungreased baking sheet. Sprinkle with the Parmesan cheese. Season lightly with salt and pepper. Bake until crisp and golden, about 12 minutes. Transfer to a wire rack to cool. If the toasts soften, recrisp them in a 400°F (200°C) oven for 1–2 minutes.

In a large saucepan over medium-low heat, warm the oil. When the oil is hot, add the shallot, carrot, celery, and mushrooms. Cook gently, stirring frequently, until the vegetables have softened slightly, about 5 minutes. Add the stock, dried thyme, and reserved chickpeas. Raise the heat to medium-high, bring to a boil, and reduce the heat to low. Cover and simmer until the ingredients are soft, 40 minutes.

In batches, purée the soup in a food mill, a food processor, or a blender. Return the purée to the pan and season to taste with salt and pepper. Reheat gently over low heat without boiling, then ladle into warmed bowls. Serve immediately, with the pita toasts. Garnish with thyme leaves, if desired.

Serves 6

1 cup (7 oz/220 g) dried chickpeas (garbanzo beans) or 3 cups (21 oz/655 g) drained canned chickpeas

FOR THE PITA TOASTS:

3 pita breads, whole wheat (wholemeal) or plain

3 teaspoons olive oil

3 tablespoons grated Parmesan cheese

Salt and freshly ground pepper

FOR THE SOUP:

1 tablespoon olive oil

4 shallots, chopped, or 2 green (spring) onions, chopped

1 *each* carrot and celery stalk, thinly sliced

1/2 cup (1 1/2 oz/45 g) thinly sliced fresh white mushrooms

5 cups (40 fl oz/1.25 l) Vegetable Stock (page 316)

1 teaspoon dried thyme

Salt and freshly ground pepper

Fresh thyme leaves (optional)

Gazpacho

This chilled soup tastes as fresh as a salad, highlighting ripe summertime vegetables. For a spicy version, add a green chile when you purée the vegetables, or stir in a few drops of hot-pepper sauce before serving.

In a food processor, combine the bread crumbs, oil, and garlic. Process until they form a smooth paste, stopping 2 or 3 times to scrape down the bowl. Set aside a small handful each of the onion, cucumber, and bell pepper. Refrigerate in a tightly covered container. Add the remaining onion, cucumber, and bell pepper and all the tomatoes to the food processor. Process until smooth. Transfer to a bowl. Cover tightly and refrigerate until well chilled, about 2–3 hours. Chill individual soup bowls in the refrigerator.

Using a whisk, stir the tomato juice, water, and vinegar into the chilled soup. Season to taste with salt and white pepper. Ladle into the chilled bowls. Garnish with the reserved vegetables, sour cream, croutons, and chopped eggs.

Serves 6–8

1½ cups (3 oz/90 g) fresh sourdough or coarse country bread crumbs

½ cup (4 fl oz/125 ml) extra-virgin olive oil

2 cloves garlic

1 red onion, finely chopped

1 cucumber, peeled, seeded, and finely chopped

1 green bell pepper (capsicum), seeded, deribbed, and finely chopped

4 tomatoes, peeled (page 329) and coarsely chopped

2 cups (16 fl oz/500 ml) tomato juice, chilled

2 cups (16 fl oz/500 ml) water, chilled

¼ cup (2 fl oz/60 ml) red wine vinegar

Salt and ground white pepper

1 cup (8 oz/250 g) sour cream

1 cup (1½ oz/45 g) croutons (page 326)

2 hard-boiled eggs, whites and yolks separated and finely chopped

Tortilla Soup

This version of the classic soup makes a hearty first course or light lunch and offers an excellent way to use up day-old tortillas. In addition to the sour cream, avocado slices, and chile rings, garnish each bowl with half a lime.

2 cloves garlic

1/2 onion, cut in half

4 tomatoes

6 cups (48 fl oz/1.5 l) Vegetable Stock (page 316)

1 tablespoon corn oil or other vegetable oil, plus oil for frying

2 small fresh epazote or fresh cilantro (fresh coriander) sprigs

Salt and freshly ground pepper

8 corn tortillas

2 fresh pasilla chiles, cut into rings 1/2 inch (12 mm) wide and seeds removed

2 avocados, cut in half, pitted, thinly sliced and scooped from the skin

1 cup (5 oz/155 g) crumbled queso fresco or feta cheese

1/2 cup (4 oz/125 g) sour cream

Heat a dry, heavy frying pan or a griddle over medium heat. Place the garlic, onion, and tomatoes on the pan or griddle. Roast, turning occasionally, until well charred, about 3 minutes for the garlic and onion and 4 minutes for the tomatoes. Remove from the heat. Peel the tomatoes, coarsely chop, and place in a food processor or blender. Add the garlic and onion. Process to form a smooth, thick purée, adding 1/4 cup (2 fl oz/60 ml) of the stock if the mixture is too thick.

In a large saucepan over high heat, warm the 1 tablespoon oil. Add the tomato purée and cook, stirring, for 2 minutes. Reduce the heat to low and cook, uncovered, until the purée thickens and reduces slightly, about 5 minutes longer. Add the epazote and the remaining stock. Season to taste with salt and pepper. Cover and simmer for 15 minutes.

While the purée simmers, cut the tortillas in half, then cut each half crosswise into thin strips. In a small frying pan over high heat, pour in oil to a depth of 1/2 inch (12 mm). When the oil is hot, in batches, fry the tortilla pieces until crisp, about 3 minutes. Using a slotted spoon, transfer to paper towels to drain. Fry the chile rings in the same oil until crisp, about 1 minute. Transfer to paper towels to drain.

Add the fried tortilla strips to the simmering soup and ladle into warmed bowls. Top with some of the chile rings and avocado slices and sprinkle with the cheese. Serve immediately. Pass the sour cream and the remaining avocado slices and chile rings in separate bowls at the table.

Serves 6

Vegetarian White Bean Soup

It's surprising how much flavor vegetables and herbs bring to this robust soup. If you wish, you can add a large chunk of ham or bacon to the pot while the soup simmers, and make the soup with Chicken Stock or Meat Stock (page 317 or 318).

Pick over the beans, discarding any misshapen beans or impurities. Put the beans in a bowl, add cold water to cover, and let soak for 4–12 hours.

In a large saucepan, warm the butter over medium heat. Add the onion, garlic, carrot, and celery. Sauté until the onion is translucent, 2–3 minutes. Drain the beans and add them to the pan along with the stock, tomatoes and juice, savory, thyme, sugar, and bay leaf. Bring to a boil, reduce the heat to low, cover, and simmer, stirring occasionally to break up the tomatoes, until the beans are very tender, 2–2¹/₂ hours. Discard the bay leaf.

Purée about half of the soup in a food mill, a food processor, or a blender. Stir the purée back into the pan, then season to taste with salt and pepper. Ladle into warmed bowls and garnish with the parsley.

Serves 6–8

1 cup (7 oz/220 g) dried small white (navy) beans

¹/₄ cup (2 oz/60 g) unsalted butter or ¹/₄ cup vegetable oil or a mixture of both

1 large yellow onion, finely chopped

1 clove garlic, finely chopped

1 large carrot, finely chopped

1 celery stalk, finely chopped

5 cups (40 fl oz/1.25 l) Vegetable Stock (page 316)

1 can (1 lb/500 g) plum (Roma) tomatoes, with juice

1 teaspoon dried summer savory

1 teaspoon dried thyme

1 teaspoon sugar

1 bay leaf

Salt and freshly ground pepper

2 tablespoons finely chopped fresh flat-leaf (Italian) parsley

Leek, Celery, and Rice Soup with Egg and Lemon

The traditional Greek egg-and-lemon mixture added to this delicate vegetable soup is called *avgolemono*. It thickens the soup and also imparts a tart and rich flavor. Be sure that the soup doesn't boil, or the eggs will curdle.

Trim off the tough dark green tops and the root ends of the leeks. Cut each leek in half lengthwise and rinse well under cold running water. Chop the leeks.

In a large soup pot over medium heat, warm the oil. Add the leeks and celery. Sauté, stirring, until very tender, 15–20 minutes. Add the stock. Reduce the heat to low. Cover and simmer until all the vegetables are very soft, 30–45 minutes.

Using a slotted spoon and working in batches, transfer the vegetables to a food processor or blender. Purée until smooth, then return to the pot. Stir well and season to taste with salt and pepper. (The soup can be prepared up to this point, cooled, covered, and stored in the refrigerator for up to 3 days. Bring to a simmer over medium heat before continuing.)

Add the rice to the soup. Cover. Bring to a simmer over medium heat and cook for 10 minutes. Meanwhile, in a bowl, using a whisk or an electric mixer set on medium speed, beat the eggs until frothy. Beat in the lemon juice and continue to beat until the mixture is very frothy. Gradually beat in about 1/2 cup (4 fl oz/125 ml) of the hot soup to temper the eggs. Then gradually beat in up to about 3 cups (24 fl oz/750 ml) of the hot soup until the eggs are warm.

Whisk the egg mixture back into the rest of the soup. Immediately ladle into warmed bowls. Garnish with the parsley, if desired.

Serves 6–8

3 lb (1.5 kg) leeks

1/4 cup (2 fl oz/60 ml) olive oil

1 bunch celery including leaves, about 1 1/2 lb (750 g), trimmed and chopped

8 cups (64 fl oz/2 l) Vegetable Stock (page 316) or water

Salt and freshly ground pepper

2–3 cups (10–15 oz/315–470 g) cooked long-grain white rice

3 eggs, at room temperature

Juice of 2 large lemons

3 tablespoons chopped fresh flat-leaf (Italian) parsley or dill (optional)

Fresh Tomato Soup

Removing the skin and seeds from fresh tomatoes before adding them to the soup ensures a smooth texture. Feel free to substitute chopped fresh basil or flat-leaf (Italian) parsley for the oregano.

2 lb (1 kg) tomatoes

2 tablespoons unsalted butter

1 yellow onion, finely diced

1/2 cup (2 1/2 oz/75 g) chopped celery leaves

1 bay leaf

2 cups (16 fl oz/500 ml) Vegetable Stock (page 316)

Salt and ground white pepper

2 tablespoons cornstarch (cornflour)

1 cup (8 fl oz/250 ml) low-fat milk

1 tablespoon chopped fresh oregano

Bring a saucepan three-fourths full of water to a boil. Cut out the core from the stem end of each tomato, then cut a shallow X in the base. In batches, blanch the tomatoes for 15–20 seconds, then peel, halve crosswise and seed, and cut into large dice. You should have about 3 cups (18 oz/555 g). Set aside.

In a heavy-bottomed saucepan over medium heat, melt the butter. Add the onion, celery leaves, and bay leaf. Cover, reduce the heat to very low, and cook until softened but not browned, about 10 minutes. Add the tomatoes and stock. Season to taste with salt and white pepper. Bring to a boil, reduce the heat to low, cover partially, and simmer, stirring occasionally, until the flavors have blended, about 30 minutes. Discard the bay leaf.

In a small bowl, stir the cornstarch into the milk until dissolved and then add the mixture to the hot soup. Simmer, stirring, for 5 minutes. The soup will thicken and lighten in color. Stir in the oregano, then taste and adjust the seasoning. Ladle into warmed bowls and serve hot.

Serves 4–6

Cream of Asparagus Soup

Just a little onion, celery, and basil are all that is needed to show off fresh asparagus in this luxurious soup. Garnish with asparagus tips, if you like. It is also excellent served chilled.

In a large saucepan over medium-low heat, melt the butter. Add the onion and celery and sauté until translucent, 2–3 minutes. Add the stock, all the asparagus stalks and two-thirds of the tips, the potatoes, and basil. Raise the heat to medium and bring to a boil, skimming away any foam from the surface. Reduce the heat to low, cover, and simmer gently until the vegetables are tender, 20 minutes.

In small batches, purée the soup in a food mill, a food processor, or a blender. If you use a processor or blender, force the purée through a strainer with a wooden spoon to remove any fibers. Return the purée to the pan. Stir in the cream, season to taste with salt and white pepper, and gently rewarm over low heat.

While the soup is warming, bring a small saucepan filled with lightly salted water to a boil. Add the reserved asparagus tips and cook just until tender-crisp, 3–4 minutes. Drain well. Ladle the soup into warmed bowls.

Serves 6–8

¼ cup (2 oz/60 g) unsalted butter

1 mild white onion, finely chopped

1 celery stalk with leaves, finely chopped

4 cups (32 fl oz/1 l) Vegetable Stock (page 316)

3 lb (1.5 kg) asparagus, trimmed and cut into 1-inch (2.5-cm) pieces, tips reserved

2 baking potatoes, peeled and cut into 1-inch (2.5-cm) chunks

2 tablespoons finely chopped fresh basil or 1 teaspoon dried basil

2 cups (16 fl oz/500 ml) heavy (double) cream

Salt and ground white pepper

Vegetable Soup with Basil and Garlic

Called *soupe au pistou*, this is a Provençal mélange of spring vegetables and pasta in a fragrant broth. If you like, drizzle each serving with extra-virgin olive oil and top with a little grated Parmesan cheese to complement the flavors.

½ cup (3½ oz/105 g) dried cannellini beans

Salt

3 tablespoons olive oil

4 yellow onions, diced

6 carrots, peeled and sliced

4 celery stalks, diced

1 lb (500 g) tomatoes, peeled, seeded, and diced (page 329)

8 cups (64 fl oz/2 l) Vegetable Stock (page 316) or water

6 new potatoes, diced

½ lb (250 g) green beans, trimmed and cut into 1-inch (2.5-cm) lengths

4 zucchini (courgettes), cut in half lengthwise, then sliced crosswise ½ inch (12 mm) thick

4 cups (8 oz/250 g) Swiss chard, carefully rinsed and sliced ½ inch (12 mm) wide

¼ lb (125 g) dried macaroni or small pasta shells

Freshly ground pepper

1 cup (8 fl oz/250 ml) Pesto (page 318)

Pick over the cannellini beans, discarding any misshapen beans or impurities. Rinse well and place in a saucepan with water to cover. Bring to a boil over high heat, boil for 2 minutes, remove from the heat, and let stand for 1 hour. Drain and return to the saucepan. Add fresh water to cover by 2 inches (5 cm) and bring to a boil over medium-high heat. Reduce the heat to low, cover, and simmer until the beans are cooked through but not falling apart, about 1 hour. Add salt to taste during the last 15 minutes of cooking. Remove from the heat, drain, and set aside.

In a large soup pot over medium heat, warm the oil. Add the onions and sauté, stirring occasionally, until tender, about 8–10 minutes. Add the carrots and celery. Cook, stirring, for about 5 minutes. Then add the tomatoes and stock, reduce the heat to low, and simmer for 10 minutes.

Add the potatoes and continue to simmer until the potatoes are tender, about 15 minutes. Add the cooked cannellini beans, green beans, zucchini, Swiss chard, and pasta during the last 10 minutes of cooking. Season to taste with salt and pepper.

Remove from the heat and stir in the pesto. Ladle into warmed bowls and serve.

Serves 6–8

Carrot Soup
with Caraway–Bread Crumb Topping

Bread crumbs sautéed with caraway seeds provide a crisp, flavorful topping for the slightly sweet carrot purée. Choose slender medium-sized carrots; avoid larger woody carrots. Enrich the soup, if you like, with a splash of cream after puréeing.

FOR THE CARROT PURÉE:

¹/₄ cup (2 oz/60 g) unsalted butter

2 yellow onions, thinly sliced

2 lb (1 kg) carrots, thinly sliced

1 fresh tarragon sprig or 1 teaspoon dried tarragon

4 cups (32 fl oz/1 l) Vegetable Stock (page 316)

¹/₃ cup (3 fl oz/80 ml) fresh orange juice

2 tablespoons fresh lemon juice

Salt and ground white pepper

FOR THE TOPPING:

¹/₄ cup (2 oz/60 g) unsalted butter

2 teaspoons caraway seeds

²/₃ cup (1¹/₃ oz/45 g) fresh white bread crumbs

2 tablespoons finely chopped fresh flat-leaf (Italian) parsley

For the carrot purée, in a large saucepan over medium heat, melt the butter. Add the onions and sauté until translucent, 2–3 minutes. Add the carrots and tarragon. Reduce the heat to low, cover, and cook, stirring occasionally, about 10 minutes. Add the stock and the orange and lemon juices. Bring to a boil, reduce the heat to low, cover, and simmer until the carrots are very tender, 10–15 minutes.

Discard the tarragon sprig, if using. In small batches, purée the soup in a food mill, a food processor, or a blender. Return the purée to the pan, season to taste with salt and white pepper, and rewarm gently over low heat.

For the topping, in a frying pan over medium-low heat, melt the butter. Add the caraway seeds and sauté for about 1 minute. Add the bread crumbs, raise the heat slightly, and sauté, stirring until golden brown, 2–3 minutes. Ladle the soup into warmed bowls and scatter the bread crumb mixture generously on top. Garnish with the parsley.

Serves 6–8

Pumpkin Soup with Gruyère

For a special occasion, you can serve the soup in one large pumpkin shell. Cut off the stem end of the pumpkin and carefully scoop out the flesh, leaving a shell ½ inch (12 mm) thick. Fill the shell with the soup and scatter crisp croutons (page 326) on top.

Cut the pumpkin in half and scoop out any strings and seeds. With a sturdy knife, cut away the hard peel. Coarsely chop the flesh; you should have about 8 cups (4 lb/2 kg).

In a large saucepan, melt the butter over medium heat. Add the onion and sauté until it begins to turn golden, 4–5 minutes. Add the stock, chopped pumpkin, and bay leaf. Bring to a boil, reduce the heat to low, cover, and simmer until tender, 15–30 minutes. Discard the bay leaf.

In small batches, purée the soup in a food mill, a food processor, or a blender. Return the purée to the pan and stir in the cream, orange zest, orange and lemon juices, nutmeg, and ginger.

Reserve a handful of the cheese for garnish and sprinkle the rest into the soup. Stir over low heat until the cheese melts and blends in. Season to taste with salt and white pepper. Pour into a warmed tureen, or ladle into warmed individual bowls and garnish with the remaining cheese and the chives.

Serves 10–12

1 pumpkin, 5–6 lb (2.5–3 kg)

¼ cup (2 oz/60 g) unsalted butter

1 large yellow onion, finely chopped

6 cups (48 fl oz/1.5 l) Vegetable Stock (page 316)

1 bay leaf

1½ cups (12 fl oz/375 ml) light (single) cream

2 tablespoons grated orange zest

2 tablespoons fresh orange juice

1 tablespoon fresh lemon juice

1 teaspoon freshly grated nutmeg

1 teaspoon ground ginger

¾ lb (375 g) Gruyère or Swiss cheese, shredded

Salt and ground white pepper

2 tablespoons finely chopped fresh chives

Hungarian Cauliflower Soup

This rich soup becomes even heartier with the addition of ham. Add 6 oz (185 g) cooked ham, cut into small dice, to the pot with the onion and carrot, and proceed with the recipe.

8 cups (64 fl oz/2 l) milk

1 yellow onion, finely chopped

1 carrot, finely chopped

1 head cauliflower

1/2 cup (4 fl oz/125 ml) sour cream

2 teaspoons salt

Freshly ground white pepper

In a saucepan, bring the milk to a boil. Pour the milk through a fine-mesh strainer into a large pot. Add the onion and carrot. Cover partially and simmer gently over medium heat for 10 minutes, taking care that it does not boil over.

Meanwhile, remove the florets from the cauliflower head and chop them coarsely. Measure 4 cups (10 oz/315 g) and add to the soup. Simmer for 15 minutes longer.

In a bowl, stir a little of the hot soup into the sour cream until smooth. Add this mixture to the remaining soup along with the salt and pepper to taste. Simmer briefly, stirring well. Taste and adjust the seasoning and ladle into warmed bowls.

Serves 4–6

Yankee Corn Chowder

Fresh in-season corn is essential for this simple soup. For a smoky flavor, sauté some chopped bacon or ham with the onion and shallot. Swirled red pepper (capsicum) purée makes an attractive garnish.

In a large saucepan, melt the butter over medium-low heat. Add the onion and shallot and sauté until translucent, about 5 minutes. Add the cream and three-fourths of the corn kernels. Raise the heat to medium, bring to a boil, and reduce the heat to low. Simmer, uncovered, until the corn is tender and the liquid thickens slightly, about 10 minutes.

In small batches, purée the soup in a food mill, food processor, or a blender. If you use a processor or blender, force the purée through a strainer, pressing the solids with a wooden spoon. Return the purée to the pan over medium-low heat and add the remaining corn kernels. Simmer until the kernels are tender-crisp, about 5 minutes. Season to taste with salt and white pepper.

Ladle into warmed bowls. Garnish with the chives. If you like, spoon a swirl of puréed bell pepper atop each bowl.

Serves 4–6

2 tablespoons unsalted butter

1 yellow onion, coarsely chopped

1 large shallot, finely chopped

6 cups (48 fl oz/1.5 l) light (single) cream

8 ears of corn, kernels removed with a sharp knife

Salt and ground white pepper

2 tablespoons finely chopped fresh chives

1 red bell pepper (capsicum), roasted, peeled, seeded (page 324), and puréed in a food processor or blender (optional)

Cream of Broccoli Soup
with Aged Cheddar

Broccoli and Cheddar appear together in many classic dishes. Both their colors
and flavors make them ideal companions. Try cauliflower in place of the broccoli.
If you like, sauté some chopped bacon along with the onion.

Reserve ½ cup (1 oz/30 g) small broccoli florets for garnish. Coarsely chop the
remaining broccoli and set aside.

In a large saucepan, melt the butter over medium heat. Add the onion and sauté
until it begins to brown, 5–7 minutes. Sprinkle in the flour and sauté, stirring, for
about 1 minute. Whisking continuously, slowly pour in the stock. Add the chopped
broccoli, thyme, and lemon juice and bring to a boil. Reduce the heat to low, cover,
and simmer until the broccoli is very tender, about 20 minutes.

About 5 minutes before the broccoli is done, bring a small saucepan of lightly salted
water to a boil. Add the reserved broccoli florets and simmer until tender-crisp,
3–5 minutes. Drain and keep warm.

In small batches, purée the soup in a food mill, a food processor, or a blender.
Return the purée to the pan, stir in the milk, and bring to a simmer over low heat.

Reserve a small handful of the cheese for garnish and sprinkle the rest into the soup.
Stir over low heat until the cheese melts and blends in. Season to taste with salt
and white pepper. Ladle into warmed bowls and garnish with the cooked broccoli
florets and remaining cheese.

Serves 6–8

1½ lb (750 g) broccoli,
trimmed and tough stems
peeled

2 tablespoons unsalted butter

1 yellow onion, finely chopped

¼ cup (1½ oz/45 g)
all-purpose (plain) flour

5 cups (40 fl oz/1.25 l)
Vegetable Stock (page 316),
heated

½ teaspoon dried thyme

1 tablespoon lemon juice

2 cups (16 fl oz/500 ml) milk

½ lb (250 g) aged sharp
Cheddar cheese, shredded

Salt and ground white pepper

Fresh Tomato Cream Soup

Make this soup in high summer, with vine-ripened tomatoes. A little grated fresh ginger, grated orange zest, or a splash of orange juice or sherry can also be added for additional flavor. Serve with crackers or buttered toast.

¼ cup (2 oz/60 g) unsalted butter

1 red onion, finely chopped

1 small carrot, finely chopped

4 lb (2 kg) tomatoes, peeled (page 329) and coarsely chopped

3 cups (24 fl oz/750 ml) Vegetable Stock (page 316)

1 fresh basil sprig

½ teaspoon dried thyme

1 bay leaf

1½ cups (3 oz/90 g) fresh white bread crumbs

1 cup (8 fl oz/250 ml) light (single) cream

Salt and ground white pepper

2 tablespoons finely shredded fresh basil leaves

In a large saucepan, melt the butter over medium heat. Add the onion and carrot and sauté until the onion is translucent, 2–3 minutes. Add the tomatoes, stock, basil sprig, thyme, and bay leaf. Bring to a boil, reduce the heat to low, cover, and simmer for about 30 minutes.

Discard the bay leaf and stir in the bread crumbs. In small batches, purée the soup in a food mill, a food processor, or a blender. If you use a processor or blender, force the purée through a strainer using a wooden spoon. Return the purée to the pan, stir in the cream, and warm thoroughly over low heat.

Season to taste with salt and white pepper. Ladle into warmed bowls and garnish with the shredded basil.

Serves 6–8

Roasted Eggplant Soup with Mint

Roasted eggplant (aubergine) has an earthy, slightly smoky flavor that is highlighted in this simple soup. For an edge of sweetness, swirl some roasted red bell pepper (capsicum) purée into each serving. The soup may also be served chilled.

Preheat the oven to 375°F (190°C).

Put the eggplants in a baking dish and puncture their skins several times with a fork. Roast in the oven, turning occasionally, until the skins are evenly browned and deeply wrinkled, 1–1 1/2 hours. Let stand at room temperature until cool enough to handle, then peel.

In a large saucepan, melt the butter over medium heat. Add the onion and garlic. Sauté until golden, 3–5 minutes. Add the eggplants, breaking them up with a wooden spoon, and sauté for 2–3 minutes. Add the stock and mint. Bring to a boil. Reduce the heat to low, cover, and simmer for about 20 minutes.

In small batches, purée the soup in a food mill, food processor, or blender. Return the purée to the pan, stir in the cream, and heat gently over medium-low heat. Season to taste with salt and white pepper. Ladle into bowls and garnish with mint sprigs.

Serves 4–6

1 1/2 lb (750 g) small- to medium-sized eggplants (aubergines)

2 tablespoons unsalted butter

1 small yellow onion, finely chopped

1 clove garlic, finely chopped

2 1/2 cups (20 fl oz/625 ml) Vegetable Stock (page 316)

1/2 tablespoon finely chopped fresh mint

1 cup (8 fl oz/250 ml) heavy (double) cream

Salt and ground white pepper

Fresh mint sprigs for garnish

Chilled Beet Borscht
with Sour Cream and Vodka

Beet soups, served hot or cold, are popular throughout Eastern Europe. This version gains extra spark from the addition of a shot of vodka. Of course, you can leave the vodka out. Serve with sliced pumpernickel and butter.

6 cups (48 fl oz/1.5 l) Vegetable Stock (page 316)

2 lb (1 kg) beets, peeled and coarsely shredded

1 bay leaf

1/2 cup (4 fl oz/125 ml) fresh orange juice

1 cucumber

2 green (spring) onions

2 cups (16 fl oz/500 ml) sour cream

1/3 cup (3 fl oz/80 ml) vodka

Salt and ground white pepper

2 tablespoons finely chopped fresh dill

In a large pot, combine the stock, beets, and bay leaf. Bring to a boil over medium heat. Reduce the heat to low. Cover and simmer gently for about 30 minutes. Remove from the heat, stir in the orange juice, and let cool to room temperature. Discard the bay leaf, cover the soup, and refrigerate until well chilled, 2–3 hours, or for up to 2–3 days. Chill individual soup bowls in the refrigerator.

Peel the cucumber and cut in half lengthwise. Remove the seeds and discard. Dice the cucumber, place in a small bowl, cover, and refrigerate. Trim the green onions and slice thinly, including the tender green parts. Place in another small bowl, cover, and refrigerate.

Shortly before serving, remove the soup from the refrigerator and spoon off any solidified fat from its surface. Put 1 1/2 cups (12 oz/375 g) of the sour cream into a bowl. Stir in the vodka and a ladleful of the chilled beet broth until thoroughly blended, then stir the sour cream mixture back into the soup. Season to taste with salt and white pepper.

Distribute the chilled cucumber and green onions evenly among the chilled bowls. Ladle in the soup and garnish with dollops of the remaining 1/2 cup (4 oz/125 g) sour cream and a sprinkle of dill.

Serves 6–8

Cold Cream of Cucumber Soup with Dill and Yogurt

Inspired by two Indian dishes—raita, a yogurt-and-vegetable salad, and lassi, a yogurt drink—this refreshing soup is perfect for lunch on a hot summer day. Try adding finely shredded carrot or a little finely chopped sweet red onion.

Combine the cucumbers, pickles, yogurt, cream, lemon juice, and the chopped dill in a food processor or blender. Process until the vegetables are finely chopped. If using a blender, you may have to process in small batches. Season to taste with salt and white pepper.

Cover the soup tightly and refrigerate until well chilled, 2–3 hours. Chill individual soup bowls in the refrigerator.

Taste and adjust the seasoning. Ladle the soup into the chilled bowls and garnish with dill sprigs.

Serves 6–8

6 pickling cucumbers, each about 5 inches (13 cm) long, ends trimmed, unpeeled, cut into large chunks

3 or 4 sour dill pickles (pickled cucumbers)

2 cups (1 lb/500 g) low-fat plain yogurt

2 cups (16 fl oz/500 ml) heavy (double) cream

2 tablespoons fresh lemon juice

2 tablespoons finely chopped fresh dill or 1 tablespoon dried dill, plus fresh dill sprigs or dried dill for garnish

Salt and white pepper

Iced Melon Soup
with Champagne and Ginger

Make this soup with the sweetest and juiciest cantaloupe or honeydew
melon you can find. For a special occasion, serve the soup in decoratively cut
melon shells, surrounded by sliced strawberries and whole raspberries.

5 cups (30 oz/940 g) coarsely
chopped fresh cantaloupe or
honeydew melon

1 tablespoon grated fresh
ginger

1 tablespoon fresh lemon juice

3 cups (24 fl oz/750 ml) dry
Champagne or sparkling wine,
well chilled

1–2 tablespoons confectioners'
(icing) sugar

Fresh mint sprigs

Purée the melon and ginger in a food mill, a food processor, or a blender. If you use
a processor or blender, force the purée through a strainer set inside a bowl, pressing
the solids with a wooden spoon. Stir in the lemon juice. Cover tightly and refrigerate
until well chilled, at least 2 hours, or for up to 12 hours. Chill individual soup bowls
in the refrigerator.

Just before serving, stir the Champagne into the chilled melon purée. Then stir in
just enough of the sugar to emphasize the melon's flavor without making the soup
overly sweet. Ladle into the chilled bowls and garnish with the mint sprigs.

Serves 4–6

Cold Cherry Soup with Kirsch

This soup makes a refreshing appetizer or light dessert. If you wish, leave out the kirsch. Try substituting plain yogurt for the sour cream. The soup is fine if made with frozen pitted cherries; just omit the first 5 minutes of simmering.

In a large saucepan, combine the cherry pits, water, wine, sugar, and lemon juice. Bring to a boil over medium heat, reduce the heat to low, and simmer, uncovered, for about 5 minutes. Remove from the heat. Cover and let steep for 5 minutes. Pour the liquid through a strainer set inside a bowl. Discard the pits.

Return the liquid to the pan. Add the pitted cherries, reserving about $1/3$ cup ($1 1/2$ oz/45 g) in a covered bowl in the refrigerator. Over medium heat, return the liquid to a boil, reduce the heat to low, and simmer gently for 5 minutes.

In small batches, purée the soup in a food mill, a food processor, or a blender. Transfer the purée to a bowl and stir in the kirsch and 1 tablespoon lemon zest. Let the soup cool to warm room temperature. Cover tightly and refrigerate until well chilled, 2–3 hours. Chill individual soup bowls in the refrigerator.

Before serving, put 2 cups (16 fl oz/500 ml) of the sour cream in a tureen and whisk briskly to liquefy it slightly. Then gradually whisk in the chilled soup. Ladle into the chilled bowls and garnish with dollops of the remaining sour cream, the reserved cherries, lemon zest, and mint sprigs.

Serves 6–8

2 lb (1 kg) red cherries, pitted, with pits reserved

1 cup (8 fl oz/250 ml) water

1 cup (8 fl oz/250 ml) medium-dry Riesling, Gewürztraminer, or other white wine

1/4 cup (2 oz/60 g) sugar

1/4 cup (2 fl oz/60 ml) fresh lemon juice

1/4 cup (2 fl oz/60 ml) kirsch

1 tablespoon grated or shredded lemon zest, plus extra for garnish

2 1/2 cups (20 fl oz/625 ml) sour cream

Fresh mint sprigs

Meat, Poultry & Seafood Soups

Mussels Provençale

Clams can be substituted for the mussels in this simple yet flavorful dish
from Provence. Garnish with lemon wedges, and serve with crusty French
bread for soaking up all the tasty juices. If you like, pour a crisp white wine.

3 lb (1.5 kg) mussels,
debearded and well scrubbed
(page 327)

1/2 cup (4 fl oz/125 ml) dry
white wine

1 small yellow onion, chopped

3 cloves garlic, coarsely
chopped, plus 2 cloves garlic,
minced

6 fresh parsley stems, plus
1/3 cup (1/2 oz/15 g) chopped
fresh parsley, preferably
flat-leaf (Italian)

Pinch of fresh or dried thyme

1 bay leaf

3–4 tablespoons fresh
lemon juice, or to taste

1/2 cup (4 fl oz/125 ml)
extra-virgin olive oil

Salt and freshly ground pepper

Discard any mussels that do not close to the touch. In a saucepan, bring the wine
to a boil. Add the mussels, onion, coarsely chopped garlic, parsley stems, thyme,
and bay leaf. Reduce the heat to medium, cover, and simmer, shaking the pan
periodically, until the mussels open, 2–4 minutes. Using a slotted spoon, transfer
the mussels to a large bowl and let cool. Discard any mussels that failed to open.

Strain the cooking liquid through a sieve lined with several layers of cheesecloth
(muslin) or a coffee filter into a small, clean saucepan. Reduce the liquid over high
heat by half to about $^1/_2$ cup (4 fl oz/125 ml). Let cool.

In a small bowl, whisk together the lemon juice, olive oil, minced garlic, reduced
cooking liquid, and salt and pepper to taste.

Add the dressing and the chopped parsley to the mussels. Toss well. Transfer to a
platter and serve.

Serves 6

Gazpacho with Shrimp

For a colorful presentation that also adds additional texture and flavor, prepare a variety of garnishes including croutons (page 326); finely diced green bell pepper; peeled, seeded, and diced cucumber; diced tomato; and finely diced red onion.

In a frying pan, bring the stock to a boil. Add the shrimp, reduce the heat to low, cover, and simmer for 1 minute. Uncover, stir lightly, re-cover, and simmer until the shrimp curl and are firm, 1 minute longer. Using a slotted spoon, transfer the shrimp to a bowl. Cover the shrimp and broth separately and refrigerate until cool.

In a large bowl, stir together the cooled broth, tomatoes, bell pepper, onion, cucumber, 5 tablespoons (2 1/2 fl oz/80 ml) of the vinegar, garlic, tomato juice, oil, and bread. In batches, purée the mixture in a blender on high speed until very smooth, 3–4 minutes. Pass the purée through a coarse-mesh sieve into another large bowl. Season to taste with salt, pepper, and vinegar. Chop the shrimp coarsely and stir into the purée. Cover and refrigerate until well chilled, about 3 hours.

To serve, ladle the soup into bowls and garnish.

Serves 6

1 cup (8 fl oz/250 ml) Fish Stock (page 317) or bottled clam juice

1/2 lb (250 g) shrimp (prawns), peeled and deveined (page 328)

3 cups (18 oz/560 g) peeled, halved, seeded, and chopped tomatoes (fresh or canned)

1 green bell pepper (capsicum), seeded, deribbed, and coarsely chopped

1 red onion, coarsely chopped

1 large cucumber, peeled, seeded, and coarsely chopped

5–6 tablespoons (2 1/2–3 fl oz/ 80–90 ml) red wine vinegar

3 large cloves garlic, minced

1 1/4 cups (10 fl oz/310 ml) tomato juice

1/4 cup (2 fl oz/60 ml) extra-virgin olive oil

1 slice coarse country white bread, crust removed, soaked in water to cover for 10 seconds, and squeezed dry

Salt and freshly ground pepper

Scallops à la Nage

The French phrase *à la nage* translates as "in the swim," describing a light bath of white wine, fish stock, and vegetables in which the bay scallops are poached and served.

3 cups (24 fl oz/750 ml)
Fish Stock (page 317) or water

3 cups (24 fl oz/750 ml) dry
white wine

1 small leek, including
tender green parts, trimmed,
carefully washed, and
thinly sliced

1 small yellow onion,
finely diced

1 small carrot, finely diced

1 small celery stalk,
finely diced

Salt and ground white pepper

1 lb (500 g) bay scallops

Fresh chervil or flat-leaf
(Italian) parsley sprigs

In a large saucepan over medium heat, combine the stock, wine, leek, onion, carrot, and celery. Bring to a boil. Reduce the heat to low. Simmer gently, uncovered, skimming off any foam that forms on the surface, until the vegetables are tender, about 10 minutes. Season to taste with salt and white pepper.

Add the scallops and simmer until just cooked through, 2–3 minutes. Ladle into warmed shallow soup plates or bowls and garnish with chervil.

Serves 4–6

Consommé with Grilled Seafood

Serve this soup at the start of an elegant dinner. If your market has fresh shiitake mushrooms, add them to the grill along with the seafood. Garnish with fresh chives cut into 1-inch (2.5 cm) lengths, if you like.

Preheat the broiler (grill) or a gas or electric grill until very hot, or prepare a fire in a charcoal grill.

In a saucepan, bring the stock to a boil over medium heat. Reduce the heat to very low and cover the pan.

Brush the scallops and shrimp with the melted butter and season lightly with salt and white pepper. Place them on a broiler tray or grill rack. Broil (grill) close to the heat source until well seared and barely cooked through, 1–2 minutes per side.

When the scallops and shrimp are almost done, ladle the hot stock into warmed large, shallow soup plates, taking care not to fill them all the way. Neatly place the scallops and shrimp in the stock; they should protrude slightly above the surface of the liquid. Float chives in the stock (see note), if desired. Serve immediately.

Serves 4–6

6 cups (48 fl oz/1.5 l)
Fish Stock (page 317)

1/2 lb (250 g) sea scallops

1/2 lb (250 g) shrimp (prawns), peeled and deveined (page 328)

2 tablespoons unsalted butter, melted

Salt and white pepper

Fresh chives, cut into 1-inch (2.5 cm) lengths (optional)

Tomato Soup with Mussels

3 tablespoons olive oil

2 large yellow onions, sliced

2 cloves garlic, minced

Pinch of cayenne pepper

1/4 cup (1/3 oz/10 g) chopped fresh flat-leaf (Italian) parsley

3 lb (1.5 kg) tomatoes, thickly sliced or cut into chunks

1 thin strip orange zest (optional)

30–36 mussels, debearded and well scrubbed (page 327)

1 cup (8 fl oz/250 ml) dry white wine or water

Salt and freshly ground pepper

Pinch of sugar, if needed

1/2 cup (4 fl oz/125 ml) heavy (double) cream (optional)

1/4 cup (3/8 oz/10 g) chopped fresh basil or flat-leaf (Italian) parsley or 6 tablespoons (3 fl oz/90 ml) Pesto (page 318) (optional)

In a large, heavy pot over medium heat, warm the oil. Add the onions and sauté, stirring occasionally, until tender, 8–10 minutes. Add the garlic, cayenne, and parsley. Cook for 1–2 minutes to release their flavors. Add the tomatoes and the orange zest, if using. Reduce the heat to low, cover, and cook, stirring often to prevent scorching, until the tomatoes have released their juices and are very tender, about 30 minutes.

Meanwhile, place the mussels in a large, wide saucepan, discarding any that do not close tightly when touched. Add the wine. Cover and place over high heat. Cook, shaking the pan occasionally, until the mussels open, 3–4 minutes. Using a slotted spoon, transfer the mussels to a colander placed over a bowl. Discard any mussels that did not open. Reserve the cooking liquid. When cool enough to handle, separate the mussels from their shells, carefully removing any remaining beards. Put the mussels in a small bowl and discard the shells. Position a sieve lined with cheesecloth (muslin) over another bowl and pour the reserved cooking liquid through it. Add the liquid to the mussels.

Remove the tomato mixture from the heat and let cool slightly. Working in batches, pass the mixture through a food mill or coarse sieve placed over a saucepan. Season to taste with salt and pepper. If the tomatoes are tart, add the sugar. For a smoother, sweeter soup, stir in the cream.

Place the tomato mixture over medium heat. When hot, add the mussels with their strained liquid, reduce the heat to low, and heat through. Season to taste with salt and pepper. Ladle into warmed bowls and garnish each serving with basil or parsley or a dollop of pesto, if desired.

Serves 6

Oyster Stew

Quick to prepare and wonderfully rich and delicious, this stew is a perfect recipe for oyster lovers. Serve the dish with oyster crackers and offer a dry white wine.

24 small oysters in the shell or bottled shucked oysters with their liquor

1/4 cup (2 oz/60 g) unsalted butter

1 small yellow onion, minced

1 celery stalk, chopped

Pinch of celery seeds, ground in a spice grinder or in a mortar with a pestle

2 cups (16 fl oz/500 ml) heavy (double) cream

2 cups (16 fl oz/500 ml) milk

1/4 teaspoon paprika

Salt and freshly ground pepper

If using oysters in the shell, shuck them as directed on page 257, reserving their liquor. Set aside.

In a soup pot over medium heat, melt the butter. Add the onion, celery, and celery seeds. Stir well, cover, and cook, stirring occasionally, until the vegetables are soft, about 12 minutes.

Add the cream, milk, paprika, and salt and pepper to taste. Heat just until bubbles form around the edge of the pot. Add the oysters and their liquor and simmer gently until the oysters are cooked, 1–2 minutes; they should be slightly firm to the touch. Do not allow to boil. Ladle the stew into warmed bowls and serve immediately.

Serves 6

Sherried Crab Bisque

A good seafood merchant will sell cooked, cracked crab in the shell. The shells are essential to enhance the flavor and color of this soup. Garnish with finely chopped fresh chives or tarragon, if desired.

In a large, heavy saucepan, melt the butter over medium-low heat. Add the shallots, onion, carrot, celery, bay leaf, and tarragon. Sauté until the vegetables begin to soften, 5–7 minutes. Add the crab shells and sauté, stirring, about 5 minutes longer.

Add the sherry, raise the heat to medium, stir briefly, and then add the white wine, water, and half of the crabmeat. Bring to a boil, reduce the heat to medium-low, and simmer briskly until the liquid reduces by about half, about 20 minutes.

Remove the crab shell pieces and discard. Transfer the pan contents to a food mill set inside a bowl and purée. Alternatively, pour the contents into a fine-mesh strainer set inside a bowl and press with a wooden spoon to extract all the liquid. Discard the solids.

Rinse the saucepan, return the purée to it, and bring to a boil over medium heat. Reduce the heat to low and stir in the cream, then the bread crumbs. Simmer briskly until thick, stirring occasionally, for about 10 minutes. Stir in the reserved crabmeat, simmer about 5 minutes longer, and season to taste with salt and white pepper. Ladle into warmed bowls, garnish (see note), and serve.

Serves 4–6

1/4 cup (2 oz/60 g) unsalted butter

2 shallots, finely chopped

1 large yellow onion, finely chopped

1 large carrot, finely chopped

1 celery stalk, finely chopped

1 bay leaf, crumbled

1 teaspoon finely chopped fresh tarragon or 1/2 teaspoon dried tarragon

2 whole steamed cracked crabs, meat removed and flaked, and shells broken into several pieces and reserved

3/4 cup (6 fl oz/180 ml) dry sherry

2 cups (16 fl oz/500 ml) dry white wine

2 cups (16 fl oz/500 ml) water

2 cups (16 fl oz/500 ml) heavy (double) cream

1 1/2 cups (3 oz/90 g) fresh bread crumbs

Salt and ground white pepper

Shellfish Gumbo

This hearty soup begins with a roux—a cooked mixture of flour and oil—which serves as a thickening agent. For additional flavor, add 6 green (spring) onions, sliced, and 3 tablespoons chopped fresh parsley with the shellfish.

1/2 cup (4 fl oz/125 ml) vegetable oil

1/4 cup (1 1/2 oz/45 g) all-purpose (plain) flour

3 yellow onions, chopped

4 cloves garlic, minced

1 celery stalk, chopped

1 green bell pepper (capsicum), seeded, deribbed, and chopped

1 lb (500 g) okra, trimmed and cut crosswise into slices 1/2 inch (12 mm) thick

1 cup (6 oz/185 g) peeled, halved, seeded, and chopped tomatoes (fresh or canned)

4 cups (32 fl oz/1 l) Fish Stock (page 317)

2 cups (16 fl oz/500 ml) water

1/4 teaspoon red pepper flakes

2 bay leaves

1 teaspoon chopped thyme

1/2 lb (250 g) cooked crabmeat

1 lb (500 g) prawns, peeled and deveined (page 328)

1/2 lb (250 g) bay scallops

Salt and freshly ground pepper

In a large soup pot over medium-low heat, warm the vegetable oil. Add the flour and cook, stirring, until the mixture is golden brown, about 10 minutes.

Add the yellow onions, garlic, celery, and bell pepper. Cook, stirring, until the vegetables soften, about 10 minutes. Add the okra and tomatoes, cover, and simmer gently, stirring occasionally until thickened slightly, about 10 minutes.

In a bowl or another vessel, combine the fish stock and water. Slowly add this mixture to the vegetables, a ladleful at a time, stirring constantly until all of the liquid has been used. Add the red pepper flakes, bay leaves, and thyme. Simmer gently, uncovered, for 30 minutes.

Add the crabmeat, prawns, scallops, and salt and pepper to taste. Simmer until the shellfish are cooked and the flavors are blended, about 10 minutes.

Discard the bay leaves. Ladle the gumbo into warmed bowls and serve immediately.

Serves 6

Creamy Crab Bisque

This rich and creamy soup is ideal for an elegant gathering. Garnish it with chopped fresh chives or parsley, and for a special treat, serve it with a glass of Champagne.

Clean and crack the crabs (page 322). Remove the meat from the body and legs as directed and set aside. Remove the meat from each large claw in a single piece, slice it, and set aside. Using heavy shears, cut the shells into small pieces. Set aside.

In a saucepan over low heat, melt the butter. Add the onion, carrot, celery, and tarragon. Sauté, stirring, until soft, about 15 minutes. Add the crab shells, tomatoes, bay leaf, bell pepper, and wine. Raise the heat to medium, bring to a boil, reduce the heat to low, cover, and simmer for 20 minutes. Remove from the heat and let cool.

In a large bowl, combine the fish stock and the water. Place one-third of the stock mixture and about one-third of the shell mixture in a blender. Pulse a few times until the shells break up. Line a fine-mesh sieve with cheesecloth (muslin) and place over a bowl. Pour the contents of the blender into the sieve. Repeat with the remaining stock and shell mixtures in 2 more batches.

Transfer 2 cups (16 fl oz/500 ml) of the strained mixture to a saucepan and bring to a boil. Add the rice, reduce the heat to low, cover, and simmer until very tender, about 20 minutes. Transfer the rice to the blender, add the remaining strained mixture, and blend until very smooth, 1–2 minutes.

Return the purée to the saucepan and bring to a simmer over low heat. Add the cream, lemon juice, and salt and pepper. Strain again through the fine-mesh sieve into a saucepan over low heat. Add the reserved crabmeat and stir to heat through. Ladle into bowls and garnish with the reserved claw meat. Serve immediately.

Serves 6–8

2 whole steamed crabs,
1–1 1/2 lb (500–750 g) each

3 tablespoons unsalted butter

1 yellow onion, diced

1 carrot, peeled and diced

2 celery stalks, diced

1/2 teaspoon chopped fresh tarragon or 1/4 teaspoon dried tarragon

1 1/2 cups (9 oz/280 g) chopped tomatoes (fresh or canned)

1 bay leaf

1 small red bell pepper (capsicum), seeded and coarsely chopped

1 cup (8 fl oz/250 ml) dry white wine

3 cups (24 fl oz/750 ml) Fish Stock (page 317) or bottled clam juice

1 1/2 cups (12 fl oz/375 ml) water

1/4 cup (3 oz/90 g) white rice

1 cup (8 fl oz/250 ml) heavy (double) cream

1 teaspoon fresh lemon juice

Salt and freshly ground pepper

Oyster Cream Soup

Fresh oysters and their liquor need only a few embellishments to produce a rich-tasting soup. Many fish markets will sell you shucked fresh oysters in their liquor, or you can shuck them yourself (page 257).

¹/₄ cup (2 oz/60 g) unsalted butter

1 boiling potato, peeled and cut into ¹/₄-inch (6-mm) dice

1 carrot, cut into ¹/₄-inch (6-mm) dice

1 celery stalk, cut into ¹/₄-inch (6-mm) dice

1 small onion, finely chopped

3 cups (1¹/₂ lb/750 g) shucked oysters with their liquor

2 cups (16 fl oz/500 ml) milk

2 cups (16 fl oz/500 ml) light (single) cream

1 teaspoon finely chopped fresh thyme

¹/₂–1 teaspoon hot-pepper sauce

Salt and freshly ground pepper

1 tablespoon chopped fresh chives

In a large saucepan, melt the butter over medium-low heat. Add the potato, carrot, celery, and onion and sauté until the onion is translucent, 2–3 minutes. Pour the oyster liquor through a fine-mesh sieve into the pan. Add the milk, cream, and thyme. Bring to a boil, reduce the heat to low, and simmer gently, uncovered, stirring frequently, until the vegetables are tender, 7–10 minutes.

Add the oysters and cook just until they turn tan and their edges curl, 2–3 minutes. Season to taste with hot-pepper sauce, salt, and pepper. Ladle into warmed shallow soup plates and garnish with the chives.

Serves 4–6

Lobster and Corn Chowder

Two live crabs can be substituted for the lobster, but should be cooked for 12 minutes. Clean and crack the crabs and remove the meat from the shells as directed on page 322, then use the shells for the broth.

In a stockpot, bring the water to a boil. If using water, add 1 tablespoon salt when it boils. Add the lobsters and cook until the shells are red, about 7 minutes. Using tongs, lift out the lobsters and let cool. Reserve the lobster broth.

Remove the lobster meat from the shells as directed on page 323. Dice the meat into $^1/_2$-inch (12-mm) pieces and set aside. Reserve the shells but discard the green tomalley, black intestinal vein, and any other organs. Cut the head section into small pieces and add them, along with all the shells and the wine, to the reserved lobster broth. Simmer over medium heat, uncovered, for 20 minutes. Strain through a fine-mesh sieve lined with cheesecloth (muslin) and reserve. While the lobster broth simmers, bring a saucepan three-fourths full of salted water to a boil. Add the potatoes and boil until tender. Drain and set aside. Using a sharp knife, cut the kernels from the ears of corn. You should have 2–2$^1/_2$ cups (12–15 oz/375–470 g). Set aside.

Rinse the stockpot, place over medium heat, and melt the butter. Add the onion and sauté, stirring, until soft, about 10 minutes. Set aside 1 cup (6 oz/185 g) of the corn kernels. Add the remaining corn to the pot along with the lobster broth. Simmer uncovered for 20 minutes, then transfer to a blender and purée until smooth. Pass the purée through a fine-mesh sieve into a clean saucepan.

Place the pan over medium heat. Add the cream, lobster meat, and reserved corn and potatoes. Season to taste with salt and pepper. Simmer for 5 minutes to heat through; do not boil. Ladle into warmed bowls and garnish with the parsley.

Serves 6

7 cups (56 fl oz/1.75 l) water or Court Bouillon (page 316)

Salt

2 live lobsters, about 1$^1/_4$ lb (625 g) each

$^1/_2$ cup (4 fl oz/125 ml) dry white wine

$^1/_2$ lb (250 g) potatoes, peeled and cut into $^1/_2$-inch (12-mm) dice

6 small ears of corn, husks and silk removed

1 tablespoon unsalted butter

1 yellow onion, finely chopped

$^1/_2$ cup (4 fl oz/125 ml) heavy (double) cream

Freshly ground pepper

1 tablespoon coarsely chopped fresh parsley or 6 parsley sprigs

Steamed Clams in Garlic Seafood Broth

Both a simple soup and a classic seafood appetizer, this dish satisfies shellfish lovers with its utter simplicity. Try cooking mussels the same way. Serve with plenty of crusty bread to sop up the broth.

4 dozen clams in the shell

1 tablespoon olive oil

4 cloves garlic, minced

4 cups (32 fl oz/1 l) Fish Stock (page 317)

1 cup (8 fl oz/250 ml) dry white wine

2 tablespoons unsalted butter

¹/₄ cup (¹/₃ oz/10 g) coarsely chopped fresh flat-leaf (Italian) parsley

2 large lemons, cut into wedges

Discard any clams that are cracked or that do not close to the touch. Clean the clams by soaking them for several minutes in cold water to cover generously. Under cold running water, scrub the shells clean with a small, stiff-bristled brush.

In a large pot, warm the oil over medium-low heat. Add the garlic and sauté for 1–2 minutes. Add the stock and wine, raise the heat to medium, and bring to a boil. Reduce the heat to medium-low, add the clams, cover, and steam just until they open, 7–10 minutes.

Line a strainer with cheesecloth (muslin) and set inside a large bowl. Pour the contents of the pot into the strainer. Discard any clams that failed to open.

Return the strained liquid to the pot over medium heat. Add the butter and parsley and stir until the butter melts. Arrange the clams in warmed shallow soup plates and ladle the broth over them. Serve with the lemon wedges.

Serves 6–8

Provençal Fish Soup

With its aromatic combination of saffron, olive oil, garlic, and tomatoes, this soup resembles the traditional bouillabaisse of the south of France. For a more elaborate soup, add fresh shrimp (prawns) or scallops.

Put the saffron threads and a pinch of salt in a metal kitchen spoon. Hold the spoon over heat for a few seconds, then use the back of a teaspoon to crush the threads into a powder. Set aside.

In a large pot over medium heat, warm the oil. Add the garlic, onion, leek, celery, and paprika. Sauté, stirring continuously, for 2–3 minutes. Add the potatoes, tomatoes, parsley, thyme, orange zest, and bay leaf. Cook, stirring occasionally for 5 minutes. Stir in the crushed saffron and salt, water, and wine. Season to taste with salt and pepper, cover, and simmer for about 15 minutes.

Add the fish to the pot and simmer, uncovered, until cooked through, 10–15 minutes. Add more water, if necessary, to keep the fish covered.

Discard the bay leaf. Taste and adjust the seasoning. Serve in warmed bowls.

Serves 4–6

1/2 teaspoon saffron threads

Salt and freshly ground pepper

3 tablespoons olive oil

3 cloves garlic, finely chopped

1 yellow onion, finely chopped

1 leek, trimmed, carefully washed, and thinly sliced

1 celery stalk, diced

1/4 teaspoon hot paprika

3 boiling potatoes, cubed

3 tomatoes, peeled (page 329) and coarsely chopped

3 fresh flat-leaf (Italian) parsley sprigs

2 fresh thyme sprigs

2 long, thin strips orange zest

1 bay leaf

5 cups (40 fl oz/1.25 l) water

1 cup (8 fl oz/250 ml) dry white wine

2 1/2 lb (1.25 kg) assorted white fish fillets, cut into 2-inch (5-cm) pieces

Fennel, Celery, and Oyster Soup

There is an appealing delicacy to the flavors of this creamy soup. If you like, substitute 6 leeks, including 3 inches (7.5 cm) of the tender green tops, carefully washed and chopped, in place of the fennel and celery.

If using oysters in the shell, shuck them as directed on page 257, reserving their liquor. Refrigerate the oysters. Set the liquor aside.

Cut off the feathery tops from the fennel bulbs and set aside. Remove the stalks and any tough or bruised outer leaves and discard. Coarsely chop 2 of the fennel bulbs.

In a soup pot over medium heat, melt 2 tablespoons of the butter. Add the onion and sauté until soft, about 10 minutes. Add the chopped fennel, celery, fish stock, water, and fresh oyster liquor. Bring to a boil, reduce the heat to medium-low, and simmer uncovered until the vegetables are very soft, about 30 minutes. Remove from the heat and let cool slightly.

Purée in a blender until very smooth, 3–4 minutes. Pass the purée through a fine-mesh sieve into a clean saucepan. Set aside.

Using a knife, cut the remaining fennel bulb into paper-thin slices. In a frying pan over low heat, melt the remaining 1 tablespoon butter. Add the sliced fennel, cover, and cook, stirring occasionally, until tender-crisp, about 10 minutes. Season to taste with salt and pepper.

Place the pan of purée over medium heat. Add the cream, oysters, and sautéed fennel. Bring to a gentle simmer and simmer uncovered until the oysters are slightly firm to the touch, 1–2 minutes. Add lemon juice to taste.

Chop the reserved fennel tops. Ladle the soup into warmed bowls, sprinkle with the fennel tops, and serve immediately.

Serves 6

18 small oysters in the shell or bottled shucked oysters, drained

3 large fennel bulbs, with stems and feathery tops intact

3 tablespoons unsalted butter

1 yellow onion, coarsely chopped

3 celery stalks, coarsely chopped

3 cups (24 fl oz/750 ml) Fish Stock (page 317) or bottled clam juice

2 cups (16 fl oz/500 ml) water

Salt and freshly ground pepper

1/2 cup (4 fl oz/125 ml) heavy (double) cream

1–2 teaspoons fresh lemon juice

Baja Seafood Chowder

Use whatever fresh seafood looks good at the market for this chowder. If you like, sauté 1 jalapeño chile, seeded and chopped, with the garlic, onion, bell pepper (capsicum), and red pepper flakes.

2 tablespoons olive oil

2 cloves garlic, finely chopped

1 yellow onion, finely chopped

1 large green bell pepper (capsicum), seeded, deribbed, and coarsely chopped

1 teaspoon red pepper flakes

1 cup (8 fl oz/250 ml) Fish Stock (page 317)

³/₄ cup (6 fl oz/180 ml) red wine

2 cans (1 lb/500 g each) tomatoes, coarsely chopped, with juice

2 tablespoons tomato paste

1¹/₂ tablespoons sugar

1 teaspoon *each* dried oregano and dried basil

1 bay leaf

1 baking potato, peeled and cut into ¹/₂-inch (12-mm) pieces

Salt and freshly ground pepper

12 small clams in the shell

¹/₂ lb (250 g) sea bass fillets

¹/₂ lb (250 g) small shrimp (prawns), peeled and deveined (page 328)

¹/₂ cup (³/₄ oz/ 20 g) cilantro (coriander), chopped (optional)

In a large pot, heat the oil over medium heat. Add the garlic, onion, bell pepper, and red pepper flakes. Sauté until the onion is translucent, 2–3 minutes. Add the stock, wine, tomatoes and their juice, tomato paste, sugar, oregano, basil, bay leaf, and potato. Bring to a boil, reduce the heat to low, cover, and simmer, stirring occasionally, until the soup is thick but still fairly liquid, about 30 minutes. Season to taste with salt and pepper.

Scrub the clams, discarding any that are cracked or that fail to close to the touch. Cut the fish into 1- to 2-inch (2.5- to 5- cm) pieces. Add the clams to the pot, along with the fish and shrimp. Raise the heat to medium-low, cover, and cook until the clams open, the fish flakes and the shrimp turn pink, 7–10 minutes. Discard any clams that failed to open.

Ladle into warmed bowls, garnish with cilantro, if desired, and serve.

Serves 8–10

Cream of Shrimp

A few aromatic vegetables, simple herbs, and cream highlight the natural sweetness of shrimp (prawns) in this rich yet light-bodied soup. For a spicier version, stir in some cayenne pepper to taste.

3 tablespoons unsalted butter

2 carrots, finely chopped

1 yellow onion, finely chopped

1 celery stalk, finely chopped

1 small baking potato, peeled and finely chopped

2 lb (1 kg) small shrimp (prawns), peeled and deveined (page 328), shells reserved

2 cups (16 fl oz/500 ml) Fish Stock (page 317)

2 cups (16 fl oz/500 ml) light (single) cream

1/2 tablespoon dried thyme

1 bay leaf, crumbled

Salt and ground white pepper

1 tablespoon fresh chervil or flat-leaf (Italian) parsley leaves

In a large saucepan, melt the butter over medium heat. Add the carrots, onion, celery, potato, and shrimp shells. Sauté until the onion is translucent and the shells turn pink, 2–3 minutes.

Add the stock, cream, thyme, bay leaf, and all but a handful of the shelled shrimp. Bring to a boil, reduce the heat to low, cover, and simmer for about 20 minutes.

In small batches, purée the soup in a food mill, a food processor, or a blender. If you use a processor or blender, force the purée through a strainer, pressing the solids with a wooden spoon. Return the soup to the pan and season to taste with salt and white pepper.

Add the remaining shrimp to the soup, cutting it into bite-sized chunks if you'd like. Simmer gently until cooked through, 2–3 minutes. Garnish with the chervil.

Serves 4–6

New England Clam Chowder with Leeks and Bacon

The flavor of the leeks and bacon highlight the natural sweetness of fresh clams. Fresh bay scallops would also be good prepared this way. Garnish with finely chopped fresh chives and parsley.

Discard any clams that are cracked or that fail to close to the touch. In a large pot, melt 1 tablespoon of the butter over medium-low heat. Add the garlic and sauté until it begins to soften, 1–2 minutes. Add the water and wine, raise the heat to medium, and bring to a boil. Reduce the heat to medium-low, immediately add the clams, cover, and steam just until they open, 7–10 minutes.

Line a strainer with cheesecloth (muslin) and set inside a large bowl. Pour the contents of the pot into the strainer. Discard any clams that failed to open. Set the clams and strained liquid aside separately.

Rinse out the pot, add the remaining 1 tablespoon butter, and place over medium heat. Add the bacon and sauté until it just begins to brown. Add the leek and sauté until it begins to soften, 2–3 minutes. Sprinkle in the flour and cook, stirring, for 1 minute.

Stirring continuously, pour in the reserved clam liquid and the cream. When the liquid reaches a boil, reduce the heat to a simmer. Add the potatoes and thyme.

Remove the clams from the shells. If they are large, cut them into $^1/_2$-inch (12-mm) pieces. When the potatoes are tender, after about 15 minutes, add the clams and simmer for 1–2 minutes. Season to taste with pepper. Ladle into warmed bowls and serve.

Serves 4–6

3 dozen clams in the shell, well scrubbed

2 tablespoons unsalted butter

1 clove garlic, minced

2 cups (16 fl oz/500 ml) water

1 cup (8 fl oz/250 ml) dry white wine

$^1/_4$ lb (125 g) lean bacon, rind removed, coarsely chopped

1 leek, including tender green parts, trimmed, carefully washed, and thinly sliced

1 tablespoon all-purpose (plain) flour

2 cups (16 fl oz/500 ml) light (single) cream

1 lb (500 g) red potatoes, peeled or unpeeled, cut into $^1/_2$-inch (12-mm) cubes

$^3/_4$ teaspoon dried thyme

Freshly ground pepper

Greek Chicken and Lemon Soup with Orzo

This fresh-tasting soup is thickened and flavored with a mixture of beaten egg and lemon juice. If you cannot find orzo, substitute an equal amount of long-grain white rice. Serve with toasted pita or hunks of sesame bread.

8 cups (64 fl oz/2 l) Chicken Stock (page 317)

3/4 cup (5 oz/155 g) orzo or other rice-shaped pasta

1 skinless, boneless chicken breast, 1/2 lb (250 g), cut crosswise into slices 1/4 inch (6 mm) thick

3 eggs

1/3 cup (3 fl oz/80 ml) fresh lemon juice

1 tablespoon grated lemon zest

Salt and ground white pepper

2 tablespoons finely chopped fresh flat-leaf (Italian) parsley

In a large saucepan, bring the stock to a boil over medium heat. Reduce the heat to medium-low, add the orzo, and cook, uncovered, until very tender, 15–20 minutes. About 5 minutes before the pasta is done, add the chicken slices.

Place the eggs in a bowl and whisk while pouring in the lemon juice. Stir in the zest. Whisking continuously, slowly pour a ladleful of the hot stock into the egg mixture. Reduce the heat to very low. While whisking the soup in the pan, slowly pour in the egg mixture; the soup should thicken slightly.

Season to taste with salt and white pepper. Remove from the heat, ladle immediately into warmed bowls, and garnish with the parsley.

Serves 6–8

Classic Deli Matzo Ball Soup

This soup of chicken broth with dumplings is traditionally served at the Passover feast. To add a little color to the matzo balls, stir 1–2 tablespoons finely chopped fresh parsley into the matzo-meal mixture.

Pour the 3 qt (3 l) stock into a large pot and add the carrots, celery, onion, and parsley. You should have a depth of at least 4 inches (10 cm) of liquid for the matzo balls to float in. Bring to a boil over medium heat and reduce the heat to maintain a bare simmer.

In a bowl, combine the matzo meal, the remaining 1 cup stock, egg yolks, chicken fat, salt, and white pepper, stirring well. In a separate bowl, beat the egg whites with a whisk until very frothy but still liquid. Using a rubber spatula, fold the whites into the matzo-meal mixture until blended smoothly.

Moistening your hands with cold water, gently and quickly shape the matzo mixture into smooth balls 2–3 inches (5–7.5 cm) in diameter. As the balls are formed, gently drop them into the simmering soup. Cover partially and cook for about 30 minutes.

Ladle the stock into warmed bowls, adding matzo balls and a few pieces of vegetables to each portion.

Serves 8–10

3 qt (3 l) plus 1 cup (8 fl oz/250 ml) Chicken Stock (page 317)

2 large carrots, cut into 1-inch (2.5-cm) chunks

2 large celery stalks, cut into 1-inch (2.5-cm) chunks

1 large yellow onion, cut into 1-inch (2.5-cm) chunks

1/2 cup (3/4 oz/20 g) coarsely chopped fresh flat-leaf (Italian) parsley

2 cups (9 oz/280 g) matzo meal

8 eggs, separated

1/2 cup (4 fl oz/125 ml) rendered chicken fat (schmaltz) or vegetable oil

1 teaspoon salt

1/2 teaspoon ground white pepper

Thai Spicy Chicken Soup with Lemongrass and Chiles

This simple clear soup, called *tom yum kai*, makes a satisfying light meal when served with steamed rice. The dried lime leaves, lemongrass, and the fish sauce, *nam pla*, are available in Southeast Asian food stores.

6 cups (48 fl oz/1.5 l) Chicken Stock (page 317)

6 dried lime leaves

2 stalks lemongrass, each about 8 inches (20 cm) long, cut into 1-inch (2.5-cm) pieces, or 2 long, thin strips lemon zest

2–4 small fresh hot green chiles, halved lengthwise

2–3 tablespoons Thai fish sauce

1/2–1 tablespoon hot chile oil

1 lb (500 g) skinless, boneless chicken breasts, cut crosswise into slices 1/4 inch (6 mm) thick

1 can (15 oz/470 g) straw mushrooms, drained

About 1/2 cup (4 fl oz/125 ml) fresh lime juice

1/2 cup (2/3 oz/20 g) roughly chopped fresh cilantro (fresh coriander) leaves (optional)

Combine the stock, lime leaves, and lemongrass in a large saucepan and bring to a boil over medium heat. Reduce the heat to low and simmer, uncovered, for about 10 minutes. Add the chiles and simmer for 5 minutes.

Stir in the fish sauce and chile oil to taste, then add the chicken slices and straw mushrooms. Simmer gently, skimming any foam from the surface, until the chicken is cooked through, about 5 minutes. Stir in the lime juice to taste. Immediately ladle into warmed bowls. Garnish with the cilantro, if desired.

Serves 4–6

Turkey and Root Vegetable Soup

When you roast a holiday turkey, use the carcass a day or two later in this robust soup. Vary the staple autumn vegetables according to what is available. If you like, serve the soup over steamed white or brown rice.

In a large pot, combine the carrots, parsnips, potatoes, onions, bay leaves, parsley, and thyme. Arrange the turkey carcass pieces on top and pour in the stock. Bring to a boil over medium heat, skimming away the foam from the surface. Reduce the heat to low, cover, and simmer gently, skimming occasionally, until the vegetables are very tender, 45–60 minutes.

Discard the bay leaves. Using a slotted spoon, remove the carcass pieces. Pick off any meat clinging to the bones and return the meat to the pot. Season to taste with salt and pepper and ladle into warmed bowls.

Serves 10–12

2 large carrots, cut into slices
1/2 inch (12 mm) thick

2 large parsnips, peeled and
cut into slices 1/2 inch (12 mm)
thick

2 large boiling potatoes, cut
into slices 1/2 inch (12 mm)
thick

2 large yellow onions, thickly
sliced

2 bay leaves

1/2 cup (3/4 oz/20 g) coarsely
chopped fresh flat-leaf
(Italian) parsley

1 tablespoon dried thyme

1 roast turkey carcass, with
some meat attached, broken
into about 6 large pieces

2 1/2 qt (2.5 l) Chicken Stock
(page 317)

Salt and freshly ground pepper

Mulligatawny with Tandoori-Style Chicken

If you like, garnish this East Indian soup with mint raita, quickly made by stirring together ½ cup (4 oz/125 g) low-fat plain yogurt, 2 tablespoons finely shredded fresh mint leaves, and 1 tablespoon fresh lemon juice.

½ cup (4 oz/125 g) low-fat plain yogurt

1 tablespoon fresh lemon juice

1½ tablespoons curry powder

1 teaspoon sweet paprika

1 lb (500 g) skinless, boneless chicken breasts

2 tablespoons vegetable oil

2 tablespoons unsalted butter

1 yellow onion, finely chopped

1 clove garlic, finely chopped

1 hot fresh green chile, seeded and finely chopped

1 teaspoon peeled and grated fresh ginger

6 cups (48 fl oz/1.5 l) Chicken Stock (page 317)

4 plum (Roma) tomatoes, peeled, seeded, and finely chopped (page 329)

1 large tart green apple, cored, peeled, and finely chopped

1 carrot, coarsely chopped

Salt and freshly ground pepper

In a bowl, stir together the yogurt, lemon juice, ½ tablespoon of the curry powder, and the paprika. Turn the chicken breasts in this mixture, cover tightly, and refrigerate for 30–60 minutes.

In a large saucepan, warm the oil and butter over medium heat. Add the onion, garlic, chile, and ginger. Sauté until the onion is translucent, 2–3 minutes. Stir in the remaining 1 tablespoon curry powder and sauté for 1 minute. Add the stock, tomatoes, apple, and carrot. Bring to a boil. Reduce the heat to low, cover, and simmer for about 30 minutes.

Meanwhile, preheat the broiler (grill) or a gas or electric grill until very hot. About 10 minutes before serving, remove the chicken from the yogurt marinade and season to taste with salt and pepper. Broil or grill, close to the heat source, turning once, until cooked through and golden brown, 4–5 minutes per side.

Before serving the soup, taste and adjust the seasoning. Cut the chicken crosswise into slices ¼ inch (6 mm) thick. Ladle the soup into warmed shallow soup plates and arrange the chicken slices on top.

Serves 6–8

Lamb and Chickpea Soup

Lamb has an assertive taste and is often paired with strong sauces or spices. This rustic soup is inspired by North African cooking, which uses these ingredients in many different preparations.

Pick over the chickpeas, discarding any misshapen peas or impurities. Place the chickpeas in a bowl, add cold water to cover, and let soak for about 12 hours.

In a large pot, heat the oil over medium heat. Season the lamb with salt and pepper and sauté until evenly browned, 3–4 minutes on each side. Remove the lamb and set it aside. Pour off all but about 2 tablespoons of the fat.

Add the onion, carrot, and garlic to the pot and sauté over medium heat until the onion is translucent, 2–3 minutes. Add the coriander, cumin, and cayenne. Sauté for 1 minute. Pour in the stock and deglaze the pot by stirring and scraping to dislodge any browned bits. Return the lamb to the pot. Drain the chickpeas and add them to the pot along with the tomatoes. Add 4 of the lemon quarters. Bring to a boil, reduce the heat to low, cover, and simmer gently until the lamb and chickpeas are tender, 2–2 1/2 hours, skimming regularly.

Remove the lamb from the pot. Cut out and discard the bones and excess fat. Cut the meat into small, coarse chunks and set aside. Discard the lemon quarters. Purée about half of the chickpea mixture in a food mill, a food processor, or a blender. Stir the purée and lamb chunks back into the pot. Taste and adjust the seasoning.

Ladle into warmed bowls. Garnish with the green onions and parsley. Accompany with the remaining lemon wedges.

Serves 6–8

1 1/4 cups (7.5 oz/235 g) dried chickpeas (garbanzo beans)

2 tablespoons olive oil

1 1/2 lb (750 g) lamb shoulder, in one piece

Salt and freshly ground pepper

1 yellow onion, finely chopped

1 carrot, finely chopped

1 clove garlic, finely chopped

3/4 teaspoon ground coriander

3/4 teaspoon ground cumin

1/4 teaspoon cayenne pepper

5 cups (40 fl oz/1.25 l) Chicken or Meat Stock (page 317 or 318)

2 large plum (Roma) tomatoes, coarsely chopped

3 large lemons, cut into quarters

2 green (spring) onions, including tender green parts, thinly sliced

1/4 cup (1/3 oz/10 g) coarsely chopped fresh flat-leaf (Italian) parsley

Sweet-and-Sour Cabbage Soup with Flank Steak

This Eastern European favorite makes the most of economical flank steak. Serve with thick slices of rye bread and garnish with coarsely chopped fresh parsley.

1/4 cup (2 fl oz/60 ml) vegetable oil

1 large yellow onion, coarsely chopped

2 cloves garlic, coarsely chopped

1 lb (500 g) flank steak, well trimmed of fat

Salt and freshly ground pepper

8 cups (64 fl oz/2 l) Meat Stock (page 318) or water

1 can (1 lb/500 g) plum (Roma) tomatoes, with juice

1/3 cup (3 fl oz/80 ml) fresh lemon juice

1/4 cup (2 oz/60 g) sugar

1/4 cup (1 1/2 oz/45 g) golden raisins (sultanas) or dark raisins

1 head savoy cabbage, cored and cut into shreds 1/2 inch (12 mm) wide

2 bay leaves

In a large pot, warm the oil over medium-low heat. Add the onion and garlic and sauté until the onion is translucent, 2–3 minutes. Lightly season the flank steak with salt and pepper, add to the pan, and sauté, turning once, until lightly browned, 2–3 minutes on each side.

Add the stock and deglaze the pan by stirring and scraping to dislodge any browned bits. Add the tomatoes and their juice, crushing them slightly with a wooden spoon. Stir in the lemon juice, sugar, raisins, cabbage, and bay leaves. Raise the heat to medium and bring to a boil. Reduce the heat to low, cover partially, and simmer gently until the meat is tender, about 1 hour.

Discard the bay leaves. Remove the meat from the pot. Using a sharp knife and a fork, cut and tear the meat into coarse, bite-sized shreds. Stir the shreds back into the pot. Taste the soup and adjust the seasoning. Ladle the soup into warmed bowls and garnish (see note), if desired.

Serves 8–10

Albóndigas with Beef-and-Tortilla Meatballs

The Spanish word *albóndigas* refers both to the meatballs and to the soup in which they are cooked. Ground (minced) pork or turkey may be substituted for the beef. Serve with warm corn tortillas.

In a bowl, stir together the beef, eggs, onion, tortilla chips, cilantro, oregano, salt, pepper, and cumin. Cover tightly and refrigerate for 1 hour.

Pour the stock into a large saucepan. Add the tomatoes, crushing them slightly with a wooden spoon. Stir in the sugar, red pepper flakes, carrots, celery, onion, and bay leaf. Bring to a boil over medium heat, then reduce the heat to low and simmer.

Moistening your hands with cold water, form the beef mixture into balls 1–1 1/2 inches (2.5–4 cm) in diameter and slip them carefully into the simmering stock. Cover and simmer gently until the meatballs are cooked through and the vegetables are tender, about 20 minutes.

Discard the bay leaf. Taste the soup and adjust the seasoning. Ladle into warmed bowls and serve.

Serves 8–10

1 lb (500 g) lean ground (minced) beef

4 eggs, lightly beaten

1/2 small red onion, finely chopped

3/4 cup (3 oz/90 g) crushed tortilla chips

1/4 cup (1/3 oz/10 g) chopped fresh cilantro (fresh coriander)

1 tablespoon dried oregano

1 teaspoon salt

1/2 teaspoon freshly ground black pepper

1/2 teaspoon ground cumin

7 cups (56 fl oz/1.75 l) Meat Stock (page 318)

1 can (1 lb/500 g) tomatoes

2 teaspoons sugar

1 teaspoon red pepper flakes

2 carrots, coarsely chopped

2 celery stalks, chopped

1 onion, coarsely chopped

1 bay leaf

Lamb and Bean Soup

The combination of lentils, lamb, and spices makes this a distinctly Middle Eastern dish. Fresh lemon juice is an important last-minute addition. It lightens the soup and balances both the vibrant spices and the strong flavor of the lamb.

½ cup (3½ oz/105 g) dried chickpeas (garbanzo beans)

Salt

2 tablespoons unsalted butter

1 tablespoon olive oil

½ lb (250 g) boneless lamb from leg or shoulder, cut into ½-inch (12-mm) cubes

2 yellow onions, chopped

2 cloves garlic, minced

1 teaspoon ground cinnamon

½ teaspoon ground ginger

½ teaspoon ground turmeric

6 cups (48 fl oz/1.5 l) water, or more as needed

⅔ cup (5 oz/155 g) dried lentils

1½ cups (9 oz/280 g) canned plum (Roma) tomato purée

½ cup (¾ oz/20 g) chopped fresh flat-leaf (Italian) parsley

¼ cup (⅓ oz/10 g) chopped fresh cilantro (fresh coriander)

Freshly ground pepper

2–3 tablespoons fresh lemon juice

Pick over the chickpeas, discarding any misshapen peas or impurities. Rinse well and place in a saucepan with plenty of water to cover. Bring to a boil over high heat, boil for 2 minutes, remove from the heat, and let stand for 1 hour.

Drain the chickpeas and transfer to a saucepan. Add fresh water to cover by 2 inches (5 cm) and bring to a boil over medium heat. Reduce the heat to low, cover, and simmer until cooked through but not falling apart, about 1 hour. Add salt to taste during the last 15 minutes of cooking. Remove from the heat, drain, and set aside. You should have about 1½ cups (10½ oz/330 g).

In a large sauté pan over high heat, melt the butter with the oil. When hot, add the lamb and brown well on all sides, 8–10 minutes. Reduce the heat to medium and add the onions, garlic, cinnamon, ginger, and turmeric. Cook, stirring, until the onions are soft, about 3 minutes. Add 3 cups (24 fl oz/750 ml) of the water or more as needed to cover the lamb. Bring to a boil over medium heat, reduce the heat to low, and simmer, uncovered, for 30 minutes.

In a large saucepan over high heat, bring the remaining 3 cups (24 fl oz/750 ml) water to a boil. Add the lentils, reduce the heat to low, and simmer, uncovered, for 20 minutes. Add the lamb mixture, drained chickpeas, tomato purée, parsley, and cilantro. Continue to simmer for 20 minutes longer. Add salt to taste and a generous amount of pepper; the soup should be peppery.

Remove from the heat. Stir in 2 tablespoons of the lemon juice. Taste and adjust the seasoning with more lemon juice, if desired. Ladle into warmed bowls and serve.

Serves 6–8

Chinese Hot-and-Sour Soup with Duck

One of the great specialties of Chinese cuisine, hot-and-sour soup may also be made with lean pork loin, beef steak, or chicken breast in place of the duck used here. All the special ingredients are readily found in Asian food shops.

Put the tree fungus, lily buds, and shiitake mushrooms in separate bowls and cover each generously with cold water. Let soak for about 30 minutes.

Using a sharp knife, cut the duck breast lengthwise into thin slices. Cut the slices lengthwise into thin strips, then cut the strips crosswise into pieces about 2 inches (5 cm) long. In a bowl, combine half each of the soy sauce, cornstarch (cornflour), sesame oil, and pepper with all of the rice wine and sugar. Add the duck pieces, toss, and marinate at room temperature for 15–30 minutes.

Drain the tree fungus, lily buds, and shiitakes. Rinse well to remove any grit. Cut off and discard the shiitake stems. Cut the tree fungus and shiitakes into thin strips; leave the lily buds whole.

In a large saucepan, bring the stock to a boil over medium heat, then reduce the heat until the stock simmers. Add the tofu, tree fungus, lily buds, and shiitakes. In a small bowl, stir together the vinegar, chile oil, and the remaining soy sauce and cornstarch until smoothly blended. Stir the vinegar mixture into the stock along with the duck pieces and their marinade and the remaining pepper. Pour in the egg and stir immediately so it forms thin wisps. Stir in the remaining sesame oil, ladle the soup immediately into warmed bowls, and garnish with the green onions.

Serves 4–6

1/4 cup (1 oz/30 g) small dried black tree fungus

2 tablespoons dried lily buds

6 dried shiitake mushrooms

1 skinless, boneless duck breast, 4–6 oz (125–185 g)

2 tablespoons soy sauce

2 tablespoons cornstarch (cornflour)

2 teaspoons sesame oil

1/2 tablespoon freshly ground pepper

1 teaspoon Chinese rice wine or dry sherry

1/2 teaspoon sugar

5 cups (40 fl oz/1.25 l) Chicken Stock (page 317)

1/2 lb (250 g) firm tofu, well drained and cut into 1/2-inch (12-mm) cubes

1/3 cup (3 fl oz/80 ml) rice vinegar or cider vinegar

1/2–1 teaspoon hot chile oil

1 egg, beaten

2 large green (spring) onions, including tender green parts, thinly sliced

Sausage and Black Bean Soup

In parts of the Caribbean and Latin America, black beans are enjoyed in appetizer and main-course dishes. You may vary this soup by substituting smoked ham or smoked turkey for the sausage.

3 cups (21 oz/655 g) dried black beans

1³/4 lb (875 g) chorizo, andouille, or other spicy sausages

1 tablespoon olive oil

4 cloves garlic, finely chopped

2 yellow onions, finely chopped

2 celery stalks, finely chopped

2¹/2 qt (2.5 l) Chicken or Meat Stock (pages 317 or 318)

¹/4 cup (¹/3 oz/10 g) finely chopped fresh flat-leaf (Italian) parsley

1 teaspoon dried oregano

¹/2 teaspoon ground cumin

2 bay leaves

¹/2 tablespoon salt

¹/2 cup (4 oz/125 g) sour cream

2 tablespoons finely chopped fresh chives

2 tablespoons finely chopped fresh cilantro (fresh coriander)

Pick over the beans, discarding any misshapen beans or impurities. Set aside.

Remove the casings from 1 lb (500 g) of the sausages. In a large saucepan, warm the oil over medium heat. Add the sausage and sauté, coarsely breaking up the meat with a wooden spoon, until lightly browned, about 5 minutes. Pour off all but about 3 tablespoons of the fat. Return the pan to medium heat, add the garlic, onions, and celery, and sauté until the onions are translucent, 2–3 minutes.

Add the beans, stock, parsley, oregano, cumin, and bay leaves and bring to a boil. Reduce the heat to low, cover, and simmer gently until the beans are very tender, 2–2¹/2 hours, adding half of the salt halfway through the cooking and a little water, if necessary, to keep the beans moist.

Discard the bay leaves. Purée a few ladlefuls of beans in a food mill, food processor, or a blender. Stir the purée back into the pan with the remaining salt. Taste and adjust the seasoning.

Cut the remaining sausages into slices ¹/2 inch (12 mm) thick. Sauté in a nonstick frying pan over medium heat until browned, about 3 minutes per side. Ladle the soup into warmed bowls. Garnish each serving with the sour cream, sausage slices, chives, and cilantro.

Serves 6–8

Hungarian Pork Goulash

True Hungarian *gulyás* is a rustic peasant soup or stew of meat, onions, and potatoes, seasoned with earthy hot paprika — its unmistakable signature — and caraway seeds. Serve over egg noodles.

In a large saucepan, warm the butter and oil over medium heat. Add the onion and garlic and sauté until the onion is translucent, 2–3 minutes. Raise the heat to medium-high, add the pork, and sauté until it is lightly browned, 3–5 minutes. Sprinkle in the paprika and caraway seeds and sauté for 1 minute longer.

Add the stock, wine, and potatoes. Bring to a boil and deglaze the pan by stirring and scraping to dislodge any browned bits. Reduce the heat to medium and simmer, uncovered, until the pork and potatoes are tender, about 30 minutes.

Season to taste with salt and pepper, ladle into warmed bowls, and garnish with the sour cream and chives.

Serves 6–8

1/4 cup (2 oz/60 g) unsalted butter

2 tablespoons vegetable oil

1 yellow onion, finely chopped

2 cloves garlic, finely chopped

1 lb (500 g) pork tenderloin, trimmed of fat and cut into 1/4- to 1/2-inch (6- to 12-mm) cubes

2 tablespoons hot paprika

1/2 tablespoon caraway seeds

8 cups (64 fl oz/2 l) Meat Stock (page 318)

1 cup (8 fl oz/250 ml) dry white wine

2 boiling potatoes, peeled and cut into 1/4- to 1/2-inch (6- to 12-mm) cubes

Salt and freshly ground pepper

3/4 cup (6 oz/180 g) sour cream

1/4 cup (1/3 oz/10 g) chopped fresh chives

Fruit & Vegetable Salads

Tossed Green Salad with Vinaigrette

The classic vinaigrette combines 1 part vinegar with 4 or more parts oil. Mustard, herbs, or anchovy can be added for extra flavor. Include any variety of fresh greens such as butter (Boston) lettuce, frisée, arugula (rocket), and mixed baby lettuces.

4 cups (4 oz/125 g) loosely packed, assorted salad greens (see note)

FOR HERB VINAIGRETTE:

1 tablespoon wine vinegar

$1/8$–$1/4$ teaspoon salt

1 teaspoon *each* finely chopped fresh flat-leaf (Italian) parsley, chives, chervil, and tarragon

Freshly ground pepper

$1/4$ cup (2 fl oz/60 ml) olive oil, preferably extra-virgin

Rinse the salad greens thoroughly, drain, and spin dry in a salad spinner or blot dry between 2 kitchen towels. Tear into bite-sized pieces, if necessary, and place in a salad bowl.

To make the herb vinaigrette, pour the vinegar into a small bowl, add the salt to taste, and stir to dissolve. Add the herbs, pepper to taste, and whisk in the olive oil.

(Alternatively, you can make a mustard or anchovy vinaigrette. To make the mustard vinaigrette, substitute the herbs with $1/2$ teaspoon dry mustard, add pepper to taste, then whisk in the olive oil. To make the anchovy vinaigrette, omit the salt. Using 2 anchovy fillets packed in olive oil and drained, crush to a paste with a spoon. Stir in the anchovies with the pepper to taste, then whisk in the olive oil.)

Pour the vinaigrette over the salad greens and toss gently. Serve immediately.

Serves 4

Watercress and Orange Salad

For this sunny Mediterranean salad, use only pale, very tender celery stalks and the small leaves of the watercress. Avocado slices can be used in place of the orange slices. For a more substantial dish, add smoked herring fillet and a few olives.

Remove and discard the tough stems and large leaves from the watercress. Arrange in a salad bowl.

Cut a slice off the top and bottom of each orange, cutting deeply enough to reveal the fruit. Place each orange upright on a cutting board and cut off the peel in strips, removing all the white pith and membrane. Cut the peeled oranges crosswise into $1/8$-inch-thick slices. Pick out and discard any seeds. Add the orange slices to the salad bowl, along with the celery.

In a small bowl, stir together the lemon juice, vinegar, curry powder, and salt and pepper to taste until well mixed. Add the oil and stir vigorously until blended. Pour the dressing over the salad, toss well, and serve.

Serves 4

1¼ lb (625 g) watercress

2 large oranges

4 celery stalks, thinly sliced crosswise

1 tablespoon fresh lemon juice

1 tablespoon white wine vinegar

1 tablespoon curry powder

Salt and freshly ground pepper

⅓ cup (3 fl oz/80 ml) extra-virgin olive oil

Broccoli and Avocado Salad

Nutritious and flavorful, this simple and attractive salad pairs well with pork, poultry, or game, and it is also easily doubled for large gatherings. To serve as a main dish, add crab or lobster meat.

1¹/₂ lb (750 g) young, tender broccoli

1 avocado

2 tablespoons fresh lemon juice

¹/₂ cup (2 oz/60 g) pecans, coarsely chopped

1 tablespoon Dijon mustard

Salt

¹/₄ cup (2 fl oz/60 ml) extra-virgin olive oil

1 tablespoon finely chopped fresh flat-leaf (Italian) parsley

Cut the broccoli florets from the large stems. (Reserve the large stems for making soup or another use.) Bring a saucepan of salted water to a boil. Add the florets and boil until barely tender, about 3 minutes. Drain, cool under cold running water, and drain again. Set aside.

Peel and pit the avocado and cut it into cubes. Place in a small bowl and toss with 1 tablespoon of the lemon juice to prevent darkening. Place the avocado and broccoli in a salad bowl and add the pecans.

In a small bowl, stir together the remaining 1 tablespoon lemon juice, the mustard, and salt to taste until well mixed. Add the oil and parsley and stir vigorously until blended. Pour the dressing over the salad, toss gently, and serve.

Serves 4

Roasted Bell Pepper Salad

This salad can be kept in a tightly sealed container in the refrigerator for a few days, enhancing the flavor even more. If you like, increase the quantity of garlic and add some finely chopped fresh basil.

Preheat the oven to 350°F (180°C).

Arrange the bell peppers in a shallow baking dish. Bake, turning them often, until they become completely soft, about 30 minutes.

Remove from the oven. While the bell peppers are still warm, peel them, if desired. Split in half lengthwise and remove and discard the stems, seeds, and ribs. Cut them into long, narrow strips.

Rub the inside of a shallow serving bowl with the cut sides of the garlic clove. Arrange the bell pepper strips in the bowl and season to taste with salt and pepper. Sprinkle with the parsley and lightly drizzle with the oil. Stir well. Let stand at room temperature for about 2 hours before serving, to allow the flavors to blend.

Serves 4

2 large yellow bell peppers (capsicums)

2 large red bell peppers (capsicums)

1 clove garlic, cut in half

Salt and freshly ground pepper

1 tablespoon finely chopped fresh flat-leaf (Italian) parsley

6 tablespoons (3 fl oz/90 ml) extra-virgin olive oil

Goat Cheese, Mushroom, Endive, and Radicchio Salad

Beautiful and very satisfying, this stylish salad takes advantage of the quality goat cheeses now available at most supermarkets. It also makes a great main course to a light brunch. Serve with hot crusty bread.

2 heads radicchio, leaves separated

2 tablespoons sherry vinegar or balsamic vinegar

1/2 teaspoon salt

1/4 teaspoon freshly ground pepper

1 1/2 tablespoons Dijon mustard

1/4 cup (2 fl oz/60 ml) walnut oil

1/4 cup (2 fl oz/60 ml) olive oil

1/2 lb (250 g) creamy fresh goat cheese, in a log 1 1/2–2 inches (4–5 cm) in diameter

2 heads Belgian endive (chicory/witloof), trimmed and thinly sliced crosswise

1/4 lb (125 g) fresh white mushrooms, thinly sliced

1 red bell pepper (capsicum) roasted, peeled, and cut lengthwise into thin strips (page 324)

Preheat the broiler (grill).

Arrange the radicchio leaves on individual salad plates to form cups. Set aside.

In a small bowl, stir together the vinegar, salt, and pepper until the salt dissolves. Stir in the mustard. Beating continuously with a fork or small whisk, pour in the walnut and olive oils in a thin, steady stream, and beat until emulsified. Set aside.

Grease a flameproof baking dish with nonstick cooking spray. Cut the goat cheese into 4 equal rounds and place them in the prepared baking dish. Broil until golden brown, 2–3 minutes.

While the cheese is broiling, combine the endive and mushrooms in another bowl. Toss well with enough of the dressing to coat them evenly. Arrange the mixture in mounds atop the radicchio on each salad plate.

As soon as the cheese is done, use a spatula to transfer each round to a salad plate, placing it atop the endive-mushroom salad. Spoon a little more dressing on top and garnish with the roasted bell pepper strips. Serve immediately.

Serves 4

Grapefruit, Black Olive, and Mint Salad

The idea for this unusual salad comes from cookbook author Marion Cunningham. The clear, fresh flavors of this dish complement a main course of fish or chicken.

2 large grapefruits, preferably pink

1 cup (1 oz/30 g) fresh mint leaves, stems removed

1/2 cup (2 1/2 oz/75 g) sliced black olives

2 tablespoons olive oil

1 teaspoon fresh lemon juice

1/4 teaspoon salt

Several leaves of butter (Boston) lettuce or iceberg lettuce

Using a small, sharp knife, cut a slice off the top and the bottom of each grapefruit, cutting deeply enough to expose the fruit. Place each grapefruit upright on a cutting board and slice off the peel in strips, removing all of the white pith and exposing the fruit all around. Working over a sieve set in a large bowl and using a small, sharp knife, remove the grapefruit sections by cutting them away from the membrane, first on one side of each section and then on the other. Let the whole sections fall into the sieve. Remove any seeds and discard.

Pour off any juice in the bowl and reserve for another use (it makes a refreshing drink). In the bowl, combine the grapefruit sections, mint, olives, oil, lemon juice, and salt. Toss gently to combine, taking care not to break the grapefruit sections.

To serve, line a platter or individual plates with the lettuce leaves and spoon the grapefruit mixture on top. Serve immediately.

Serves 4

Cucumber Salad with Dill

This lovely summertime salad is typical of the southern Mediterranean region. It can be enjoyed as a side dish or an appetizer, served with a few slices of red onion on a bed of greens.

Peel and thinly slice the cucumbers, then place the slices on a flat plate. Salt lightly and tilt the plate so that excess water will drain off easily. Let stand for about 1 hour.

Pass the garlic cloves through a garlic press into a small bowl. Add the yogurt, lemon juice, and dill. Add salt and white pepper to taste. Stir until well mixed. Add the oil and stir vigorously until blended.

Place the drained cucumber slices in a salad bowl, pour the dressing over the top, and toss gently to coat the slices evenly. Refrigerate for about 1 hour to allow the flavors to blend before serving.

Serves 4

4 cucumbers

Salt

3 cloves garlic

²/₃ cup (5 oz/155 g) plain yogurt

1 tablespoon fresh lemon juice

2 tablespoons finely chopped fresh dill

Ground white pepper

3 tablespoons extra-virgin olive oil

Butter Lettuce and Tarragon Salad

Fresh and light, this salad makes a nice side dish to fish or meat. If it is served with fish, substitute lemon juice for the vinegar. Fresh finely chopped basil and flat-leaf (Italian) parsley can be added to the dressing.

Discard the largest and darkest lettuce leaves; use only the most tender ones. If the leaves are large, tear them into pieces. Arrange in a salad bowl and sprinkle with the tarragon and chives.

In a small bowl, stir together the vinegar, mustard, and salt to taste until well mixed. Add the oil and stir vigorously with a fork until blended. Pour the dressing over the lettuce and herbs, toss well, and serve.

Serves 4

2 small heads butter (Boston) lettuce, separated into leaves

2 tablespoons fresh tarragon leaves

2 tablespoons finely chopped fresh chives

1 tablespoon red wine vinegar

1 tablespoon Dijon mustard

Salt

¼ cup (2 fl oz/60 ml) extra-virgin olive oil

Artichoke Heart and Orzo Salad

This refreshing pasta salad takes well to the addition of neatly cut leftover vegetables. It can also stand on its own at a springtime buffet or dinner party. For a bright accent, add roasted yellow bell pepper (capsicum) with the diced red pepper.

2¹⁄₂ qt (2.5 l) water

¹⁄₃ cup (3 fl oz/80 ml) fresh lemon juice, plus the juice of 1 lemon

14–16 baby artichokes, about 1 lb (500 g) total weight

¹⁄₂ lb (250 g) orzo or other rice-shaped pasta

2 tablespoons olive oil

¹⁄₄ cup (1¹⁄₂ oz/45 g) red bell pepper (capsicum) roasted, peeled (page 324), and diced

2 tablespoons Dijon mustard

2 tablespoons white wine vinegar

2 tablespoons fresh tarragon or flat-leaf (Italian) parsley or ¹⁄₂ teaspoon dried tarragon, chopped

Salt and freshly ground pepper

In a large saucepan, combine the water and the ¹⁄₃ cup lemon juice and bring to a rolling boil over high heat.

Meanwhile, add the juice of 1 lemon to a bowl of water. Working with 1 artichoke at a time, pull off and discard the tough outer leaves until you reach the more tender yellow-green leaves. Cut off about 1 inch (2.5 cm) from the top to remove the thorny tips of the leaves. Cut off the stem end even with the bottom. Cut the trimmed artichokes into halves or quarters, depending on their size, and trim away any thorny choke. The pieces should be about ¹⁄₂ inch (12 mm) thick. As each artichoke is finished, drop it into the bowl of lemon water.

Drain the artichoke pieces. Add the artichokes and orzo to the boiling water. Boil until the orzo is al dente and the artichokes are tender when pierced with the tip of a sharp knife, about 8–10 minutes. Drain the artichokes and orzo well and place in a large bowl. Add the oil. Using a fork, toss to coat evenly. Let cool, stirring and tossing occasionally.

While the salad cools, in a small bowl, combine the roasted bell pepper, mustard, vinegar, and tarragon. Using a fork, stir to combine. Add to the orzo mixture and stir and toss to coat the ingredients evenly. Season to taste with salt and pepper. Serve immediately.

Serves 4

Creamy Red Potato Salad with Celery Seeds

The red skins on the potatoes add extra color and texture to this salad. Fresh celery and celery seeds add a double dose of flavor. Serve on a bed of mixed greens. This salad is perfect with cold roast beef or chicken.

3 lb (1.5 kg) red potatoes, unpeeled and well scrubbed

3/4 cup (6 fl oz/180 ml) sour cream

3/4 cup (6 fl oz/180 ml) Mayonnaise (page 318)

2 celery stalks, finely diced

1 tablespoon celery seeds

2 tablespoons chopped plus 1 tablespoon minced green (spring) onion

5 tablespoons (1/2 oz/15 g) chopped fresh flat-leaf (Italian) parsley

1 teaspoon dry mustard

1/2 teaspoon salt

1/4 teaspoon ground white pepper

Bring a large pot three-fourths full of salted water to a boil over high heat. Add the potatoes and cook until tender but slightly resistant when pierced with a fork, 25–30 minutes. Drain and let cool, then cut the unpeeled potatoes into 1-inch (2.5-cm) cubes. Place in a bowl.

To make the dressing, in a small bowl, combine the sour cream, mayonnaise, celery, celery seeds, the chopped green onion, 4 tablespoons of the parsley, the mustard, salt, and white pepper. Mix well.

Pour the dressing over the potatoes and mix gently until evenly coated. Taste and adjust the seasoning. Transfer to a serving bowl and garnish with the remaining 1 tablespoon parsley and the minced green onion.

Before serving, cover and refrigerate for 1–2 hours to chill and blend the flavors.

Serves 6–8

Cabbage Salad with Cumin Seeds

A chopped apple and 2 tablespoons raisins are possible additions here. An alternative dressing can be made using extra-virgin olive oil, pressed garlic, anchovy paste, and vinegar.

Remove and discard the larger leaves from the cabbage, then cut it lengthwise into quarters. Cut each quarter into long, very thin strips. Set aside.

In a salad bowl, stir together the cream, vinegar, and sugar. Add salt and white pepper to taste. Add the cabbage and mix gently. Sprinkle with the cumin seeds and let stand for 30 minutes to allow the flavors to blend before serving.

Serves 4

1 head savoy cabbage, about 13 oz (410 g)

1/2 cup (4 fl oz/125 ml) heavy (double) cream

1 tablespoon red wine vinegar

1 tablespoon sugar

Salt and ground white pepper

1 tablespoon cumin seeds

Eggplant and Tomato Salad

This Moroccan eggplant salad is best made in the summertime, when tomatoes are ripe and flavorful. For a smoky flavor, grill the eggplants (aubergines) over a charcoal fire, turning frequently to prevent burning. For a milder taste, roast them in the oven.

Preheat the broiler (grill).

Prick each eggplant in a few places with a fork. Place on a baking sheet and slip under the broiler (grill). Broil (grill), turning often, until blistered and charred on all sides and soft throughout, 15–20 minutes. If the eggplants darken too quickly and are not yet soft, finish cooking them in a 400°F (200°C) oven. (Alternatively, bake the eggplants in a preheated 400°F/200°C oven, turning often, for 45 minutes.) Remove the eggplants from the broiler or oven. Slit open and scoop the pulp into a colander. Discard the skins and any large seed pockets. Let the pulp stand for about 15 minutes to drain off the bitter juices.

If using cumin seeds, in a small frying pan over low heat, toast the seeds, stirring occasionally, until fragrant, 2–3 minutes. Transfer to a spice grinder or a mortar and pestle and grind to a powder. If using ground cumin, in a small frying pan over low heat, warm the cumin, stirring occasionally, until fragrant, 1–2 minutes.

Chop the eggplant pulp coarsely and place in a bowl. Fold in the cumin, garlic, 2 tablespoons of the lemon juice, 1/3 cup of the oil, paprika, and cayenne. Then fold in the tomatoes and the cilantro. Add more oil and lemon juice to adjust the taste and texture. Season to taste with salt and pepper. Serve at room temperature.

Serves 6

3 eggplants (aubergines), about 1 lb (500 g) each

3 tablespoons cumin seeds or 2 tablespoons ground cumin

4 cloves garlic, minced

2–3 tablespoons fresh lemon juice

1/3–1/2 cup (3–4 fl oz/ 80–125 ml) olive oil

2 teaspoons paprika

1/4 teaspoon cayenne pepper

2 tomatoes, peeled, seeded and chopped (page 329)

3 tablespoons finely chopped fresh cilantro (fresh coriander) or flat-leaf (Italian) parsley

Salt and freshly ground pepper

Apple and Chicory Salad

Quick and easy to prepare, this perfect summer salad can be enriched with cubed Swiss cheese and tossed with Mayonnaise (page 318) in place of the sour cream dressing. Another pleasant addition is a thick slice of ham, cut into small pieces.

Fill a large bowl with water and add the lemon juice. Core the apples, but do not peel them. Cut them into 1-inch (2.5-cm) chunks, dropping them into the bowl of water as they are cut to prevent darkening. Drain well and transfer to a salad bowl along with the celery and chicory.

In a small bowl, stir together the sour cream, yogurt, horseradish, and salt and pepper to taste until well mixed. Pour the dressing over the salad, add the walnuts, toss well, and serve.

Serves 4

1 tablespoon fresh lemon juice

3 red apples

3 celery stalks, thinly sliced crosswise

1 small heart of chicory (curly endive), torn into pieces

2/3 cup (5 oz/155 g) sour cream

2 tablespoons plain yogurt

1 tablespoon freshly grated horseradish

Salt and freshly ground pepper

6 walnut halves, coarsely chopped

Two-Color Salad

This salad can be enjoyed warm or cold. Delicate and slightly sweet, it goes well with meats, fish, or cheeses. Mayonnaise (page 318) flavored with fresh mint and chives can be used in place of the cream dressing.

1¼ cups (6 oz/185 g) shelled English peas

¼ lb (125 g) green beans, trimmed

2 carrots, about 6 oz (185 g) total weight, peeled and cut into long, thin strips

2 zucchini (courgettes), about 6 oz (185 g) total weight, cut into small cubes

1 tablespoon dry white wine

1 tablespoon tarragon vinegar

2 tablespoons heavy (double) cream

2 tablespoons sunflower oil

Salt

Arrange the peas and beans on a steamer rack, place over a pan of boiling water, cover, and steam for 5 minutes. Add the carrots and steam for 2–3 minutes longer. Add the zucchini and steam until all the vegetables are tender, 2–3 minutes longer. Transfer to a serving plate.

Meanwhile, in a small bowl, stir together the wine, vinegar, cream, oil, and salt to taste until well blended. Pour over the vegetables and serve.

Serves 4

Spinach and Pear Salad

The spinach leaves should be young and tender — the smaller the better. If they are large, pull off the stems and tear the leaves into smaller pieces. You can also use watercress leaves in place of the spinach.

To make the vinegar-mustard dressing, in a small bowl, combine the vinegar and mustard. Using a whisk or fork, stir until smooth. Add the oil and sugar and whisk or stir until blended. Add salt and pepper to taste and mix well. Set aside.

To make the chutney dressing, in another small bowl, combine the chutney and yogurt. Stir until blended. (If the chutney contains large, irregular pieces of fruit, purée the dressing in a food processor or blender, if you wish.) Set aside.

Carefully rinse the spinach leaves, and gently spin or pat dry. Place in a large bowl.

Peel, halve, and core the pears. Cut each pear half crosswise into thin slices, cutting all the way through but keeping each half intact.

To assemble the salad, drizzle the vinegar-mustard dressing over the spinach leaves and toss to coat the spinach evenly. Divide the spinach among individual plates. Arrange the pear halves, fanning the slices slightly, on top of the spinach. Spoon the chutney dressing over each pear half. Serve immediately.

Serves 4

FOR THE VINEGAR–MUSTARD DRESSING:

2 tablespoons raspberry vinegar or balsamic vinegar

1 tablespoon Dijon mustard

1 tablespoon walnut oil or olive oil

2 teaspoons sugar

Salt and freshly ground pepper

FOR THE CHUTNEY DRESSING:

1/4 cup (2 1/2 oz/75 g) store-bought mango or peach chutney

1/4 cup (2 oz/60 g) low-fat plain yogurt

8 cups (8 oz/250 g) loosely packed spinach leaves (see note)

2 pears such as Bosc or Bartlett (Williams')

Orange and Fennel Salad

Fennel is a pale green, bulbous vegetable with a feathery top and a delicious licorice-like flavor. It is available in most supermarkets. Sweet orange slices, trimmed of their bitter skin and pith, offer a perfect foil to fennel's assertive taste.

4 navel oranges or large Valencia oranges

4 small fennel bulbs, about 1½ lb (750 g) total weight

2 green (spring) onions, white part only, thinly sliced

2 cups (2 oz/60 g) loosely packed baby spinach leaves, carefully rinsed and dried

1 tablespoon red wine vinegar

1 teaspoon salt

Freshly ground pepper

¼ cup (2 fl oz/60 ml) olive oil

Using a small, sharp knife, cut a slice off the top and bottom of each orange, cutting deeply enough to reveal the fruit. Then cut off the peel, removing all the white pith and membrane. Holding the fruit over a bowl to catch the juices, cut along both sides of each segment to free it from the membrane, letting the segments drop into the bowl. Pick out and discard any seeds. Finally, squeeze any remaining juice from the empty membranes into the bowl before discarding the membranes.

Trim off any feathery tops from the fennel bulbs and discard. Cut away any discolored areas from the bulbs. Cut the bulbs and tender stalks crosswise into very thin slices and add to the orange sections, along with the green onions. Divide the spinach leaves among 4 salad plates.

In a small bowl, combine the vinegar and salt. Stir to dissolve the salt. Add pepper to taste and then slowly whisk in the olive oil to form an emulsion. Pour the vinaigrette over the orange mixture and toss gently. Spoon over the spinach leaves, dividing evenly, and serve.

Serves 4

Grapefruit and Olive Salad
with Red-Leaf Lettuce

This tasty salad goes well with chicken or fish. Select an aromatic mustard for the dressing. In the colder months, the salad can be made heartier with the addition of cooked beets, red cabbage, red onion, and some pomegranate seeds.

If the lettuce leaves are large, tear them into pieces. Place in a salad bowl.

Cut a slice off the top and bottom of each grapefruit, cutting deeply enough to reveal the fruit. Then cut off the peel, removing all the white pith and membrane. Cut along both sides of each segment to free it from the membrane, letting the segments drop into a bowl. Pick out and discard any seeds. Add the grapefruit segments to the salad bowl along with the olives.

In a small bowl, stir together the mustard, vinegar, sugar, and salt and white pepper to taste until well mixed. Add the oil and stir vigorously until blended. Pour the dressing over the salad, toss well, and serve.

Serves 4

1 head red-leaf lettuce, separated into leaves

2 grapefruits

12 black olives, pitted

2 tablespoons strong-flavored mustard

1 teaspoon cider vinegar

1 teaspoon sugar

Salt and ground white pepper

1/4 cup (2 fl oz/60 ml) extra-virgin olive oil

Artichoke and Fennel Salad

Use the most tender part of the artichoke — the heart and the pale leaves that surround it. For a richer salad, use Yogurt Dressing (page 142) in place of the olive oil.

2 tablespoons fresh lemon juice

4 young, tender artichokes, about 5 oz (155 g) each

2 fennel bulbs, thinly sliced crosswise

1 tablespoon finely chopped fresh dill

1 handful of finely chopped fresh mint

Salt and ground white pepper

¼ cup (2 fl oz/60 ml) extra-virgin olive oil

Yogurt Dressing, optional (page 142)

Fill a large bowl with water and add 1 tablespoon of the lemon juice. Trim off the stem and remove the outer leaves from each artichoke until you reach the pale, tender inner leaves. As each artichoke is stripped, cut it in half lengthwise, trim away any fuzzy choke, and drop the halves into the lemon water to prevent darkening. Drain, pat dry with paper towels, and cut lengthwise into thin slices. Place the slices in a salad bowl, add the remaining 1 tablespoon lemon juice, and toss to coat the slices evenly.

Arrange the fennel slices in the bowl with the artichokes. Scatter the dill and mint over the top. Sprinkle with salt and white pepper to taste. Drizzle with the oil and serve immediately.

Serves 4

Asparagus and Red Pepper Salad

Green asparagus spears contrast with bright red bell pepper (capsicum) strips in this springtime salad, which makes a fitting first course for an elegant supper. Offer it as a prelude to roast chicken or baked pasta.

To make the dressing, in a food processor or blender, combine $^1/_2$ cup (3 oz/90 g) of the bell pepper strips with the vinegar and mustard. Purée until smooth. Add the tarragon and season to taste with salt and pepper.

Toss $^1/_4$ cup (2 fl oz/60 ml) of the dressing with the remaining bell pepper strips. Set aside the dressed pepper strips and the remaining dressing.

Cut or snap off the tough, pale, fibrous bottoms from the asparagus spears. If the spears are especially large, peel the tough skin: Using a vegetable peeler and starting about halfway down from the tip, peel away the thin outer skin. Choose a frying pan large enough to hold the asparagus flat and fill three-fourths full with water. Bring to a boil, add the asparagus spears, and boil until just tender, 3–5 minutes. The timing will depend on the size of the spears. Drain, pat dry with paper towels, and let cool.

To serve, spread the asparagus on a platter or divide among individual plates. Top with the dressed bell pepper strips. Spoon the remaining dressing over the top. Garnish with the herb sprigs and serve.

Serves 4

4 large red bell peppers (capsicums), roasted, peeled, and cut lengthwise into strips about $^1/_4$ inch (6 mm) wide (page 324)

2 tablespoons red or white wine vinegar

1 tablespoon Dijon mustard

2 tablespoons chopped fresh tarragon or $^1/_2$ teaspoon dried tarragon

Salt and freshly ground pepper

1 lb (500 g) asparagus (16–20 spears)

4 fresh tarragon, flat-leaf (Italian) parsley, or watercress sprigs

Mixed Green Salad with Country Dressing

All kinds of greens work with this salad: butter (Boston) lettuce, Bibb lettuce, escarole, oakleaf lettuce, tender spinach leaves, dandelion, watercress, and radicchio. If you prefer, substitute Yogurt Dressing (page 142) for the country dressing.

FOR THE COUNTRY DRESSING:

2 cloves garlic, thinly sliced or passed through a garlic press

1 tablespoon honey

Salt

1 tablespoon red wine vinegar or balsamic vinegar

¼ cup (2 fl oz/60 ml) extra-virgin olive oil

1 large handful of green-leaf lettuce leaves, about 3 oz (90 g), torn if large

1 large handful of romaine (cos) lettuce leaves, about 3 oz (90 g), torn if large

1 small bunch arugula (rocket), stemmed

1 cucumber, peeled and thinly sliced

1 green bell pepper (capsicum), seeded, deribbed, and finely chopped

To make the country dressing, in a small bowl, stir together the garlic, honey, and salt to taste until well mixed. Add the vinegar and then the oil, stirring vigorously until blended. Let stand for about 10 minutes to allow the flavors to blend.

Arrange the lettuces and arugula in a salad bowl. Add the cucumber and bell pepper. Pour the dressing over the salad, toss, and serve.

Serves 4

Warm Potato and Chicory Salad

The pleasure of this salad is the combination of hot onions and potatoes with cold chicory. It makes an excellent accompaniment to grilled or roasted meats and fish. To serve it as a main course, add some flaked tuna and capers.

2 white onions, about
6 oz (185 g) total weight,
unpeeled

2 russet potatoes, about
10 oz (315 g) total weight

1 heart of chicory (curly
endive), torn into pieces

1 tablespoon finely chopped
fresh oregano

1 tablespoon white wine
vinegar

Salt and freshly ground pepper

3 tablespoons extra-virgin
olive oil

Preheat the oven to 350°F (180°C).

Place the onions in a small, shallow baking dish and bake until they are completely soft, about 1 hour.

When the onions have been cooking for 30 minutes, begin to prepare the potatoes. Peel them and cut into 1-inch (2.5-cm) cubes. Arrange on a steamer rack above boiling water, cover, and steam until tender, about 20 minutes.

Place the chicory in a salad bowl. As soon as the onions are cooked, remove and discard the skins, chop the onions coarsely, and add them while still hot to the chicory. Then add the warm potatoes and sprinkle with the oregano.

In a small bowl, stir together the vinegar and salt and pepper to taste until well mixed. Add the oil and stir vigorously until blended. Pour the dressing over the salad, toss well, and serve immediately.

Serves 4

Orange, Fennel, and Endive Salad

Colorful and refreshing, this salad combines tart-sweet oranges, licorice-flavored fennel, and slightly bitter endive with a walnut-and-orange vinaigrette. It is excellent in the wintertime when oranges are at their peak.

To make the vinaigrette, in a bowl, whisk together the walnut and olive oils, vinegar, orange and lemon juices, and salt and pepper to taste. Taste and add the sugar if needed to balance the tartness of the citrus juice.

To make the salad, cut a slice off the top and bottom of each orange, cutting deeply enough to reveal the fruit. Then cut off the peel, removing all the white pith and membrane. Cut along both sides of each segment to free it from the membrane, letting the segments drop into a bowl. Pick out and discard any seeds.

In a small bowl, combine the walnuts with a few tablespoons of the vinaigrette and let stand for 10 minutes.

Trim off any stems and feathery tops from the fennel bulbs and discard. Cut any bruised outer stalks. Cut each bulb in half lengthwise and remove the tough core. Thinly slice each half lengthwise and place in a large bowl. Remove the cores from the endives and separate the leaves. Add to the bowl holding the fennel.

Add the remaining vinaigrette to the endive and fennel and toss well. Divide evenly among individual plates and distribute the orange segments on top. Sprinkle with the walnuts and serve.

Serves 6

FOR THE VINAIGRETTE:

1/3 cup (3 fl oz/80 ml) walnut oil

3 tablespoons olive oil

1 tablespoon balsamic vinegar

1/4 cup (2 fl oz/60 ml) fresh orange juice

1 tablespoon fresh lemon juice

Salt and freshly ground pepper

Pinch of sugar, if needed

3 large oranges

1/2 cup (2 oz/60 g) walnuts, toasted (page 328) and coarsely chopped

3 small fennel bulbs

3 heads Belgian endive (chicory/witloof)

Carrot and Cumin Salad with Yogurt Dressing

This tasty salad goes well with simple dishes such as grilled meats or omelets. Celery makes an interesting alternative to carrots. Sesame, poppy, or mustard seeds can replace the cumin seeds.

FOR THE YOGURT DRESSING:

1 tablespoon Dijon mustard

Salt and white pepper

1 tablespoon fresh lemon juice

2/3 cup (5 oz/155 g) plain yogurt

2 tablespoons extra-virgin olive oil

1 tablespoon finely chopped fresh flat-leaf (Italian) parsley

1 lb (500 g) carrots, peeled and thinly sliced

1 tablespoon cumin seeds

To make the dressing, in a small bowl, stir together the mustard and salt and white pepper to taste. Add the lemon juice. Stir well to dissolve and blend all the ingredients. Mix in the yogurt until thoroughly incorporated, then vigorously stir in the oil. Sprinkle the parsley over the top, then mix it in well. Cover and refrigerate for 30 minutes.

To serve, arrange the carrots in a serving bowl, pour the dressing over the top, toss, and sprinkle with the cumin seeds.

Serves 4

Zucchini and Mint Salad

It is important to use very young, tender zucchini (courgettes) in this salad. The result will be a delicate, refreshing flavor that complements omelets, fish, or cheeses.

Fill a bowl with water and ice cubes, add the zucchini, and refrigerate for 2 hours. (This makes the zucchini crunchy and easier to cut.)

Drain the zucchini and dry well, then cut crosswise into very thin slices. Arrange the slices on a serving plate.

In a small bowl, stir together the lemon juice and mint. Add salt and cayenne to taste and stir until well mixed. Add the oil and stir vigorously until blended. Pour the dressing over the zucchini and serve.

Serves 4

8 baby zucchini (courgettes), about 3/4 lb (375 g) total weight

2 tablespoons fresh lemon juice

1 tablespoon finely chopped fresh mint leaves

Salt

Cayenne pepper

1/4 cup (2 fl oz/60 ml) extra-virgin olive oil

Beet Salad with Feta

In Mediterranean countries, salads made with beets are dressed simply with olive oil and vinegar, or, as here, sprinkled with feta cheese. Reserve the beet greens, boil until tender, and use in place of the watercress, if you like.

If the greens are still attached to the beets, cut them off, leaving about 1 inch (2.5 cm) of the stem intact. Scrub the beets well under cold running water but do not break the skin, or the color will bleed as they are boiled. Place in a saucepan with water to cover. Bring to a boil over high heat, cover partially, reduce the heat to low, and simmer until tender, 30–40 minutes for large beets or 15–20 minutes for small beets. Drain the beets and put them briefly in a bowl of cold water to cool. Peel the beets and slice them or cut them into quarters, depending on their size. Place in a bowl.

In a small bowl, whisk together the oil, vinegar, garlic, half of the mint, the allspice, and salt and pepper to taste to form a vinaigrette.

Place the onion slices in a small bowl and dress with a few tablespoons of the vinaigrette. Let stand for 15 minutes.

Add 1/4 cup (2 fl oz/60 ml) of the vinaigrette to the beets and toss well. Add the onion and toss to mix. In a separate bowl, toss the watercress with the remaining vinaigrette and arrange on a platter. Distribute the beets and onion evenly over the greens. Sprinkle with the feta cheese and the remaining 1/4 cup (1/3 oz/10 g) mint. Serve immediately.

Serves 4

4 large or 8 small beets

1/2 cup (4 fl oz/125 ml) extra-virgin olive oil

3 tablespoons red wine vinegar or 1/4 cup (2 fl oz/ 60 ml) fresh lemon juice

1 clove garlic, minced

1/2 cup (2/3 oz/20 g) chopped fresh mint

1/2 teaspoon ground allspice

Salt and freshly ground pepper

1 red onion, thinly sliced

6–7 cups (6–7 oz/185–220 g) young, tender watercress sprigs (about 4 bunches) or baby spinach leaves, carefully rinsed

1 cup (5 oz/155 g) crumbled feta cheese

German Potato Salad

Serve this salad warm for a comforting wintertime lunch. Another version of this salad could include 6 slices of bacon, cut into 1-inch (2.5-cm) pieces and sautéed until crisp. Add the bacon to the warm dressing, when you add the vinegar.

2 lb (1 kg) red or white potatoes, unpeeled and well scrubbed

6 tablespoons (3 fl oz/90 ml) olive oil

1 yellow onion, thinly sliced

2 teaspoons all-purpose (plain) flour

1 tablespoon sugar

1/2 teaspoon salt

1/4 teaspoon freshly ground pepper

1/2 cup (4 fl oz/125 ml) water

1/4 cup (2 fl oz/60 ml) cider vinegar

6 tablespoons (1/2 oz/15 g) finely chopped fresh flat-leaf (Italian) parsley

Bring a large pot three-fourths full of salted water to a boil over high heat. Add the potatoes and cook until tender but slightly resistant when pierced with a fork, 25–30 minutes. Drain and let cool slightly, then peel and cut into slices 1 inch (2.5 cm) thick. Place in a serving bowl.

In a frying pan, heat the oil over medium heat. Add the onion and sauté until soft and lightly browned, about 5 minutes. Stir in the flour, sugar, salt, pepper, and water. Continue to cook until the dressing begins to thicken, 3–5 minutes. Add the vinegar and 4 tablespoons of the parsley and cook for 1 minute longer. Taste and adjust the seasoning.

Pour the dressing over the potatoes and mix gently to coat evenly. Garnish with the remaining 2 tablespoons parsley and serve immediately.

Serves 4–6

Fresh Fruit Salad in Melon Boat

Use only the finest seasonal fruits for this salad. Cherries, strawberries, figs, mangoes, and pears can be added to or substituted for the fruits listed here. For a richer dressing, use light (single) cream in place of the citrus juices.

1 cantaloupe

2 peaches, peeled if desired

6 apricots, peeled if desired

1 small bunch seedless grapes, about 6 oz (185 g), stemmed

2 tablespoons confectioners' (icing) sugar

Juice of 1 orange

Juice of 1 lemon

Thin strips lemon zest for garnish (optional)

Cut off about 2 inches (5 cm) of the stem end of the melon. Remove the seeds and discard. Scoop out the flesh in small balls and place in a bowl. Cover and refrigerate the carved-out melon boat.

Pit the peaches and apricots and cut them into thin slices or cubes. Add them to the bowl holding the melon balls along with the grapes. Sift the sugar over the top and then sprinkle with the orange and lemon juices. Stir well.

Spoon the fruit mixture into the melon boat and garnish with lemon zest, if desired. Serve immediately or refrigerate for 30 minutes before serving.

Serves 4

Orange and Date Salad

Dates are a good source of protein and iron and they pair nicely with many types of fruits and nuts. Chopped unsalted pistachios or hazelnuts (filberts) can be strewn over the top of this simple, sweet, and flavorful mélange.

Cut a slice off the top and bottom of each orange, cutting deeply enough to reveal the fruit. Place each orange upright on a cutting board and cut off the peel in strips, removing all the white pith and membrane. Cut crosswise into thin slices and remove any seeds. Arrange on a serving platter. Top with the banana slices and then with the date halves.

In a small bowl, stir together the honey and lemon juice until well mixed. Add the cinnamon and stir well, then pour evenly over the fruit. Cover and refrigerate for about 2 hours before serving.

Serves 4

4 oranges

2 bananas, peeled and sliced crosswise

12 dates, pitted and halved lengthwise

3 tablespoons honey

Juice of 2 lemons

1 teaspoon ground cinnamon

Grapefruit and Fennel Salad

Apples or strawberries go well alongside or in place of the grapefruit, in which case fresh mint should be used instead of parsley. Pine nuts are an elegant substitute for the almonds.

2 pink grapefruits

2 fennel bulbs, thinly sliced crosswise

1/2 cup (3 oz/90 g) almonds, coarsely chopped

3 tablespoons apple juice

1/4 cup (2 oz/60 g) plain yogurt

Salt

Freshly ground green peppercorns

1 tablespoon chopped fresh flat-leaf (Italian) parsley

Cut a slice off the top and bottom of each grapefruit, cutting deeply enough to reveal the fruit. Then cut off the peel in strips, removing all the white pith and membrane. Cut along both sides of each segment to free it from the membrane, letting the segments drop into a bowl. Pick out and discard any seeds. Place the grapefruit segments in a salad bowl and add the fennel and almonds.

In a small bowl, stir together the apple juice, yogurt, and salt and ground green peppercorns to taste until well mixed. Pour the dressing over the salad and toss well. Sprinkle with the parsley and serve.

Serves 4

Grape and Carrot Mold

Very refined, this exquisite molded salad can be served as an appetizer course for an elegant meal — perhaps prepared in individual molds — or between courses. It can also accompany meat and cheese dishes.

Pour half of the stock into a small saucepan and add the gelatin. Let stand to soften for 3 minutes. Place the pan over low heat and stir until the gelatin dissolves. Remove from the heat and pour into a bowl. Add the remaining stock, the lemon juice, Worcestershire sauce, parsley, and salt and white pepper to taste. Stir well.

Rinse a 1-qt (1-l) mold or 4 small individual molds in cold water and pour in enough of the stock mixture to form a thin layer in the bottom of the dish(es). Let stand for 30 minutes.

Add the grapes and carrots to the mold(s) and then pour in the remaining stock mixture. Cover and refrigerate for a few hours until set.

Carefully run a knife tip around the edge of the mold(s). Dip the mold(s) briefly in hot water, place an inverted serving plate or individual plates on top, and invert the plate and mold(s) together. Serve immediately.

Serves 4

2 cups (16 fl oz/500 ml) Vegetable Stock (page 316)

1 packet plus 1 teaspoon unflavored powdered gelatin

1/4 cup (2 fl oz/60 ml) fresh lemon juice

1 tablespoon Worcestershire sauce

2 tablespoons finely chopped fresh flat-leaf (Italian) parsley

Salt and ground white pepper

1 bunch seedless green grapes, about 10 oz (315 g), stemmed and cut in half

4 carrots, about 6 oz (185 g) total weight, peeled and cut lengthwise into thin strips

White Wine and Peach Salad

In wintertime, use red wine in place of white and substitute apples or pears for the peaches. These winter fruits will need to be simmered in the red wine—sugar mixture over low heat until they are tender, about 10 minutes, then cooled before serving.

Place the peaches in a salad bowl. In a separate bowl, stir together the sugar and wine until the sugar is thoroughly dissolved. Pour the dressing over the peaches, cover, and refrigerate for at least 1 hour, or for up to 12 hours, before serving.

Serves 4

6 white peaches, peeled, pitted, and cut lengthwise into thin slices

1¼ cups (5 oz/155 g) confectioners' (icing) sugar

2 cups (16 fl oz/500 ml) dry white wine

Berry and Banana Salad

For a luxurious touch, wash the berries with a little white wine instead of water, to preserve their perfume. This salad can also be dressed with white wine and sugar or, if you prefer, with cream and sugar.

½ lb (250 g) strawberries, stemmed and thinly sliced lengthwise

½ lb (250 g) blueberries

2 bananas, peeled and thinly sliced

1 cup (4 oz/125 g) confectioners' (icing) sugar

Juice of 1 orange

Juice of ½ lemon

Combine the berries and bananas in a salad bowl. In a small bowl, stir together the sugar and the orange and lemon juices until the sugar dissolves. Pour the dressing over the fruit and serve.

Serves 4

Meat, Poultry & Seafood Salads

Shrimp Caesar Salad

Here is a delicious variation on a classic salad. Two types of olive oil are used to give the dressing a more balanced flavor. Marinating the shrimp (prawns) briefly in the dressing helps to meld the flavors of the salad.

1/2 cup (4 fl oz/125 ml)
Fish Stock (page 317)
or bottled clam juice

1 lb (500 g) shrimp (prawns),
peeled and deveined
(page 328)

1/2 baguette, about 1 1/2 inches
(4 cm) in diameter

3 tablespoons plus 1/4 cup
(2 fl oz/60 ml) olive oil

2 cloves garlic

1 teaspoon Dijon mustard

3 tablespoons fresh lemon
juice

3 anchovy fillets, soaked
in cold water to cover for
5 minutes, drained, patted
dry, and mashed

1 egg yolk

1/4 cup (2 fl oz/60 ml)
extra-virgin olive oil

Salt and freshly ground pepper

2 heads romaine (cos) lettuce,
separated into leaves

1/2 cup (2 oz/60 g) grated
Parmesan cheese

Preheat the oven to 350°F (180°C). Oil a baking sheet.

In a frying pan, bring the fish stock to a boil. Add the shrimp, reduce the heat to low, cover, and simmer for 1 minute. Uncover, stir lightly, re-cover, and cook until the shrimp curl and are firm, 1 minute longer. Using a slotted spoon, transfer the shrimp to a bowl and let cool slightly. Cover and refrigerate. Raise the heat to high and reduce the cooking liquid to 2 tablespoons. Cover and refrigerate.

Cut the baguette into slices 1/4 inch (6 mm) thick. Using a pastry brush, lightly brush the slices with the 3 tablespoons olive oil. Place in a single layer on the prepared baking sheet and bake, turning occasionally, until golden on both sides, 7–10 minutes. Remove from the oven and rub the top of each crouton with 1 of the garlic cloves. Set aside.

Mince the remaining garlic clove. In a large bowl, whisk together the minced garlic, the mustard, lemon juice, anchovies, and egg yolk. In a small bowl, combine the 1/4 cup (2 fl oz/60 ml) each olive oil and extra-virgin olive oil. Whisking constantly, pour the oils in a steady stream into the anchovy mixture. Whisk in the reduced cooking liquid and then add the shrimp, stirring to coat. Let marinate for 10 minutes. Season to taste with salt and pepper. Add the lettuce and half of the Parmesan to the bowl and toss until all of the leaves are evenly coated.

Divide the salad evenly among individual salad plates. Garnish with the croutons and sprinkle with the remaining Parmesan. Serve immediately.

Serves 6

Shrimp and Asparagus Salad

Arrange this elegant salad on a large platter, and choose attractive lettuce leaves of the same size for the best presentation. If it is difficult to find asparagus, you can substitute avocado, sliced and moistened with a little lemon juice.

Bring a saucepan of salted water to a boil. Boil the shrimp until they turn pink and curl slightly, 2–3 minutes. Drain, place under cold running water, and drain again. Peel and devein the shrimp (page 328) and set aside.

Bind the asparagus together into a bundle with kitchen string. Fill a tall, narrow saucepan halfway with water and stand the asparagus in it, with the tips above the waterline. Bring to a boil. Boil until just tender when pierced with a knife, about 8 minutes. Remove from the pan and discard the string. Let cool. Cut off the top 2 inches (5 cm) and set aside. (Reserve the stalks for another use.)

In a food processor or blender, combine the egg yolk and salt and cayenne to taste and process briefly. With the motor running, add the olive and sesame oils in a thin stream. When the mixture thickens to a mayonnaise consistency, transfer to a bowl and stir in the lemon juice. Reserve 2 or 3 of the nicest-looking shrimp for a garnish; mix the remaining shrimp into the mayonnaise.

Arrange the lettuce leaves on a serving platter and spoon the shrimp mixture on top. Decorate with the asparagus tips and reserved shrimp. Serve immediately.

Serves 4

1 lb (500 g) shrimp (prawns)

24 slender stalks of asparagus

1 egg yolk

Salt

Cayenne pepper

1/3 cup (3 fl oz/80 ml) extra-virgin olive oil

1/3 cup (3 fl oz/80 ml) sesame oil

1 tablespoon fresh lemon juice

8 leaves green-leaf lettuce

Smoked Trout, Avocado, and Orange Salad

This salad can start a meal or serve as a centerpiece for a light summer lunch. Increase the amount of trout if you want a more filling salad. The vinaigrette can be made up to 6 hours in advance of serving.

FOR THE GINGER VINAIGRETTE:

1/3 cup (1 1/2 oz/45 g) peeled and sliced fresh ginger

1/4 cup (2 fl oz/60 ml) fresh lemon juice

2 tablespoons white wine vinegar, or to taste

1 teaspoon sugar

2/3 cup (5 fl oz/160 ml) peanut oil

Salt and freshly ground pepper

2 smoked trout, about 7 oz (220 g) each

1 red onion, sliced paper thin

2 avocados

6 cups (6 oz/185 g) loosely packed spinach or watercress leaves or assorted greens, carefully washed

2 large navel oranges, peeled, white membrane removed, and sectioned

To make the vinaigrette, place the ginger in a food processor or blender and chop finely. Add the lemon juice and vinegar and process to a fine purée. Transfer to a bowl and whisk in the sugar, oil, and salt and pepper to taste. You should have about 1 1/4 cups (10 fl oz/310 ml) vinaigrette.

To assemble the salad, skin and bone the trout. Separate the fillets, then tear them into bite-sized pieces. Set aside.

In a bowl, combine the onion and 1/4 cup (2 fl oz/60 ml) of the vinaigrette. Set aside for 15 minutes.

Cut the avocados in half. Remove the pits and peel the halves. Cut the avocado halves into long slices 1/4 inch (6 mm) thick. Place in a bowl and drizzle with 1/4 cup (2 fl oz/60 ml) of the vinaigrette.

In a large bowl, toss together the spinach and the onion slices in vinaigrette with 1/2 cup (4 fl oz/125 ml) of the remaining vinaigrette. Distribute the greens among 4 salad plates. Combine the orange segments and trout in the large bowl, drizzle with the remaining vinaigrette, and toss well. Arrange the avocado slices, trout pieces, and orange segments atop the greens and serve.

Serves 4

Niçoise Salad

This classic Provençal salad has the true flavor of the sea. Toss the salad or, to show off its striking colors, arrange the ingredients on individual plates. Herb Vinaigrette (page 108) can be used in place of the dressing.

Put the potatoes in a saucepan, add salted water to cover, and bring to a boil. Cook over medium heat until tender when pierced with a fork, 15–20 minutes. Drain and peel the potatoes while still hot. Let cool, then cut into 1-inch (2.5-cm) cubes. Place in a salad bowl.

Meanwhile, fill another saucepan with salted water and bring to a boil. Add the green beans and boil just until tender, about 5 minutes. Drain, place under cold running water, and drain again. Add to the salad bowl.

Rinse the capers under cold running water, drain, and pat dry with paper towels. Add to the salad bowl along with the tomatoes and tuna. Sprinkle the oregano over the top.

In a small bowl, stir together the mustard, vinegar, and salt to taste until well blended. Vigorously stir in the olive oil until well mixed. Pour the dressing over the salad and toss well. Garnish with the olives and serve.

Serves 4

2 boiling potatoes, about
³/4 lb (375 g) total weight

1/2 lb (250 g) green beans,
trimmed

2 tablespoons capers

4 tomatoes, about ³/4 lb
(375 g) total weight,
cut into 6–8 wedges

1 can (7 oz/220 g) tuna in
olive oil, drained and flaked

1 tablespoon finely chopped
fresh oregano

1 tablespoon Dijon mustard

2 tablespoons white
wine vinegar

Salt

¹/3 cup (3 fl oz/80 ml)
extra-virgin olive oil

¹/4 lb (125 g) black olives
for garnish

Crabmeat and New Potato Salad with Lemon-Dill Dressing

Surprisingly restrained in its flavors, this simple yet elegant salad is a lovely dish to serve for a special brunch. If crab is not available, you can use precooked bay shrimp, salmon poached in court bouillon, or even canned tuna.

1½ lb (750 g) red new potatoes

¼ cup (2 fl oz/60 ml) fresh lemon juice

1 teaspoon sugar

½ teaspoon salt

¼ teaspoon ground white pepper

2 tablespoons finely chopped fresh dill

¾ cup (6 fl oz/180 ml) extra-virgin olive oil

1 lb (500 g) cooked lump crabmeat

2 heads butter (Boston) lettuce, separated into leaves

Fresh chervil leaves and sprigs

Place the potatoes in a large saucepan with lightly salted cold water to cover. Bring to a boil over medium-high heat. Boil until tender when pierced with the tip of a small, sharp knife, 10–15 minutes.

While the potatoes are cooking, make the dressing: In a bowl large enough to hold the potatoes, stir together the lemon juice, sugar, salt, and white pepper until the sugar and salt dissolve. Stir in the dill. Whisking continuously, pour in the olive oil in a thin, steady stream and whisk until emulsified.

In another bowl, lightly toss the crabmeat with 2 tablespoons of the dressing. Set aside.

As soon as the potatoes are done, drain them. Holding the hot potatoes with a folded kitchen towel to protect your hand and using a small, sharp knife, cut the potatoes, one at a time, into slices about ½ inch (12 mm) thick, letting the slices fall into the bowl of dressing. Toss the potatoes gently with the dressing and let stand at room temperature until barely warm.

Arrange the lettuce leaves in a bed on a serving platter or individual plates. Spoon the potato salad on top of the lettuce and arrange the crabmeat on top of the potatoes. Garnish with chervil and serve at once.

Serves 6–8

Pasta, Shrimp, and Salmon Salad

Curry powder imparts an intense yellow hue that contrasts beautifully with the pinks of the shrimp (prawns) and salmon. The pasta should be very firm to the bite, or the salad will not have the proper texture.

Bring a saucepan of salted water to a boil. Boil the shrimp until they turn pink and curl slightly, 2–3 minutes. Drain, place under cold running water, and drain again. Peel and devein the shrimp (page 328) and set aside.

Bring a large saucepan of salted water to a boil. Add the curry powder, let it dissolve, and then add the pasta. Cook until just al dente, about 9 minutes. Drain and then cool under cold running water. Drain again thoroughly and place in a salad bowl. Add the shrimp, salmon, and chickpeas.

In a small bowl, stir together the tarragon, lemon juice, and salt and pepper to taste until well mixed. Add the oil and stir vigorously until blended. Pour the dressing over the salad, toss well, and serve.

Serves 4

3/4 lb (375 g) shrimp (prawns) in the shell

3 tablespoons curry powder

1/2 lb (250 g) farfalle

1/4 lb (125 g) smoked salmon, thinly sliced and cut into long, narrow strips

1 1/2 cups (10 1/2 oz/330 g) well-drained cooked or canned chickpeas (garbanzo beans)

1 tablespoon finely chopped fresh tarragon

1 teaspoon fresh lemon juice

Salt and freshly ground pepper

3 tablespoons extra-virgin olive oil

Tuna and Chicory Salad with Romesco Vinaigrette

Pale green and white chicory (curly endive) is the foundation for *xato*, a specialty of Barcelona. The salad is dressed with a piquant almond vinaigrette based on the classic Catalan *romesco* sauce.

½ lb (250 g) tuna fillet, about 1 inch (2.5 cm) thick

FOR THE ROMESCO VINAIGRETTE:

1 cup (5½ oz/170 g) blanched almonds, toasted (page 328)

1 tablespoon minced garlic

2 dried red chiles, seeded, or 2 teaspoons red pepper flakes

1 large red bell pepper (capsicum), roasted and peeled (page 324), then chopped

½ cup (4 fl oz/125 ml) red wine vinegar

¾ cup (6 fl oz/180 ml) olive oil

Salt and freshly ground pepper

3 heads chicory (curly endive)

2 hard-boiled eggs, peeled and cut into quarters

½ cup (2½ oz/75 g) Moroccan, Gaeta, or other Mediterranean-style oil-cured black olives

Preheat the broiler (grill).

Place the tuna fillet on a broiler pan and slip under the broiler about 3 inches (7.5 cm) from the heat source. Broil (grill), turning once, until lightly browned on the outside but still pink in the center, 3–5 minutes on each side, or until done to your liking. Remove from the broiler and let cool.

To make the vinaigrette, in a food processor, combine the almonds, garlic, and chiles. Process until reduced to fine crumbs. Add the bell pepper and pulse to combine. Add the vinegar and purée until smooth. Pour the mixture into a bowl and, using a whisk, gradually beat in the oil until the mixture has the consistency of thick cream. Season to taste with salt and pepper. Set aside.

Cut out the cores from the heads of chicory and distribute the greens evenly among 6 individual plates. Break up the tuna into bite-sized morsels and scatter over the top. Drizzle the vinaigrette evenly over the salads and garnish with the eggs. Sprinkle the olives on top and serve.

Serves 6

Lobster and Fava Bean Salad

If young fava beans are unavailable, substitute 1 pound (500 g) asparagus or green beans, trimmed, cut into ¾-inch (2-cm) pieces, and simmered in salted water to cover until tender-crisp, about 5 minutes.

In a stockpot, bring the water or court bouillon to a boil. If using water, add 1 tablespoon salt once it boils. Add the lobsters and boil until dark red and fully cooked, about 10 minutes. Using tongs, remove the lobsters from the pot and set aside to cool. Discard the cooking liquid.

When the lobsters are cool, remove the meat from the tails and claws as directed on page 323. Reserve the body meat for other uses. Dice the tail and claw meat into ½-inch (12-mm) pieces and place in a large salad bowl. Set aside.

Remove the tough outer pods from the fava beans. Bring a saucepan three-fourths full of water to a boil. Add the fava beans and boil for 30 seconds. Drain and let cool. Remove the thin skin covering each bean by making a small slit in the skin and then popping out the tender bean. Discard the skins. Add the fava beans to the salad bowl along with the lettuce.

In a small bowl, whisk together the orange juice, vinegar, orange zest, oil, garlic, parsley, and salt and pepper to taste.

Add the dressing to the salad bowl and toss well. Serve immediately.

Serves 6

7 cups (56 fl oz/1.75 l) water or Court Bouillon (page 316)

Salt

2 live lobsters, about 1¼ lb (625 g) each

4 lb (2 kg) young, tender fava (broad) beans in the shell

½ small head romaine (cos) lettuce, tender leaves only, carefully washed, dried, and cut crosswise into strips ½ inch (12 mm) wide

¼ cup (2 fl oz/60 ml) fresh orange juice

1 tablespoon balsamic vinegar

½ teaspoon finely grated orange zest

½ cup (4 fl oz/125 ml) extra-virgin olive oil

1 clove garlic, minced

2 tablespoons chopped fresh flat-leaf (Italian) parsley

Freshly ground pepper

Poached Shrimp and Scallop Salad with Mango Salsa

The fresh flavors of this fruit-and-shellfish combination make it an ideal luncheon salad. If you like, substitute a small papaya for the mangoes. To prepare the papaya, peel and seed it, then cut the flesh into 1/2-inch (12-mm) dice.

In a frying pan, bring the fish stock to a boil. Add the shrimp, reduce the heat to low, cover, and simmer for 1 minute. Stir lightly, re-cover, and cook until the shrimp curl and are firm, about 1 minute for medium shrimp and 2 minutes for large shrimp. Using a slotted spoon, transfer the shrimp to a bowl. Maintain the pan of cooking liquid at a simmer.

If you are using sea scallops, cut them horizontally into slices 1/4 inch (6 mm) thick. Leave bay scallops whole. Add the scallops to the simmering liquid, cover, and simmer until almost firm, about 2 minutes, turning the sea scallops halfway through the cooking process. Using the slotted spoon, transfer to the bowl holding the shrimp. Cover and refrigerate. Discard the cooking liquid.

Working with 1 mango at a time, cut off the flesh lengthwise from each side of the large, flat mango pit, to form 2 large pieces. Discard the pit. Using a knife, score the flesh lengthwise and then crosswise through to the skin. Turn the mango half inside out and slip the blade between the skin and the flesh to cut away the cubes of flesh, dropping them into a large bowl. Add the bell pepper, jalapeño chile, lime zest, lime juice to taste, the chopped mint, oil, and salt and pepper to taste. Mix well. Add the shrimp and scallops and toss gently.

Arrange the salad on a platter. Garnish with mint sprigs and serve with lime wedges.

Serves 6

1/2 cup (4 fl oz/125 ml) Fish Stock (page 317) or bottled clam juice

3/4 lb (375 g) medium or large shrimp (prawns), peeled and deveined (page 328)

3/4 lb (375 g) sea or bay scallops

2 large mangoes

1/2 red bell pepper (capsicum), seeded, deribbed, and cut into 1/4-inch (6-mm) dice

1 fresh jalapeño chile, seeded and minced (optional)

1 teaspoon grated lime zest

Juice of 2–3 limes

3 tablespoons chopped fresh mint leaves, plus mint sprigs for garnish

2 tablespoons extra-virgin olive oil

Salt and freshly ground pepper

Lime wedges

Warm Scallop and Asparagus Salad with Orange Dressing

This salad is great in the springtime, when fresh asparagus is at its peak. Try to avoid stalks that are too thick, as they can be woody and fibrous. Substitute thinly sliced green (spring) onions for the sesame seed garnish, if you prefer.

3 large navel oranges

1/2 teaspoon peeled and grated fresh ginger

3 tablespoons balsamic vinegar

1/2 teaspoon sesame oil

6 tablespoons (3 fl oz/90 ml) olive oil

Salt and freshly ground pepper

1 tablespoon sesame seeds

1 lb (500 g) asparagus, trimmed and cut on the diagonal into 1 1/2-inch (4-cm) lengths

1 1/2 lb (750 g) sea scallops, cut horizontally into slices 1/2 inch (12 mm) thick

Holding 1 orange over a small bowl, grate enough zest to measure 1 teaspoon. Cut the orange in half crosswise and add the juice of half of the orange to the bowl. Set aside the remaining half. Add the ginger, vinegar, sesame oil, and two-thirds of the olive oil. Add salt and pepper to taste, stir well, and set aside.

Using a sharp knife, cut the tops and bottoms off the 2 whole oranges and the top off the reserved orange half to reveal the fruit. Trim all the peel so that no white pith remains. Cut the oranges crosswise into slices 1/4 inch (6 mm) thick and then cut the slices in half. Set aside.

In a small, dry frying pan over medium heat, toast the sesame seeds until golden, about 1 minute. Set aside.

Bring a saucepan three-fourths full of salted water to a boil. Add the asparagus and boil uncovered until tender-crisp, about 5 minutes. Drain well and set aside.

In a frying pan, heat 1 tablespoon of the oil over high heat. Add half of the scallops and cook, stirring occasionally, until almost firm, about 2–3 minutes. Season to taste with salt and pepper. Transfer to a plate. Repeat with the remaining scallops, using the remaining 1 tablespoon oil. Return the first batch of scallops to the pan, along with the dressing and asparagus. Warm gently over low heat, stirring occasionally, about 1 minute.

Line a platter or individual plates with the orange slices. Spoon the scallops and asparagus over and garnish with the sesame seeds.

Serves 6

Fennel, Radish, and Scallop Salad with Dill Dressing

This salad has a crisp texture, attractive colors, and refreshingly light flavors. Enjoy it as a first course or as a light main course. If you like, garnish with fresh dill sprigs or lemon slices.

1/2 cup (4 fl oz/125 ml) Fish Stock (page 317) or bottled clam juice

1 1/2 lb (750 g) sea scallops, cut horizontally into slices 1/4 inch (6 mm) thick

2 fennel bulbs, with feathery tops intact

3–5 tablespoons (1 1/2–3 fl oz/ 45–75 ml) fresh lemon juice

6 tablespoons (3 fl oz/90 ml) extra-virgin olive oil

1 clove garlic, minced

3 tablespoons chopped fresh dill

Salt and freshly ground pepper

1 bunch radishes, trimmed and thinly sliced

In a frying pan, bring the fish stock to a boil. Add the scallops, reduce the heat to medium, cover, and simmer for 1 minute. Turn the scallops over and continue simmering until almost firm, about 1 minute longer. Using a slotted spoon, transfer the scallops to a large bowl. Cover and refrigerate. Discard the cooking liquid.

Cut off the feathery tops from the fennel bulbs and set aside. Remove the stalks and any tough or bruised outer leaves from the bulbs and discard. Using a sharp knife, cut each bulb in half lengthwise and then slice the bulb halves crosswise into paper-thin slices. Place the slices in a large bowl and add 1 tablespoon of the lemon juice. Toss well. Cover and refrigerate. Chop 1 tablespoon of the fennel tops and set aside. Discard the remaining fennel tops.

In a small bowl, whisk together the oil, 2 tablespoons of the lemon juice, the garlic, fennel tops, and dill. Season to taste with salt and pepper. Taste and adjust the seasoning with more lemon juice, if needed.

Add the sliced fennel and radishes to the scallops. Add the dressing and toss gently to mix well. Transfer to a platter and let stand for 10 minutes at room temperature before serving.

Serves 6

Mediterranean Tuna Salad

Using a fresh tuna fillet turns this classic salad into a special treat. To achieve the correct balance of flavors, combine mild olive oil and a fruitier extra-virgin olive oil to make the vinaigrette.

Preheat the broiler (grill), or prepare a fire in a charcoal grill. Alternatively, warm a little oil in a frying pan over medium heat.

If broiling, brush the tuna fillet on both sides with oil. Place on the broiler pan or grill rack. Broil or grill, turning once, to desired doneness, 2–3 minutes on each side for medium-rare. Or sauté the tuna fillet, turning once, to desired doneness, 4–5 minutes on each side for medium-rare.

Let the tuna cool completely, then cut into 1- to 2-inch (2.5- to 5-cm) chunks. Arrange the tuna, potatoes, tomatoes, green beans, eggs, olives, and bell peppers on 4 individual plates, lined with lettuce leaves if desired. Drizzle with the vinaigrette and serve at once.

Serves 4

1 lb (500 g) tuna fillet

Olive oil for brushing

12 small new potatoes, unpeeled, boiled until tender, drained, and cut in half or into thick slices

4 tomatoes, cut into quarters

1 lb (500 g) green beans, trimmed, boiled just until tender-crisp, plunged into cold water, and drained

2 hard-boiled eggs, cut into quarters

1/2 cup (2 oz/60 g) Niçoise or Kalamata olives

2 green bell peppers (capsicums), seeded, deribbed, and sliced lengthwise

Lettuce leaves (optional)

Herb Vinaigrette (page 108)

Bean and Shrimp Salad

A classic variation on this recipe substitutes for the shrimp (prawns) a mixture of cut-up anchovy fillets, minced garlic, and parsley. If you don't have time to soak and prepare raw beans, canned beans are an acceptable substitute.

1¼ cups (8 oz/250 g) dried small white (navy) beans or cranberry (borlotti) beans

Salt

½ white onion or 2 green (spring) onions, cut into paper-thin slices

Juice of ½ lemon

Freshly ground green peppercorns

⅓ cup (3 fl oz/80 ml) extra-virgin olive oil

½ lb (250 g) shrimp (prawns)

1 tablespoon finely chopped fresh flat-leaf (Italian) parsley

1 small head Bibb lettuce, about 5 oz (155 g), separated into leaves

Place the beans in a bowl. Add water to cover by ½ inch (12 mm) and let stand for 4–12 hours. Drain the beans and put them in a saucepan. Add water to cover by 1 inch (2.5 cm) and salt lightly. Bring to a boil, reduce the heat to low, and simmer, partially covered, until tender, about 1½ hours. Drain well and let cool.

While the beans are cooking, arrange the onion slices in a salad bowl. In a small bowl, stir together the lemon juice and salt and ground green peppercorns to taste until well mixed. Add the oil and stir vigorously until well blended. Pour over the onions, toss gently, and let stand for a few hours.

Bring a saucepan of salted water to a boil. Add the shrimp and boil until they turn pink and curl slightly, 2–3 minutes. Drain, place under cold running water, and drain again. Peel and devein the shrimp (page 328) and add to the salad bowl. Add the beans and parsley and toss gently.

Arrange the lettuce leaves on a serving platter. Spoon the shrimp mixture over the top and serve.

Serves 4

Warm Potato and Shrimp Salad

If you are starting with uncooked shrimp (prawns), you will need about 1¼ pounds (625 g). Boil them until they turn pink and begin to curl, about 3 minutes. Then drain, immerse in cold water to cool, drain again, and peel and devein.

Bring a large pot three-fourths full of salted water to a boil over high heat. Add the potatoes and cook until tender but slightly resistant when pierced with a fork, 25–30 minutes. Drain and let cool slightly.

Holding the potatoes under cold water, peel them. Cut into ½-inch (12-mm) cubes and place in a bowl. Add the shrimp.

To make the dressing, in a small bowl, combine the shallot, garlic, parsley, chives, the 1 teaspoon dill, mustard, lemon juice, and vinegar. Whisk until well mixed. Slowly pour in the oil, whisking continuously until blended. Add the salt and pepper. Taste and adjust the seasoning.

Pour the dressing over the potatoes and shrimp and mix gently until evenly coated. Transfer to a serving bowl and garnish with the 2 tablespoons dill. Serve immediately.

Serves 6

2½ lb (1.25 kg) yellow-fleshed potatoes, unpeeled and well scrubbed

1 lb (500 g) shrimp (prawns) cooked, peeled, and deveined (page 328) cut into 1-inch (2.5-cm) pieces

1 shallot, finely chopped

1 clove garlic, minced

1 tablespoon chopped fresh flat-leaf (Italian) parsley

1 tablespoon chopped fresh chives

1 teaspoon plus 2 tablespoons chopped fresh dill

1 teaspoon Dijon mustard

2 tablespoons fresh lemon juice

2 tablespoons white wine vinegar

¾ cup (6 fl oz/180 ml) olive oil

½ teaspoon salt

¼ teaspoon freshly ground pepper

Italian Shellfish Salad with Salsa Verde

Each village along Italy's Amalfi coast makes its own version of this salad. Serve within an hour of making the salad. Pass grilled Italian bread rubbed with garlic for dipping, and garnish with lemon wedges.

½ cup (4 fl oz/125 ml)
Fish Stock (page 317)

½ lb (250 g) shrimp (prawns)

½ lb (250 g) sea
or bay scallops

2 lb (1 kg) *each* mussels and
clams, well scrubbed

½ cup (¾ oz/20 g) chopped
fresh flat-leaf (Italian) parsley

¼ cup (⅓ oz/ 10 g) chopped
fresh chives

½ teaspoon *each* chopped
fresh thyme and oregano

2 tablespoons well-drained
capers, chopped

2 anchovy fillets, soaked
in cold water to cover
for 5 minutes

2 cloves garlic, minced

¼ cup (2 fl oz/ 60 ml) fresh
lemon juice

½ cup (4 fl oz/125 ml)
extra-virgin olive oil

Salt and freshly ground pepper

Lemon wedges (optional)

In a sautè pan over medium heat, bring the fish stock to a boil. Add the shrimp and scallops, reduce the heat to low, cover, and simmer until almost firm, 1–2 minutes. Using a slotted spoon, transfer the shrimp and scallops to a large bowl and let cool. Maintain the pan of cooking liquid at a simmer.

Discard any mussels and clams that do not close to the touch. Clean and debeard the mussels as directed on page 327. Add the mussels to the simmering liquid, cover, and cook, shaking the pan periodically, until they open, 2–4 minutes. Using the slotted spoon, lift out the mussels as they open and set aside. Discard any unopened mussels. Cook the clams in the same way until they open, 3–5 minutes, remove them with the slotted spoon, and set aside. Discard any unopened clams. Raise the heat to high and reduce the cooking liquid to 2 tablespoons. Remove from the heat.

Peel and devein the shrimp (page 328). Return them to the bowl holding the scallops. Remove all but 6 mussels and 6 clams from their shells and add the shelled and unshelled mussels and clams to the shrimp and scallops. Add the reduced cooking liquid to the shellfish and toss to coat evenly.

In a bowl, whisk together the parsley, chives, thyme, oregano, capers, anchovies, garlic, lemon juice, and oil. Whisk in salt and pepper to taste. Pour the dressing over the shellfish, toss well, and let stand for 30 minutes.

Place the shellfish on a platter and garnish (see note). Serve immediately.

Serves 6

Tomatoes Stuffed with Eggs and Anchovies

Ideal for hot weather, these stuffed tomatoes can be served chilled, as a side dish accompanying cold meat or fish. For a simple first course, top each tomato with a generous spoonful of Mayonnaise (page 318).

Slice off the top of each tomato. Using a spoon, gently remove the pulp and seeds. (Reserve the pulp for another use.) Lightly salt the insides and then invert the hollowed-out tomatoes on a plate to drain for 30 minutes.

In a small bowl, stir together the mustard and salt to taste until well mixed. Add the oil and stir vigorously until blended. Add the flat-leaf parsley, mint, basil, anchovies, and eggs. Mix well.

Turn the tomatoes cut side up and arrange on a serving platter. Fill each tomato with one-fourth of the egg-anchovy mixture. If desired, place 1 lemon slice atop each tomato, decorate each slice with 3 capers and a curly parsley leaf, and serve.

Serves 4

4 tomatoes

Salt

1 teaspoon Dijon mustard

1/4 cup (2 fl oz/60 ml)
extra-virgin olive oil

1 teaspoon finely chopped
fresh flat-leaf (Italian) parsley

1 teaspoon finely chopped
fresh mint

1 teaspoon finely chopped
fresh basil

4 anchovy fillets in oil,
drained and cut into
small pieces

3 hard-boiled eggs,
cut into cubes

4 thin slices lemon (optional)

12 well-drained capers
(optional)

Curly-leaf parsley (optional)

Hot Shrimp Salad with Baby Spinach

This salad presents an appealing combination of colors and textures, highlighted by the sweet, vibrant strips of roasted red bell pepper (capsicum). Perfect for a light brunch main course, this salad may also be made with precooked bay shrimp.

Put the pine nuts in a small, dry frying pan over medium-low heat and toast, stirring continuously, until light golden brown, 3–5 minutes. Remove from the pan and set them aside.

Meanwhile, put the shrimp in a bowl of lightly salted cold water and let soak for 10–15 minutes. Rinse well with cool running water, then drain thoroughly and pat dry with paper towels.

Arrange the spinach in beds on individual plates or in shallow bowls. Scatter the eggs evenly on top. Set aside.

In a small bowl, stir together the lemon juice, vinegar, sugar, $1/2$ teaspoon salt, and $1/4$ teaspoon white pepper until the sugar and salt dissolve. Stir in the mustard and shallot. Whisking continuously, pour in all but 1 tablespoon of the oil in a thin, steady stream and whisk until emulsified. Transfer the dressing to a small saucepan and warm it over low heat. Keep warm.

In a large frying pan over medium heat, warm the remaining 1 tablespoon oil with the red pepper flakes, if using. Add the shrimp to the pan, season lightly with salt and white pepper, and sauté, stirring, just until the shrimp turn pink, 1–2 minutes.

Arrange the shrimp attractively atop the beds of spinach. Drizzle the dressing evenly over the shrimp and spinach leaves. Garnish each serving with the bell pepper strips and pine nuts and serve immediately.

Serves 4

1/4 cup (1 oz/30 g) pine nuts

1 lb (500 g) shrimp (prawns), peeled and deveined (page 328)

8 cups (8 oz/250 g) loosely packed baby spinach leaves or large leaves torn into bite-sized pieces

2 hard-boiled eggs, peeled and chopped

2 tablespoons fresh lemon juice

2 tablespoons balsamic vinegar

3/4 teaspoon sugar

Salt and ground white pepper

2 teaspoons Dijon mustard

2 tablespoons finely chopped shallot

2/3 cup (5 fl oz/160 ml) extra-virgin olive oil

1/2 teaspoon red pepper flakes (optional)

1 red bell pepper (capsicum), roasted, peeled (page 324), seeded, deribbed, and cut into long, narrow strips

Thai Shrimp Salad with Ginger and Mint

You can make this zesty salad a day in advance. Serve it on your choice
of salad greens as an appetizer or as part of a buffet, or pack it in a cooler
for a picnic lunch. If you like, garnish the salad with lime wedges.

1/2 cup (4 fl oz/125 ml)
Fish Stock (page 317)

1 1/2 lb (750 g) shrimp
(prawns), peeled and deveined
(page 328)

1/4 cup (2 fl oz/60 ml)
fresh lime juice

2 tablespoons fish sauce
(optional)

1 tablespoon peanut oil

1 teaspoon sugar

Tender heart of 1 lemongrass
stalk, finely chopped, or
1 teaspoon grated lemon zest

1 tablespoon peeled and
minced fresh ginger

1 fresh jalapeño or serrano
chile, seeded and minced

2 cloves garlic, minced

Salt and freshly ground pepper

1/2 English (hothouse)
cucumber

1/2 small red onion, sliced

1/4 cup (1/3 oz/10 g) fresh mint
leaves, cut into thin shreds

1/4 cup (1/3 oz/10 g) cilantro
(fresh coriander) leaves

In a frying pan, bring the fish stock to a boil. Add the shrimp, reduce the heat
to low, cover, and simmer for about 1 minute. Stir lightly, re-cover, and cook until
the shrimp curl and are firm, 1 minute longer. Using a slotted spoon, transfer the
shrimp to a bowl and let cool slightly. Cover and refrigerate until chilled. Discard
the cooking liquid.

In a large bowl, whisk together the lime juice, fish sauce (if using), oil, sugar,
lemongrass, ginger, chile, garlic, and salt and pepper to taste.

Peel the cucumber half, cut it in half lengthwise, and then cut crosswise into 1/4-inch
(6-mm) slices. Add the cucumber slices to the large bowl along with the chilled
shrimp, onion, mint, and cilantro. Toss well.

Arrange the salad on a platter and serve.

Serves 6

Caesar Salad

Capers give this famous salad an Italian accent. If possible, mellow the flavor of the garlic cloves by steeping them in the extra-virgin olive oil for at least an hour before using them.

1/3 cup (3 fl oz/80 ml) extra-virgin olive oil

4 cloves garlic, sliced lengthwise

4 thick slices coarse country bread, crusts removed and bread cut into 3/4-inch (2-cm) cubes

1 head romaine (cos) lettuce, separated into leaves

4 anchovy fillets in olive oil, drained

2 tablespoons capers

1 egg

1 tablespoon fresh lemon juice

1 tablespoon Worcestershire sauce

1 teaspoon coarse-grain mustard

1 1/2 oz (45 g) Parmesan cheese shavings

In a frying pan over high heat, combine the oil and garlic and fry the garlic until brown, 4 minutes. Remove the garlic and discard. Add the bread cubes to the pan and fry over high heat, stirring, until browned. Transfer to paper towels to drain.

Tear the large and medium-sized lettuce leaves coarsely and leave the small leaves whole. Put the lettuce in a large salad bowl. In a smaller bowl, mash the anchovies with a fork. Rinse the capers under cold running water, drain, and pat dry with paper towels. Add the capers and bread cubes to the anchovies and toss to mix.

Bring a small saucepan filled with water to a boil, gently slip in the egg, remove the pan from the heat, and let stand for 1 minute. Remove the egg from the pan, immerse it in cold water, and break it into a small bowl. Add the lemon juice, Worcestershire sauce, and mustard. Stir vigorously until well blended.

Add the anchovy mixture to the lettuce. Pour the dressing over the salad, scatter the Parmesan over the top, toss gently, and serve.

Serves 4

Turkey and Belgian Endive Salad

Other types of young seasonal salad greens can be substituted for the Belgian endive, as long as the leaves are small. You can also add crumbled Roquefort cheese, substituting sunflower oil for the olive oil.

Tear the endive leaves coarsely and arrange them in a serving bowl. Lay the turkey slices on the leaves.

In a food processor or blender, combine the nuts, oil, lemon juice, and salt to taste. Process until a smooth cream forms. Spoon the dressing over the salad. Garnish with the extra nuts and serve.

Serves 4

4 small heads Belgian endive (chicory/witloof)

1 lb (500 g) cooked turkey breast, thinly sliced

1/2 cup (2 oz/60 g) walnuts or hazelnuts (filberts), plus a few for garnish

1/4 cup (2 fl oz/60 ml) extra-virgin olive oil

1/4 cup (2 fl oz/60 ml) fresh lemon juice

Salt

Grilled Chicken Cobb Salad

This variation on the traditional Cobb salad features grilled marinated chicken
breast in place of the cooked turkey breast. Dress it with Herb Vinaigrette
(page 108) and serve it as part of an afternoon luncheon or a simple dinner.

4 skinless, boneless chicken breast halves, about 6 oz (185 g) each

2 tablespoons lemon juice

2 tablespoons extra-virgin olive oil

1 teaspoon finely chopped fresh rosemary

Salt and freshly ground pepper

3 heads romaine (cos) lettuce, coarse outer leaves removed and remaining tender inner leaves coarsely chopped

8 slices smoked bacon, fried until crisp, drained, and coarsely crumbled

3 hard-boiled eggs, peeled and coarsely chopped

6 oz (185 g) blue cheese, crumbled

3 plum (Roma) tomatoes, seeded and diced

1 large Hass avocado, pitted, cut in half, peeled, and diced

2 tablespoons coarsely chopped fresh flat-leaf (Italian) parsley

One at a time, place each chicken breast half between 2 sheets of plastic wrap.
Using a rolling pin, roll back and forth across the breast half until it is a uniform
thickness of about $1/2$ inch (12 mm).

In a small bowl, stir together the lemon juice, oil, and rosemary. Place the chicken
breasts in a shallow bowl large enough to hold them in a single layer and pour the
marinade over them. Turn to coat evenly and let stand for 15–30 minutes.

Preheat a ridged stove-top grill pan over medium-high heat, or preheat the
broiler (grill).

Season the chicken breasts with salt and pepper. Place on the preheated grill pan,
or slip under the broiler 3–4 inches (7.5–10 cm) from the heat source. Grill or broil,
turning once, until just opaque throughout, 2–3 minutes on each side.

While the chicken is grilling, combine all the remaining ingredients except the
parsley in a large bowl and toss with just enough of the dressing (see note) to coat.
Arrange in individual bowls or on plates.

When the chicken is done, cut each breast half crosswise into strips $1/2$ inch (12 mm)
wide. Keeping each breast half together, arrange on top of the salads. Spoon the
remaining dressing over the chicken. Garnish with the parsley and serve.

Serves 4

Asian Chicken Salad

The secret to preparing this light and simple salad is hand-cutting
the ingredients into matchstick-sized strips to achieve a uniform texture.
Napa cabbage can be successfully substituted for the red cabbage.

1/4 red onion, thinly sliced

2 cloves garlic, minced

2 teaspoons peeled and grated fresh ginger

1 teaspoon sugar

2 tablespoons white rice vinegar

3 tablespoons peanut oil

1 teaspoon chile oil

2 tablespoons soy sauce

Pinch of salt (optional)

3 bone-in chicken breast halves

1 cucumber, peeled, seeded, and cut into matchsticks

1 red bell pepper (capsicum), seeded, deribbed, and cut into matchsticks

1 cup (3 oz/90 g) bean sprouts

2 cups (6 oz/185 g) coarsely chopped red cabbage

2 tablespoons chopped fresh cilantro (fresh coriander)

1/2 cup (3 oz/90 g) chopped roasted peanuts

In a small bowl, combine the onion, garlic, ginger, and sugar. Stir in the vinegar, peanut and chile oils, and soy sauce until well mixed. Season with salt, if desired. Set aside.

Bring a saucepan of salted water to a boil. Add the chicken breasts, reduce the heat to medium-low, and simmer for 10 minutes. Skim any foam from the surface, remove from the heat, cover the pan, and let stand for 15 minutes.

Drain the chicken breasts and let cool completely. Bone and skin them. Cut the chicken meat into long, thin strips and place in a salad bowl. Add the cucumber, bell pepper, bean sprouts, and cabbage. Stir the dressing again, pour it over the salad, and toss well. Sprinkle with the cilantro and peanuts. Serve.

Serves 4

Smoked Chicken Salad with Grapes

You can use poached or roasted chicken in place of the smoked chicken, in which case Yogurt Dressing (page 142) should stand in for the sunflower-oil dressing.

1 small bunch seedless green or red grapes, about 1/4 lb (125 g), stemmed and cut in half

1 yellow bell pepper (capsicum), seeded, deribbed, and chopped

3 celery stalks, chopped

1 lb (500 g) boned smoked chicken, cut into small cubes

1 heart of butter (Boston) lettuce, separated into leaves

2 tablespoons fresh orange juice

1 tablespoon tarragon vinegar

Salt and ground white pepper

1/4 cup (2 fl oz/60 ml) sunflower oil

1 tablespoon finely chopped fresh tarragon

Place the grapes, bell pepper, celery, and chicken in a salad bowl. Add the lettuce, tearing any large leaves in half. Set aside.

In a small bowl, stir together the orange juice, vinegar, and salt and white pepper to taste until well mixed. Add the oil and tarragon and stir vigorously until blended. Pour the dressing over the salad, toss gently, and serve.

Serves 4

Ham and Celery Salad with Walnuts

To make this light, fresh salad more substantial, add sliced fresh mushrooms and Swiss cheese. If you like, toast the walnuts (page 328) for added texture and flavor.

Select the palest, most tender stalks of the celery bunch. (Reserve the remaining stalks for another use.) Cut the celery crosswise into thin slices and place in a salad bowl. Add the lettuce and ham and toss together.

In a small bowl, stir together the lemon juice and salt to taste until well mixed. Add the oil and stir vigorously until blended. Pour the dressing over the salad and toss well. Scatter the walnuts over the top and serve.

Serves 4

1 bunch celery, about
1¹/₄ lb (625 g)

1 head romaine (cos) lettuce, shredded

2 slices cooked ham, about
3 oz (90 g) each, cut into
long, thin strips

Juice of ¹/₂ lemon

Salt

¹/₃ cup (3 fl oz/80 ml)
extra-virgin olive oil

¹/₂ cup (2 oz/60 g) walnuts,
chopped

Spinach and Apple Salad with Bacon

Choose small, young spinach leaves for this salad, as they will be more tender than larger leaves. If only more mature leaves are available, prepare them by sprinkling with lemon juice and allowing them to marinate for a few minutes.

Peel the apples, if desired, then core and chop. Place in a bowl, sprinkle with the lemon juice, and toss lightly. Set aside.

In a frying pan over high heat, fry the bacon until crisp, about 5 minutes. Transfer to paper towels to drain. When cool, crumble into small pieces and set aside.

In a small bowl, stir together the mustard, vinegar, and salt and white pepper to taste until well mixed. Add the oil and stir vigorously until blended. Set aside for a few minutes to allow the flavors to blend.

Place the spinach in a salad bowl. Add the apples, bacon, olives, and dressing and toss well. Garnish with the egg wedges and serve.

Serves 4

2 apples

A few drops of fresh lemon juice

1/4 lb (125 g) sliced bacon

1 tablespoon Dijon mustard

1–2 tablespoons balsamic vinegar

Salt and ground white pepper

1/4 cup (2 fl oz/60 ml) extra-virgin olive oil

1/2 lb (250 g) spinach, stemmed and washed

12 black olives, pitted and chopped

2 hard-boiled eggs, peeled and cut into wedges, for garnish

Sliced Beef and Potato Salad

This salad is usually made with leftover cooked beef or roast beef. If you are making it from scratch, put 1 pound (500 g) boiling beef in a heavy pot with salted water to cover. Add onions and carrots and cook gently until very tender, about 2 hours.

2 boiling potatoes, about ³/4 lb (375 g) total weight

10 oz (315 g) boiled beef, at room temperature

2 tablespoons balsamic vinegar

Salt and freshly ground pepper

2 tablespoons extra-virgin olive oil

1 white onion, thinly sliced

4–6 cornichons, thinly sliced

2 tomatoes, thinly sliced

Put the potatoes in a saucepan, add salted water to cover, and bring to a boil. Cook over medium heat until tender when pierced with a fork, 15–20 minutes. Drain and peel while still hot. Let cool. Cut crosswise into thin slices. Set aside.

Remove any fat and gristle from the beef. Slice it thinly.

In a small bowl, stir together the balsamic vinegar and salt and pepper to taste until well mixed. Add the oil and stir vigorously until blended.

In a large, shallow bowl or on a platter, arrange the slices of beef, potatoes, onion, cornichons, and tomatoes. Stir the dressing again and slowly pour it over the slices. Serve immediately.

Serves 4

Warm Potato, Sausage, and Goat Cheese Salad

This hearty salad is ideal served alongside a bowl of hot soup on a chilly day. It is also substantial enough to stand on its own as a satisfying main course. Add the goat cheese just before serving, so that the chunks do not melt into the dressing.

1½ lb (750 g) fresh sausages, such as sweet or hot Italian or bockwurst

2 lb (1 kg) white, red, or yellow-fleshed potatoes, unpeeled and well scrubbed

1 shallot, finely chopped

1 clove garlic, minced

1 tablespoon chopped fresh flat-leaf (Italian) parsley

1 tablespoon chopped fresh chives

1 teaspoon chopped fresh basil

1 teaspoon Dijon mustard

3 tablespoons white wine vinegar

1 tablespoon fresh lemon juice

¾ cup (6 fl oz/180 ml) olive oil

Salt and freshly ground pepper

¾ cup (3 oz/90 g) crumbled fresh goat cheese

4 tablespoons (⅓ oz/10 g) chopped fresh flat-leaf (Italian) parsley

Red-leaf lettuce leaves

Preheat the broiler (grill), or prepare a fire in a charcoal grill. Place the sausages on a broiler pan or grill rack and broil or grill, turning to cook evenly, until done, about 10 minutes, depending on the sausage. Let cool, then cut on the diagonal into slices 1 inch (2.5 cm) thick. Place in a bowl and set aside.

Meanwhile, bring a large pot three-fourths full of salted water to a boil. Add the potatoes and boil until tender but slightly resistant when pierced, 25–30 minutes. Drain and let cool slightly. Holding the potatoes under cold water, peel them. Cut into 1-inch (2.5-cm) cubes and add to the sausages.

To make the dressing, in a small bowl, combine the shallot, garlic, parsley, chives, basil, mustard, vinegar, and lemon juice. Whisk to mix well. Slowly add the oil, whisking continuously. Add the salt and pepper to taste.

Pour the dressing over the potatoes and sausage. Mix gently. Taste again and adjust the seasoning. Add the cheese and 2 tablespoons of the parsley and toss gently.

Line a serving platter with lettuce leaves and spoon the salad on top. Garnish with the remaining 2 tablespoons parsley and serve immediately.

Serves 6

Cheese & Vegetable Starters

Mozzarella and Tomato Crostini

Assemble this simple and popular Italian antipasto up to 1 hour in advance and put into the oven when guests arrive. Serve the crostini hot from the oven or warm. They are also delicious with other good melting cheeses such as jack, Swiss, or Cheddar.

2 tablespoons unsalted butter

6 slices coarse country bread

3 plum (Roma) tomatoes, thinly sliced crosswise

1 tablespoon extra-virgin olive oil

Dried oregano

Salt and freshly ground pepper

10 oz (315 g) mozzarella cheese

12 anchovy fillets in olive oil, drained (optional)

Preheat the oven to 350°F (180°C). Butter the bread slices on one side and cut in half. Place the bread pieces on a baking sheet, buttered side up.

Place the tomato slices in a shallow dish and drizzle with the oil. Sprinkle with oregano, salt, and pepper to taste. Toss gently.

Cut the mozzarella into 12 thin slices to fit the bread pieces and top each piece of bread with a slice of mozzarella.

Place an anchovy fillet, if using, on top of each cheese slice. Arrange 1 or 2 tomato slices on top. Bake until the bread is thoroughly heated and the mozzarella is almost melted, about 5 minutes.

Makes 12 crostini; serves 6

Dolmas

To make the filling, drain the lentils, place in a saucepan, and add fresh water to cover by about 1 inch (2.5 cm). Bring to a boil over medium-high heat, reduce the heat to low, cover, and simmer until tender but still firm, about 20 minutes. Drain.

Meanwhile, place the rice in a bowl with water to cover and let stand for about 30 minutes. In a sauté pan over medium heat, warm the oil. Add the yellow and green onions and sauté, stirring occasionally, until tender, about 8 minutes. Add the garlic and the cinnamon and allspice, if using, and sauté for 2 minutes. Transfer to a bowl. Drain the rice and add it to the onion mixture along with the drained lentils, tomatoes, pine nuts, dill, mint, and parsley. Season with salt and a generous amount of pepper. Mix well.

Briefly rinse the grape leaves, drain well, and cut off any tough stems. Place the leaves on a work surface, smooth side down. Place about 1 teaspoon filling near the stem end of each leaf. Fold the stem end over the filling, fold the sides over the stem end, and then roll the leaf into a cylinder. Do not roll too tightly; the rice will swell during cooking. Place seam side down in a large, wide sauté pan. Repeat with the remaining leaves and filling, placing the dolmas snugly in a single layer.

Pour the oil and lemon juice over the dolmas. Add hot water to cover. Place a heavy plate (or plates) on top of the dolmas to weigh them down. Bring to a simmer over medium heat, cover, reduce the heat to low, and cook until the filling is tender, about 45 minutes. Remove from the heat, uncover, and remove the plate(s). Transfer the dolmas to platters so they will cool quickly. Serve at room temperature with lemon wedges or plain yogurt.

Makes 36 dolmas

FOR THE FILLING:

1/2 cup (3 1/2 oz/105 g) dried lentils, picked over and soaked for 1 hour in water to cover

1 cup (7 oz/220 g) long-grain white rice

3 tablespoons olive oil

1/2 yellow onion, chopped

2 green (spring) onions, chopped

3 cloves garlic, minced

1/2 teaspoon *each* ground cinnamon and ground allspice (optional)

1 tomato, peeled, seeded, and diced

1/2 cup (2 1/2 oz/75 g) pine nuts

1/3 cup (1/2 oz/15 g) *each* chopped fresh dill and fresh mint

1/4 cup (1/3 oz/10 g) chopped fresh flat-leaf (Italian) parsley

Salt and freshly ground pepper

36 brine-packed grape leaves

1 cup (8 fl oz/250 ml) olive oil

1/4 cup (2 fl oz/60 ml) fresh lemon juice

Lemon wedges or plain yogurt

Mexican Crispy Baked Potato Skins

Brushing potato skins with oil provides extra crispness. These are tasty appetizers to serve with a pitcher of frosty margaritas. Follow with chicken tostadas or carne asada.

4 baking potatoes, about ¹/₂ lb (250 g) each, unpeeled

4 teaspoons vegetable oil

2 tablespoons olive oil

1 cup (4 oz/125 g) shredded Monterey jack or sharp Cheddar cheese, or a mixture

¹/₂ cup (4 fl oz/125 ml) Fresh Mexican Salsa (page 319)

¹/₂ cup (4 oz/125 g) sour cream

Preheat the oven to 425°F (220°C). Scrub the potatoes to remove all dirt, then dry thoroughly with a kitchen towel. Prick the skin in a few places with a fork. Rub each potato with 1 teaspoon of the vegetable oil to coat evenly. Place the potatoes on an ungreased baking sheet in the middle of the oven.

Bake until tender when pierced with a knife or skewer, about 1 hour. The potatoes should be cooked through and slightly crisp on the outside.

Increase the oven temperature to 450°F (230°C).

While the potatoes are still warm, cut each one in half lengthwise. Using a spoon, scoop out the flesh from each half, leaving shells ¹/₂ inch (12 mm) thick. (Reserve the flesh for mashed potatoes or another use.) Quarter each potato half to make 32 roughly same-sized wedges.

Brush the skin side of each piece with a light coating of olive oil. Place the pieces, skin side down, on an ungreased baking sheet. Sprinkle the cheese evenly over the tops. Bake until the cheese melts, about 10 minutes.

Transfer to a warmed serving platter and top each potato evenly with the salsa and sour cream. Serve immediately.

Makes 32 pieces; serves 4–6

Mushroom Quesadillas

This recipe calls for cultivated mushrooms, but you can substitute your favorite wild variety. For cheese quesadillas, fill each tortilla with 1½ tablespoons cheese and a sprig of fresh cilantro (fresh coriander).

To make the mushroom filling, in a frying pan over medium heat, melt the butter with the olive oil. Add the garlic and onion and sauté until golden, about 2 minutes. Add the chiles, mushrooms, and cilantro and sauté until the mushrooms are tender, about 5 minutes. Season to taste with salt and pepper. Set aside.

Place the dough in a large bowl and add the flour, melted shortening, baking powder, and ½ teaspoon salt. Moisten your hands and knead the dough in the bowl until it is soft but not sticky, about 5 minutes. Cover with a damp kitchen towel and set aside for 10 minutes.

Following the directions for forming tortillas on page 320, shape the dough into 12 balls, each about 1½ inches (4 cm) in diameter. Roll the balls into tortillas about 5 inches (12.5 cm) in diameter.

Spread a spoonful of the mushroom filling on half of each tortilla, leaving a ½-inch (12-mm) border. Fold the uncovered portion over the filling and press the edges together to seal.

In a large frying pan over medium heat, pour oil to a depth of ½ inch (12 mm). When the oil is hot, slip in the filled tortillas, 1 or 2 at a time, and fry, turning once, until golden, about 2 minutes on each side. Using a slotted spoon, transfer to paper towels to drain. Serve immediately.

Makes 12 quesadillas

2 tablespoons unsalted butter

¼ cup (2 fl oz/60 ml) olive oil

3 cloves garlic, finely chopped

½ yellow onion, finely chopped

2 fresh serrano chiles, finely chopped

1 lb (500 g) fresh mushrooms, sliced

2 tablespoons finely chopped fresh cilantro (fresh coriander) or 1 tablespoon finely chopped fresh epazote

Salt and freshly ground pepper

½ recipe (1 lb/500 g) dough for Flour Tortillas (page 320)

3 tablespoons all-purpose (plain) flour

1 tablespoon melted vegetable shortening or lard

1 teaspoon baking powder

Corn oil or other vegetable oil for frying

Marinated Button Mushrooms

Rice vinegar, chile, and cloves contribute to the spicy-sweet taste of these young, tender mushrooms. Fresh cilantro (fresh coriander) can replace the parsley, in which case 1 tablespoon of coriander seeds may be added to the marinade.

Trim off and discard the stem ends from the mushrooms, then wash and pat dry.

In a large nonreactive saucepan, combine the wine and vinegar . Add the salt, pepper, chile, oregano, cloves, parsley, lemon, bell pepper, and garlic. Bring to a boil and add the mushrooms. Drizzle with the oil and boil for 7 minutes. Remove from the heat and let the mixture cool completely before serving.

Serve the mushrooms at room temperature, with toothpicks, or serve on individual plates as a first course.

Serves 4–6

1 lb (500 g) very small white button mushrooms, no larger than $1/2$ inch (12 mm) in diameter

$2/3$ cup (5 fl oz/160 ml) dry white wine

$2/3$ cup (5 fl oz/160 ml) rice vinegar

1 teaspoon fine sea salt

1 teaspoon coarsely ground pepper

1 dried hot chile pepper, crumbled

2 teaspoons dried oregano

3 whole cloves

2 tablespoons chopped fresh flat-leaf (Italian) parsley

1 lemon, thinly sliced, seeded, with slices cut into quarters

1 small red bell pepper (capsicum), stemmed, seeded, deribbed, and cut into $3/8$-inch (1-cm) squares

1 clove garlic

3 tablespoons extra-virgin olive oil

Vegetable Quesadillas

Filled with a mixture of fresh vegetables, these tortilla pockets are a specialty of the street markets in Chilapa, Guerrero. Parmesan or pecorino romano cheese is used here in place of the traditional Mexican queso fresco.

1¼ teaspoons salt

Kernels from 2 ears of fresh corn

1 cup (5 oz/155 g) finely chopped green beans

2 carrots, finely chopped

1 zucchini (courgette), finely chopped

4 tablespoons coarsely chopped fresh epazote or cilantro (fresh coriander)

2 fresh serrano chiles, finely chopped

²/₃ cup (3 oz/90 g) grated Parmesan, pecorino romano, or another firm, dry cheese

½ recipe (1 lb/500 g) dough for Flour Tortillas (page 320)

3 tablespoons all-purpose (plain) flour

Vegetable oil for frying

Tomatillo Salsa (page 319)

Shredded lettuce

3 radishes, thinly sliced

½ cup (2½ oz/75 g) crumbled feta cheese (optional)

Bring a saucepan three-fourths full of water to a boil and add 1 teaspoon of the salt. Add the corn, green beans, carrot, and zucchini. Cook, uncovered, until the vegetables are tender-crisp, 3–4 minutes. Drain well. Place in a bowl. Add the epazote, chiles, and grated cheese. Stir well. Cover to keep warm.

Place the dough in a bowl and, with your fingers, work in the flour and the remaining ¼ teaspoon salt. The dough should be soft. If it is too dry, work in 1–2 tablespoons lukewarm water.

Following the directions for forming tortillas on page 320, shape the dough into 12 balls, each about 1 ½ inches (4 cm) in diameter. Press the balls into tortillas about 5 inches (12 cm) in diameter.

Place an equal amount of the vegetable mixture atop half of each tortilla, leaving a ½-inch (12-mm) border. Fold the uncovered portion over the filling and press the edges together well.

In a large frying pan over medium-high heat, pour oil to a depth of ½ inch (12 mm). When the oil is hot, slip the filled tortillas, 1 or 2 at a time, into the oil and fry, turning once, until golden, about 2 minutes on each side. Using a slotted spoon, transfer to paper towels to drain.

Top with the salsa, shredded lettuce, radishes, and the crumbled feta cheese, if desired. Serve immediately.

Makes 12 quesadillas

Jicama, Cucumber, and Mango with Orange and Chile

Traditionally, only oranges and jicama are used in this dish, but this more elaborate version includes cucumber and slices of mango. If pineapple is in season, it may also be included. Offer margaritas, mojitos, or other refreshing cocktails.

2 large jicamas, about 1½ lb (750 g) total weight

2 large cucumbers

1 large mango

2 large seedless oranges

⅓ cup (3 fl oz/80 ml) fresh lime juice

1 teaspoon chile powder

1 teaspoon salt

1 fresh serrano chile, finely chopped (optional)

3 limes, cut into wedges

6 fresh mint sprigs

Peel and slice the jicamas ½ inch (12 mm) thick and then cut into sticks 3 inches (7.5 cm) long and ½ inch (12 mm) wide. Cut the cucumbers in half crosswise. Peel them and then cut in half lengthwise. Scoop out the seeds and discard. Cut the cucumbers into sticks the same size as the jicama sticks. Peel and pit the mango (see page 327) and then slice lengthwise. Cut a slice off the top and bottom of the oranges, cutting deeply enough to reveal the fruit. One at a time, stand the oranges upright on a cutting board and slice off the peel, pith, and membranes, exposing the fruit. Slice the oranges crosswise.

Attractively arrange the jicama, cucumber sticks, mango, and orange slices on a large platter. Pour the lime juice evenly over the top and then sprinkle with the chile powder, salt, and chopped serrano chile, if using. Garnish with lime wedges and mint sprigs.

Serves 6

Onion Tartlets

The savory topping of onions, olives, and anchovies is inspired by *pissaladière*, the Niçoise relative of the pizza. If you make the tartlets in advance, they may be reheated for 6–8 minutes in a preheated 425°F (220°C) oven.

Prepare the pizza dough. Preheat the oven to 500°F (260°C).

On a lightly floured work surface, roll out the dough 3/8 inch (1 cm) thick. With a round pastry cutter 1 1/2 inches (4 cm) in diameter, cut out 24 rounds. Roll these rounds out again until they are 1/8 inch (3 mm) thick. Place the rounds on a non-stick baking sheet.

In a nonstick frying pan, combine the oil, water, and sugar. Add salt and pepper to taste. Bring to a boil and add the onions. Cover and cook over low heat, stirring from time to time, until the onions are golden and the water evaporates, about 20 minutes. Remove from the heat. Add the olives; anchovies, if using; and pine nuts and mix well.

Divide the topping evenly among the dough rounds. Bake until the topping and the edges of the pastry are golden, about 15 minutes. Serve warm.

Makes 24 tartlets; serves 6–8

About 3/4 recipe (13 oz/410 g) Basic Pizza Dough (page 320)

2 tablespoons extra-virgin olive oil

1/2 cup (4 fl oz/125 ml) water

1/2 teaspoon sugar

Salt and freshly ground pepper

1 lb (500 g) large yellow onions, thinly sliced and cut into slivers

12 plump black olives, pitted and cut into slivers

12 anchovy fillets in olive oil, drained and cut in half crosswise (optional)

1/2 cup (2 1/2 oz/75 g) pine nuts

Stuffed Cherry Tomatoes

Two different stuffings—one based on black olives, the other on creamy goat's milk cheese—add variety in flavor and color. The fillings are also excellent served as dips for other vegetables such as celery sticks or wedges of bell pepper (capsicum).

36 large cherry tomatoes

FOR THE OLIVE STUFFING:

6 boned and skinned canned sardines in olive oil, well drained and tails removed (optional)

3 tablespoons black olive paste

1 tablespoon chopped celery leaves

3 gherkins, finely chopped

1/4 teaspoon cayenne pepper

FOR THE CHEESE STUFFING:

13 oz (410 g) fresh goat's milk cheese such as Brousse, or ricotta, drained

2 tablespoons extra-virgin olive oil

2 green (spring) onions, finely chopped

1 tablespoon finely chopped fresh summer savory or flat-leaf (Italian) parsley

Freshly ground pepper

Cut a small cap from the top of each tomato. With a small scoop or spoon, remove all of the pulp. (Reserve for another use.) Invert the hollowed-out tomatoes on a plate and let drain.

To make the olive stuffing, place the sardines in a bowl, if using, and mash them with a fork. Add the olive paste, celery leaves, gherkins, and cayenne. Mix well. Using a small spoon, fill 18 of the tomatoes with this stuffing.

To make the cheese stuffing, place the cheese in a bowl and mash it with a fork. Add the oil, green onions, savory, and pepper to taste. Mix well. Using a small spoon, fill the remaining 18 tomatoes with this stuffing.

Refrigerate until well chilled before serving.

Makes 36 stuffed tomatoes; serves 6–8

Guacamole

You may substitute mild canned green chiles for the fresh hot ones. You can also add one or two firm, ripe plum (Roma) tomatoes that have been seeded (page 329) and coarsely chopped. Serve with tortilla chips.

2 avocados, 8 oz (250 g) each

2 tablespoons fresh lime juice

2 fresh hot chiles, stemmed, seeded, and finely chopped

6 green (spring) onions, cut on the diagonal into very thin slices, including the green portions

1 tablespoon finely chopped fresh cilantro (fresh coriander)

Halve the avocados and remove the pits. With a teaspoon, scoop out the flesh from the skins. Put the flesh in a bowl. Mash the avocado roughly with a fork, sprinkling with lime juice as you mash.

Quickly mix the chiles, green onions, and cilantro into the avocado. Serve at once.

Serves 6

Tomato–Pumpkin Seed Dip

This spicy dip contains a serrano chile pepper, which can be quite hot. Serve this dip with raw vegetables, toasted bread wedges, or crackers. It can be covered and stored in the refrigerator for up to 24 hours.

In a dry, heavy frying pan over low heat, toast the pumpkin seeds, shaking the pan occasionally, until lightly browned, about 8 minutes. Watch carefully that the seeds do not burn. Remove the seeds from the pan and set aside.

In the same pan over medium heat, combine the chile and tomatoes. After 1 minute, add the garlic. Roast, turning occasionally, until well charred, about 4 minutes for the chile and tomatoes and 3 minutes for the garlic. Remove from the heat, cover, and set aside to cool. Alternatively, place the chile and tomatoes in a closed paper bag to cool.

Place the toasted pumpkin seeds in a mortar, if available, or in a spice mill or mini food processor. Grind with a pestle or process to a coarse powder.

Peel and coarsely chop the tomatoes. Place tomatoes in a food processor or blender. Add the garlic and process for a few seconds, until smooth. Transfer to a serving bowl and stir in the ground pumpkin seeds.

Peel the chile and cut in half. Remove the stem and ribs. If a milder dip is desired, remove the seeds as well. Chop the chile finely and add it, along with the onion and cilantro, to the tomato–pumpkin seed mixture. Season to taste with salt. Stir well and serve.

Serves 6–8

1 cup (5 oz/155 g) hulled raw pumpkin seeds

1 serrano or jalapeño chile

2 tomatoes

2 cloves garlic

2 tablespoons finely chopped onion

3 tablespoons chopped fresh cilantro (fresh coriander)

Salt

Blue Cheese Spread with Walnuts

Walnuts and blue cheese are a favorite European pairing. Serve with toasted whole-grain country bread, breadsticks, or fresh vegetables. If you like, offer guests a small glass of Port, which will complement the nuts and cheese.

12 walnut halves

1 lb (500 g) soft white cheese such as cream cheese or ricotta, at room temperature

5 oz (155 g) blue cheese such as Roquefort, Gorgonzola, or Stilton, at room temperature

1 tablespoon Cognac or Armagnac

Salt and freshly ground pepper

1 bunch fresh chives, finely chopped

In a food processor fitted with a shredding disk or in a rotary grater fitted with the large-holed disk, grate the walnuts. Set aside.

In a bowl, combine the white and blue cheeses and mash them together with a fork. Mix in the Cognac and salt and pepper to taste. When the mixture is smooth, add the walnuts and chives. Mix again until well blended. Spoon into a serving bowl.

Serves 8

Artichoke Hearts with Parsley

Vegetables prepared in a marinade of olive oil, garlic, and oregano are sometimes referred to as *à la grecque*—"in the Greek style." You can use the same recipe for other firm-textured vegetables such as carrots, broccoli, or cauliflower.

Working with 1 artichoke at a time, pull off and discard the tough outer leaves until you reach the more tender yellow-green leaves. Cut off about 1 inch (2.5 cm) from the top to remove the thorns and tough tips of the leaves. Cut off the stem end even with the bottom. Cut the trimmed artichokes into halves or quarters, depending on their size, and trim away any fuzzy choke. The pieces should be about ¹/₂ inch (12 mm) thick. Rub the artichokes all over with the cut lemon halves.

In a large saucepan, bring the water to a boil. Add the lemon juice and coarse salt. Drop in the artichokes and cook for 10 minutes; they should still be slightly crunchy. Drain the artichokes and place them, heads down, in a strainer to cool.

Pour the oil into a bowl. Add the garlic, chile, cloves, and oregano.

When the artichokes are thoroughly drained and cool, add them to the bowl. Mix well and add the parsley. Let stand at room temperature for up to 6 hours.

Arrange the artichokes on a platter. Serve with toothpicks or serve on individual plates as a first course.

Serves 6

18 small artichokes, about
2¹/₂ oz (75 g) each

2 lemons, cut in half

4 cups (32 fl oz/1 l) water

¹/₂ cup (4 fl oz/125 ml)
fresh lemon juice

1 teaspoon coarse salt

¹/₂ cup (4 fl oz/125 ml)
extra-virgin olive oil

2 cloves garlic,
cut into thin slivers

1 dried hot chile, crumbled

6 whole cloves

2 pinches dried oregano

36 fresh flat-leaf (Italian)
parsley leaves

Eggplant Caviar

In the Middle East, this purée is called *baba ghanoush*, or "harem girl"—no doubt a reference to its seductive texture. Prepare it up to 24 hours in advance and serve with crackers or raw vegetables.

2 eggplants (aubergines), about 9 oz (280 g) each

1 small clove garlic

1 1/2 teaspoons fresh lemon juice

1 tablespoon extra-virgin olive oil

2 or 3 pinches of ground cumin

Salt

Preheat the oven to 500°F (260°C). With a sharp knife, make 2 or 3 slashes in each eggplant so that it will not burst as it cooks. Place the eggplants on a rack in the oven and position a pan beneath them to catch any drips. Bake until they are black and wrinkled, about 45 minutes. Remove the eggplants from the oven and let cool until they can be handled.

Peel the eggplants and place the pulp in a bowl. With a fork, mash the pulp to a coarse consistency. Pass the garlic through a garlic press into the bowl and then add the lemon juice, oil, cumin, and salt to taste. Mix well.

Serve at room temperature.

Serves 4

Crisp Ricotta Rolls
with Walnuts and Chives

Specialty cheese shops and well-stocked supermarkets may offer different types of ricotta, made from cow's, sheep's, or goat's milk, which will impart subtle flavor variations to the creamy cheese mixture.

Preheat the oven to 425°F (220°C).

In a bowl, mash the ricotta with a fork. Using a rotary grater fitted with the large-holed disk, grate first the walnuts and then the Emmentaler into the bowl containing the ricotta. Alternatively, grate the walnuts and Emmentaler in a food processor fitted with a shredding disk. Add the lemon zest, nutmeg, cinnamon, chives, and salt and pepper to taste. Mix well.

Cut the filo sheets in half crosswise. Place a half sheet on a work surface, keeping the remaining sheets covered with plastic wrap and a damp kitchen towel, to prevent them from drying out. Spread about 2 tablespoons of the cheese mixture on the filo in a rectangle about 3 inches (7.5 cm) long and 3/4 inch (2 cm) wide, leaving the bottom edge and sides uncovered. Fold the bottom edge over the mixture, then fold in the sides and roll up into a cylinder about 1 1/2 inches (4 cm) in diameter. Repeat with the remaining half sheets and cheese mixture.

Using a pastry brush, lightly brush a baking sheet with some of the oil. Arrange the rolls on the baking sheet at least 1/2 inch (12 mm) apart. Lightly brush the pastries with the remaining oil. Bake until golden and crisp, 18–20 minutes. Serve while still crisp, either hot or warm.

Makes 12 rolls; serves 6

3/4 cup (6 oz/185 g) ricotta

1/4 cup (1 oz/30 g) walnut halves

2 oz (60 g) Emmentaler cheese

Freshly grated zest of 1 lemon

2 pinches of freshly grated nutmeg

4 pinches of ground cinnamon

2 tablespoons snipped fresh chives

Salt and freshly ground pepper

6 sheets filo dough

1 tablespoon peanut oil or vegetable oil

New Potatoes with Tapenade

The mild, earthy flavor of boiled potatoes is an ideal backdrop for the Provençal spread called *tapenade*, a purée of black olives and anchovies. Tapenade is also good on toast or served as a condiment with cold roasted meats or poultry.

2 lb (1 kg) small firm-fleshed new potatoes, such as red-skinned, rose fir, or white rose varieties

2/3 cup (5 fl oz/160 ml) water

1 tablespoon fine sea salt

FOR THE TAPENADE:

1 small clove garlic

2 oz (60 g) anchovy fillets in olive oil, well drained (optional)

Freshly ground pepper

2 tablespoons extra-virgin olive oil

1/2 cup (4 oz/125 g) capers in brine, rinsed and well drained

8 oz (250 g) large plump black olives, pitted

Place the unpeeled potatoes in a small, deep, heavy pot with a tight-fitting lid. Pour in the water and sprinkle the salt over the top. Cover the pot, place over medium heat, and cook for 20 minutes without touching the pot. At this point the potatoes should be cooked and all the water evaporated. To test for doneness, insert the tip of a knife into the center of one of the potatoes. Let cool to room temperature.

While the potatoes are cooking, make the tapenade. Pass the garlic clove through a garlic press into a food processor or blender. Add the anchovies, pepper to taste, and the oil and process to a fine purée. Add the capers and process again. Add the olives and process quickly to form a thick purée.

At serving time, cut the cooled potatoes into thin slices (the skins may be left on) and spread each slice with some of the tapenade. Arrange on a platter.

Serves 8

Marinated Jalapeño Chiles

Homemade pickled chiles are easy to make and keep well for up to 3 months in the refrigerator, ready to serve on an hors d'oeuvre tray, to accompany grilled steaks or chicken, or to cut into strips for tacos.

In a large saucepan over medium heat, warm the oil. Add the chiles, onion, garlic, and carrots. Sauté until tender-crisp, about 1 minute. Add the vinegar, water, oregano, brown sugar, and salt and pepper to taste. Bring to a boil, remove from the heat, cover, and let cool completely before serving.

To store, pour into glass jars and cover tightly. The pickled chiles can be refrigerated for up to 3 months.

Makes about 8 cups (64 fl oz/2 l)

1 tablespoon vegetable oil

2 lb (1 kg) fresh jalapeño chiles

1 large onion, thinly sliced

1 head garlic, cut in half vertically with loose outer peel removed

2 large carrots, peeled and thinly sliced

3 cups (24 fl oz/750 ml) distilled white vinegar

1 cup (8 fl oz/250 ml) water

3 rounded tablespoons dried oregano, crumbled

1/4 cup (2 oz/60 g) firmly packed dark brown sugar

Salt and freshly ground pepper

Pizza Margherita

A well-loved and widely traveled variety of pizza, this combination was the inspiration of nineteenth-century Neapolitan pizza maker Raffaele Esposito, who created it to honor Queen Margherita, wife of Italy's King Umberto I, on a royal visit to Naples in 1889.

Divide and shape the pizza dough into 2 equal balls and place on a floured baking sheet. Cover with a kitchen towel and let rest in the refrigerator for 30 minutes.

Preheat the oven to 500°F (260°C). Generously sprinkle a large baking sheet with cornmeal. On a lightly floured work surface, roll out each ball of dough into a round 9 inches (23 cm) in diameter. Using your hands, transfer the rounds to the prepared baking sheet.

In a bowl, combine the tomatoes, garlic, and basil and toss to mix. Spread evenly over the dough rounds. Drizzle with some of the extra-virgin olive oil and season to taste with salt and pepper. Distribute the mozzarella cheese evenly over each round and sprinkle with the Parmesan.

Bake until the crusts are golden, 10–15 minutes. Remove from the oven and brush the edge of each crust with the remaining extra-virgin olive oil. Cut into wedges and serve hot.

Serves 4–6 as an appetizer

About 1/2 recipe (3/4 lb/375 g) Basic Pizza Dough (page 320)

2 1/2 lb (1.25 kg) tomatoes, peeled (if desired), seeded and coarsely chopped (page 329)

4 cloves garlic, minced

12–16 fresh basil leaves, cut into thin strips

1/4 cup (2 fl oz/60 ml) extra-virgin olive oil

Salt and freshly ground pepper

1/2 lb (250 g) mozzarella cheese, thinly sliced

1/4 cup (1 oz/30 g) grated Parmesan cheese

Ratatouille-Stuffed New Potatoes

Tiny new potatoes make great appetizers because they are easy to eat out of hand. These luscious stuffed potatoes are also a fine side dish to grilled sea bass or halibut.

12–16 small red new potatoes, 1½ lb (750 g) total weight

2 tablespoons olive oil, plus extra for brushing

1 small yellow onion, finely chopped

1 eggplant (aubergine), 1½–2 lb (750 g–1 kg), peeled and cut into ⅛-inch (3-mm) dice

2 red bell peppers (capsicums), seeded, deribbed, and cut into ⅛-inch (3-mm) dice

2 lb (1 kg) plum (Roma) tomatoes, peeled, seeded, and finely chopped (page 329)

2 cloves garlic, minced

2 tablespoons finely chopped fresh basil

1 tablespoon balsamic vinegar

1 teaspoon salt

¼ teaspoon freshly ground pepper

½ cup (2 oz/60 g) grated Parmesan cheese

Preheat the oven to 475°F (245°C).

Place the potatoes on an ungreased baking sheet. Bake until the potatoes are tender when pierced with a knife and the skins are slightly crispy, 45–50 minutes. Remove from the oven and let cool. Leave the oven set at 475°F (245°C).

Cut each potato in half across its width. If the ends are uneven, cut off a thin slice so they will stand upright when filled. Carefully scoop out the flesh from each half, leaving only a thin shell. (Reserve the flesh for another use.) Return the potato shells to the baking sheet, hollow sides down, and brush the skins with the oil. Bake until crisp, 10–15 minutes. Remove from the oven and reduce the oven temperature to 425°F (220°C).

While the shells are baking, make the filling. In a large frying pan over medium heat, warm the 2 tablespoons oil. Add the onion and sauté, stirring frequently, until translucent, about 5 minutes. Add the eggplant and cook, stirring, until it begins to soften, 5–7 minutes. Add the bell peppers and cook, stirring, for 5 minutes. Add the tomatoes, garlic, basil, and vinegar and continue to cook until the liquid evaporates and the eggplant is soft, 5–10 minutes longer. Add the salt and pepper. Set aside.

Sprinkle the insides of the potato shells with some Parmesan cheese. Spoon in the filling and place on an ungreased baking sheet. Sprinkle with the remaining Parmesan. Bake until heated through, 10–15 minutes. Serve immediately.

Serves 10–12 as an appetizer; 6–8 as a side dish

Terrine of Mediterranean Mixed Vegetables

Think of this baked flat omelet as an elegant variation on the classic Provençal ratatouille. You may also leave the terrine slices whole and serve them as a first course.

Heat the oil in a nonstick frying pan over medium heat. Add the onions and cook until they begin to color, about 3 minutes. Add the bell peppers and cook, stirring, for 5 minutes. Add the eggplants and cook, stirring, for 5 minutes longer. Add the zucchini, tomatoes, thyme, and salt and pepper to taste. Stir well, cover, and cook, stirring occasionally, for 30 minutes.

Meanwhile, break the eggs into a bowl. Season them with salt and pepper to taste. Beat with a fork until blended.

Preheat the oven to 350°F (180°C). Oil an 8-by-12-inch (20-by-30-cm) baking dish.

When the vegetables have been cooking for 30 minutes, stir in the garlic and basil and then the eggs. Mix thoroughly and remove the pan from the heat. Pour the mixture into the prepared baking dish and cover with a sheet of aluminum foil pricked all over with the tip of a knife.

Bake until set, about 45 minutes. Remove from the oven and allow to cool completely in the dish. Refrigerate for 6 hours before serving.

Cut the terrine into slices, then into cubes, and serve.

Serves 8

3 tablespoons extra-virgin olive oil

1/2 lb (250 g) small white onions, about 3/4 inch (2 cm) in diameter, thinly sliced

1 1/4 lb (625 g) red and green bell peppers (capsicums), stemmed, seeded, deribbed, and cut into 3/8-inch (1-cm) squares

11 oz (345 g) eggplants (aubergines), trimmed and cut into 3/8-inch (1-cm) dice

13 oz (410 g) zucchini (courgettes), trimmed and cut into 3/8-inch (1-cm) dice

1/2 lb (250 g) plum (Roma) tomatoes, peeled, seeded, and cut into 3/8-inch (1-cm) dice (page 329)

1 teaspoon fresh thyme leaves or 1/4 teaspoon dried thyme

Salt and freshly ground pepper

6 eggs

1 clove garlic, finely chopped

2 tablespoons chopped fresh basil

Curried Vegetables in Filo Packets

Curry powder gives dishes a distinctly sweet and spicy flavor. Although you can find commercial curry powder in most supermarkets, the real thing is actually a combination of up to 20 different spices, and in India, it is known to vary from region to region.

3 tablespoons unsalted butter

1 zucchini (courgette), trimmed and finely chopped

1 carrot, peeled and finely chopped

3 oz (90 g) fresh button mushrooms, trimmed and finely chopped

2 shallots, finely chopped

2 tablespoons snipped fresh chives

2 teaspoons curry powder

Salt

3 tablespoons water

2¹/₂ cups (8 oz/250 g) finely chopped tender heart of green cabbage

Grated zest of ¹/₂ lemon

4 sheets filo dough, thawed in the refrigerator if frozen

In a large nonstick frying pan, melt 1 ¹/₂ tablespoons of the butter over medium heat. Add the zucchini, carrot, mushrooms, shallots, and chives. Cook, stirring, until the vegetables are golden, about 3 minutes. Add the curry powder and salt to taste and cook, stirring, for 2 minutes. Add the water to the pan and then stir in the cabbage. Cover and cook over low heat, stirring often, for 20 minutes.

While the cabbage is cooking, preheat the oven to 425°F (220°C). In a very small saucepan, melt the remaining 1 ¹/₂ tablespoons butter and let it cool. With a pastry brush, lightly brush a nonstick baking sheet with some of the melted butter.

When the vegetables are cooked, transfer them to a bowl and let them cool slightly. Stir in the lemon zest. Cut the filo sheets into quarters. Keep the sheets covered with plastic wrap and a damp kitchen towel to prevent them from drying out. Place a quarter sheet on a work surface and brush the edges with a little of the melted butter, covering a border about 1 ¹/₂ inches (4 cm) wide. Place a large spoonful of the vegetable mixture in the center and spread it into a small rectangle. Fold the sides of the pastry inward and then fold over the top edges, to form a rectangle. Place the packet, seam side down, on the prepared baking sheet. Repeat with the remaining filo sheets, butter, and vegetable mixture.

Bake until the pastry is crisp, 12–15 minutes. Serve warm.

Makes 16 packets; serves 8

Corn Pancakes with Fresh Tomato Salsa

Serve these corn-flecked pancakes as a brunch or lunch main dish, or as a side dish with meat or poultry. If you are unable to make your own salsa, look for fresh tomato salsa in the refrigerator case of well-stocked food stores.

In a food processor or blender, combine two-thirds of the corn kernels with the whole egg and egg white, buttermilk, hot-pepper sauce, flour, salt, baking powder, and baking soda. Process until the batter is blended and smooth, about 30 seconds, stopping once to scrape down the sides of the container. Scrape the batter into a bowl and stir in the parsley and the remaining corn kernels.

Coat a large nonstick frying pan with nonstick cooking spray and place over medium heat. When the pan is hot—the batter should sizzle when it hits the surface—spoon in about 2 tablespoons batter for each pancake. Do not crowd the pan. Cook the pancakes on the first side until they are dry around the edges and a few small bubbles appear on the surface, about 2 minutes. Using a spatula, turn carefully and cook until lightly browned and dry on the second side, $1–1^{1}/_2$ minutes longer. Transfer to a warmed platter and cover loosely with aluminum foil to keep warm until all the pancakes are cooked.

Serve the pancakes immediately. Accompany with the salsa and the yogurt.

Makes about 16 3-inch pancakes; serves 4

$1^{1}/_2$ cups (9 oz/280 g) corn kernels

1 whole egg plus 1 egg white

$^{2}/_3$ cup (5 fl oz/160 ml) buttermilk

Dash of hot-pepper sauce

$^{2}/_3$ cup (4 oz/120 g) all-purpose (plain) flour

$^{1}/_2$ teaspoon salt

$^{1}/_2$ teaspoon baking powder

$^{1}/_4$ teaspoon baking soda (bicarbonate of soda)

2 tablespoons chopped fresh flat-leaf (Italian) parsley

$^{1}/_2$ cup (4 fl oz/125 ml) Fresh Mexican Salsa (page 319) or purchased salsa

$^{1}/_2$ cup (4 fl oz/125 ml) nonfat plain yogurt

Cheese-Filled Filo Triangles

These favorite Greek hors d'oeuvres are formed into small triangles — hence their name, *tiropetes*, meaning "three-sided pies." Feta cheese can be quite crumbly and salty. The addition of Monterey jack gives the filling a creamier texture and a milder taste.

1 lb (500 g) feta cheese, crumbled

1/2 lb (250 g) Monterey jack cheese, finely shredded

3 eggs, lightly beaten

1/3 cup (1/2 oz/15 g) finely chopped fresh flat-leaf (Italian) parsley

3 tablespoons chopped fresh dill (optional)

1/2 teaspoon freshly grated nutmeg

1/4 teaspoon freshly ground pepper

1 lb (500 g) filo dough, thawed in the refrigerator if frozen

1 1/2 cups (12 oz/375 g) unsalted butter, clarified (page 324) and kept warm

In a bowl, combine the feta and jack cheeses, eggs, parsley, dill (if using), nutmeg, and pepper. Stir to mix well and set aside.

Place the filo dough sheets flat on a work surface. Cut lengthwise into thirds. The strips should be 2–2 1/2 inches (5–6 cm) wide. Keep the strips covered with plastic wrap and a damp kitchen towel to prevent them from drying out.

Preheat the oven to 400°F (200°C). Line the bottoms of 2 baking sheets with parchment (baking) paper or lightly brush with some of the clarified butter.

Remove 2 strips from the stack of filo sheets, then re-cover the sheets. Brush 1 strip lightly with clarified butter. Lay the second strip directly on top of the first and brush with butter. Place 1 teaspoon of the cheese mixture on the top strip about 2 inches (5 cm) from one end. Fold the end at an angle over the filling to form a triangle. Continue to fold the dough, preserving the triangle shape, until you have folded the entire strip. Place the triangular pastry on a prepared baking sheet. Repeat until all of the dough strips and filling have been used and both baking sheets are filled.

Brush the tops with butter. Bake the pastries, 1 baking sheet at a time, until golden brown, about 10 minutes. Serve hot.

Makes about 48 pastries; serves 12

Blue Cheese Tartlets

The robust flavor of spinach or Swiss chard is more than a match for the tang of blue cheese in these bite-sized tarts. The pine nuts add a mellow richness to balance the assertive flavors of the cheese.

About 3/4 recipe (8 oz/250 g) Tart Pastry dough (page 321) or purchased puff pastry

3 oz (90 g) spinach or Swiss chard, trimmed

1 egg

2/3 cup (5 fl oz/160 ml) heavy (double) cream

3/4 cup (3 oz/90 g) shredded Emmentaler cheese

1/4 teaspoon freshly grated nutmeg

Salt and freshly ground pepper

3 oz (90 g) Roquefort cheese, crumbled

2 tablespoons pine nuts

If using tart pastry, prepare the dough and refrigerate for at least 3 hours. Remove from the refrigerator 30 minutes before you are ready to roll it out. If using commercial puff pastry, defrost it in the refrigerator or at room temperature.

Preheat the oven to 425°F (220°C). Bring a large saucepan filled with water to a boil. Plunge the spinach into the boiling water and cook for 30 seconds. Immediately drain in a colander and rinse with cold water to halt the cooking. Drain again, pressing against the greens to force out as much water as possible. Set aside.

Break the egg into a bowl. Add the cream, Emmentaler cheese, nutmeg, and salt and pepper to taste. Beat with a fork until completely blended. Coarsely chop the spinach and add it to the bowl. Stir well.

On a lightly floured board, roll the dough out as thinly as possible. Sprinkle the Roquefort cheese evenly over the dough. With a fluted pastry cutter about 1 1/2 inches (4 cm) in diameter, cut out 18 dough rounds. Use the rounds to line 18 individual tartlet pans, the cups in tartlet trays, or miniature muffin pans. If using individual pans, arrange them on a large baking sheet. Fill each pastry-lined pan with some of the egg mixture and scatter a few pine nuts on top. Bake until the filling sets and the crust is golden, about 15 minutes. Serve warm.

Makes 18 tartlets; serves 6

Tex-Mex Cheese Dip
with Tortilla Chips

Tortilla chips, or *totopos*, can be easily prepared at home, although store-bought chips work just as well. This dip can also be enjoyed with vegetable sticks, such as celery or carrot.

Corn oil or other
vegetable oil for frying

6 corn tortillas,
each cut into 6 wedges

1 cup (4 oz/125 g) shredded
Cheddar cheese

1 cup (4 oz/125 g) shredded
Monterey Jack cheese

2 tablespoons finely chopped
canned, pickled jalapeño chile

2 tablespoons finely chopped
red bell pepper (capsicum)

To make the tortilla chips, in a frying pan over high heat, pour oil to a depth of about 1 1/2 inches (4 cm). Heat until the oil registers 350°F (180°C) on a deep-frying thermometer. Working in batches to avoid overcrowding, add the tortilla wedges and fry until crisp and golden, about 1 minute. Using a slotted spoon, transfer to paper towels to drain.

Combine the cheeses in the top pan of a double boiler or heatproof bowl. Place over simmering water and heat until melted, about 5 minutes. Alternatively, combine the cheeses in a microwave-safe container and heat in a microwave oven set on high until melted, 2–3 minutes.

Add the chile and bell pepper to the melted cheeses. Mix well.

To serve, place the tortilla chips on a platter. Transfer the hot cheese dip to a bowl and nest it on the platter with the chips. Serve immediately.

Serves 6

Stuffed Poblano Chiles with Jalapeño Salsa

Poblano chiles are ideal for stuffing. Wear rubber gloves, if you like, and be careful not to touch your eyes or face when handling the chiles. There are volatile oils in the seeds and ribs that can sting tender skin.

Preheat the oven to 400°F (200°C).

To remove the seeds and ribs from the poblano chiles, carefully cut off the cap from the stem end of each chile. Cut away the cluster of seeds, but reserve the cap with stem intact.

Bring a saucepan three-fourths full of water to a boil. Add the chiles and their caps and boil for 2 minutes. Using a slotted spoon, transfer to cold water to cool. Drain and blot dry.

In a bowl, combine the cheeses. Stuff the chiles with the cheese mixture and replace the caps. Pour the 2 tablespoons oil into a baking dish, roll the stuffed chiles in it to coat, and lay them on their sides. Cover with aluminum foil and bake until tender when pierced with a knife, about 30 minutes.

While the chiles bake, make the salsa. Sprinkle the tomato halves with salt. Place, cut sides down, in a colander to drain for about 20 minutes, then dice.

While the tomatoes drain, remove the seeds and ribs from the jalapeño chile. Chop finely and place in a bowl. Add the green onions, cilantro, cumin, lemon juice, 1/4 cup (2 fl oz/60 ml) oil, and diced tomatoes. Toss to mix. Season to taste with salt and pepper.

Transfer the baked chiles to warmed plates and top with the salsa. Serve immediately.

Serves 4

4 fresh poblano chiles

1/4 lb (125 g) blue cheese, crumbled

1/4 lb (125 g) Monterey jack cheese, shredded

1/4 lb (125 g) sharp Cheddar cheese, shredded

2 tablespoons olive oil

FOR THE JALAPEÑO SALSA:

2 tomatoes, peeled and seeded (page 329)

Salt

1 fresh jalapeño chile

3 green (spring) onions, chopped

3 tablespoons chopped fresh cilantro (fresh coriander)

1/2 teaspoon ground cumin

Juice of 1 lemon

1/4 cup (2 fl oz/60 ml) olive oil

Freshly ground pepper

Cheese Puffs

Pastry dough, mixed with shredded Emmentaler or Gruyère cheese and piped onto a baking sheet, puffs up to form light, flaky hors d'oeuvres that are good hot or at room temperature.

1 lb (500 g) Puff Shell Pastry (page 321)

1 cup (4 oz/125 g) shredded Emmentaler or Gruyère cheese

1/4 teaspoon freshly grated nutmeg

Freshly ground white pepper

Prepare the pastry dough. While it is still hot, vigorously beat in the cheese, nutmeg, and white pepper to taste with a rubber spatula.

Preheat the oven to 450°F (230°C). Spoon the dough into a pastry bag fitted with a plain tip 1/2 inch (12 mm) in diameter. Pipe small rounds about 1 1/2 inches (4 cm) in diameter onto a nonstick baking sheet at about 2-inch (5-cm) intervals. Alternatively, pipe the mixture into muffin-pan cups.

Bake until the pastry is puffed and golden, 15–20 minutes. If serving at room temperature, cool on wire racks.

Makes about 30 puffs; serves 6

Deep-Fried Chiles Stuffed with Cream Cheese

Although jalapeño and wax chiles are normally quite fiery, you may seed, derib, and then soak them for 24 hours to temper their heat without diminishing their flavor.

The day before serving, heat the oil in a small frying pan over high heat until very hot. Add the chiles, a few at a time, and fry until well blistered, about 3 seconds on each side. Using a slotted spoon, transfer the chiles to a large bowl filled with cold water. Remove the pan from the heat and let the oil cool. Reserve the cooled oil in a covered container to cook the stuffed chiles the next day.

With the chiles still in the water, peel off the skins with your fingers, or use a knife if necessary. Make a lengthwise slit in each chile. Remove and discard the seeds and ribs, leaving the stem intact. Discard the water.

In a medium bowl, stir together 1 cup (8 fl oz/250 ml) water, the vinegar, and the salt. Add the chiles, cover, and let soak at room temperature for about 24 hours to reduce the piquancy.

The next day, drain the chiles, rinse under cold water, drain again, and pat dry. Carefully stuff each chile with an equal amount of the cream cheese. Place the flour, egg, and Parmesan cheese in separate shallow bowls. Dip each stuffed chile first in the flour, then in the egg, and finally in the Parmesan, coating completely each time.

In a small frying pan over medium heat, heat the reserved oil. When the oil is hot, add the chiles, a few at a time, and fry until lightly golden, about 2 minutes on each side. Using a slotted spoon, transfer to paper towels to drain. Serve warm with salsa on the side.

Makes 12 stuffed chiles; serves 4

2 cups (16 fl oz/500 ml) corn oil or other vegetable oil

12 fresh jalapeño or yellow wax chiles

1/2 cup (4 fl oz/125 ml) distilled white vinegar

1/2 teaspoon salt

3 oz (90 g) cream cheese

1/3 cup (2 oz/60 g) all-purpose (plain) flour

1 egg, lightly beaten

1/2 cup (2 oz/60 g) grated Parmesan cheese

Fresh Mexican Salsa (page 319)

Mini Pizzas with Mozzarella

With their simple yet flavorful toppings, these mini pies represent pizza in its most basic and memorable Neapolitan form. The pizzas can be made in advance and reheated before serving in a preheated 425°F (220°C) oven for 6−8 minutes.

Prepare the pizza dough. Preheat the oven to 500°F (260°C).

On a lightly floured work surface, roll out the dough 3/8 inch (1 cm) thick. With a round pastry cutter that is 1 1/2 inches (4 cm) in diameter, cut out 24 rounds. Roll these rounds out again until they are 1/8 inch (3 mm) thick. Lay the rounds on a nonstick baking sheet.

Place the tomatoes in a bowl. Add the mozzarella and the anchovies, if using. Toss lightly. Drizzle with the olive oil. Sprinkle with the oregano and pepper to taste. Mix gently.

Divide the tomato mixture evenly among the dough rounds and top each with an olive. Bake the pizzas until the cheese melts and the edges of the crust are golden, about 15 minutes. Serve warm.

Makes 24 mini pizzas; serves 8

About 3/4 recipe (13 oz/410 g) Basic Pizza Dough (page 320)

1 1/4 lb (625 g) tomatoes, cut in half crosswise, seeded, and cut into thin strips

6 oz (185 g) mozzarella cheese, cut into thin strips

12 anchovy fillets in olive oil, drained and finely diced (optional)

2 tablespoons extra-virgin olive oil

1 teaspoon dried oregano

Freshly ground pepper

24 black olives, pitted

Potato Omelet

Flat vegetable omelets such as these are eaten throughout southwestern Europe. They are particularly popular in Spain, where they are often cut into wedges and served as a first course or snack, with a glass of wine.

1 lb (500 g) baking potatoes, peeled

½ cup (4 fl oz/125 ml) water

1 tablespoon unsalted butter

3 tablespoons extra-virgin olive oil

Salt

1 clove garlic

2 tablespoons finely chopped fresh flat-leaf (Italian) parsley

6 eggs

Freshly ground pepper

¼ teaspoon freshly grated nutmeg

In a food processor or with a sharp knife, cut the potatoes into matchstick lengths.

Pour the water into a small nonstick frying pan. Add the butter and 2 tablespoons of the oil. Bring to a boil over medium-high heat. Add the potatoes. Stir well. Sprinkle with salt to taste. Reduce the heat to low. Cover partially. Cook, turning often, until the potatoes are just crisp and the water evaporates, about 12 minutes. Add the garlic by passing it through a garlic press. Add the parsley. Continue to cook and stir for 3 minutes longer.

Meanwhile, break the eggs into a large bowl. Add salt and pepper to taste. Add the nutmeg and the remaining 1 tablespoon oil. Beat with a fork until the eggs are completely blended. Pour the eggs over the potatoes. When the eggs begin to set, smooth the surface with the back of a spoon and cover the pan. Cook over low heat for 8 minutes.

Lightly oil a serving plate large enough to hold the omelet. When the outer edges of the omelet are firm, invert it onto the oiled plate. Slide it back into the pan, browned side up. Cover and cook over low heat until firm and golden brown, about 8 minutes longer. Transfer the omelet to the plate and cut into cubes or small triangles. Serve warm or at room temperature, with toothpicks.

Serves 6

Marinated Bell Peppers

Most varieties of bell pepper (capsicum) turn red or yellow when they mature and develop a sweet, mellow flavor. Their tough skin can be removed by exposing it to the intense direct heat of a broiler or grill and then peeling it off.

2 red bell peppers (capsicums)

2 yellow bell peppers (capsicums)

6 anchovy fillets in olive oil, drained and chopped (optional)

1 tablespoon drained capers

Salt and freshly ground pepper

3 tablespoons olive oil

1 large clove garlic, minced

2 heads Belgian endive (chicory/witloof), separated into leaves (optional)

Fresh basil leaves (optional)

Buttered, toasted baguette slices (optional)

Preheat the broiler (grill). Line a broiler pan with parchment (baking) paper or aluminum foil, if desired, to keep the pan free of any burned-on juices.

Cut the bell peppers lengthwise into quarters, then remove the stems, seeds, and ribs. Arrange the quarters, cut sides down, on the prepared broiler pan. Broil (grill) about 4 inches (10 cm) below the heat source until the skins blacken and blister, 5–6 minutes. Remove from the broiler, cover with aluminum foil, and let stand for 10 minutes, then peel away the skins.

Preheat the oven to 400°F (200°C).

Cut each bell pepper quarter lengthwise into 4 strips. Scatter half of the strips over the bottom of a large, shallow baking dish. Sprinkle evenly with the anchovies (if using), capers, and salt and pepper to taste. Drizzle with half of the oil. Sprinkle over the garlic and the remaining bell peppers. Drizzle with the remaining oil. Bake until the bell peppers are soft, about 15 minutes. Let cool.

To serve, arrange the peppers on a platter. Or, if desired, spoon the bell peppers into the endive leaves and garnish with basil leaves; serve with baguette slices.

Makes about 16 appetizers; serves 4

Meat, Poultry & Seafood Starters

Oysters on the Half Shell with Shallot-Pepper Sauce

You can omit the shallot sauce and make a traditional cocktail sauce by seasoning ketchup with prepared horseradish, hot-pepper sauce, and fresh lemon juice. Paired with well-buttered rye bread, the oysters are a light and refreshing first course.

In a small serving bowl, stir together the wine, vinegar, shallots, and pepper to taste. Taste and adjust the seasoning with vinegar and pepper.

Place the bowl of shallot-pepper sauce in the center of a large platter. Surround the bowl with a bed of crushed or shaved ice.

To prepare the oysters, first discard any that have a bad odor or that do not close to the touch. Using a stiff-bristled kitchen brush, thoroughly scrub the shell of each oyster, rinsing it under cold water. To one side of the hinge, opposite the shell's concentric ridges, push in the tip of an oyster knife and pry upward to open the shell (during shucking, protect your hand from the sharp-edged shell by gripping the oyster flat-side up with a folded kitchen towel).

To detach the oyster, run the knife all around the oyster to cut the muscle that holds the shell halves together. Be sure to keep the blade edge against the inside of the top shell. Lift off the top shell and discard. Run the knife underneath the oyster to cut its flesh free from the bottom shell, being careful not to spill the liquor. Nest the oysters in their bottom shells on the ice.

Garnish with lemon wedges and parsley sprigs, if desired. Serve immediately.

Serves 6

1/2 cup (4 fl oz/125 ml) dry white wine

1/4 cup (2 fl oz/60 ml) Champagne vinegar or white wine vinegar, or to taste

4 shallots, minced

Coarsely ground pepper

Crushed or shaved ice

36 oysters in the shell, well scrubbed

Lemon wedges (optional)

Fresh flat-leaf (Italian) parsley sprigs (optional)

New Potatoes with Caviar

Caviar is an elegant and impressive appetizer. For an attractive presentation, use golden caviar, or salmon roe. For a special treat, use the real thing: beluga, osetra, or sevruga caviar. If you like, serve with chilled vodka or Champagne.

12–16 small red new potatoes, 1^1/$_2$ lb (750 g) total weight, unpeeled and well scrubbed

2 tablespoons vegetable oil

^{3}/$_4$ cup (6 fl oz/185 ml) sour cream or crème fraîche

2 teaspoons finely chopped fresh chives

^{1}/$_4$ teaspoon salt

Pinch of ground white pepper

2 oz (60 g) any variety caviar or fish roe (see note)

Watercress or fresh flat-leaf (Italian) parsley sprigs

Preheat the oven to 475°F (245°C).

Place the potatoes on an ungreased baking sheet. Bake until the potatoes are tender when pierced with a knife and the skin is slightly crispy, 45–50 minutes. Remove from the oven and let cool.

Cut each potato in half crosswise. If the ends are uneven, cut off a thin slice so they will stand upright when filled. Scoop out all the pulp from each half, leaving only a thin shell. Place the pulp in a bowl. Return the potato shells to the baking sheet, hollow sides down, and brush with the oil. Bake until crisp, 10–15 minutes. Remove from the oven and reduce the oven temperature to 425°F (220°C).

Add ^{1}/$_2$ cup (4 fl oz/125 ml) of the sour cream to the potato pulp along with the chives, salt, and white pepper. Mix well. Pack the potato mixture into a pastry bag fitted with a medium star tip and pipe the mixture into the potato shells. Alternatively, using a small teaspoon, spoon the mixture into the shells.

Place the filled potatoes on an ungreased baking sheet. Bake until heated through, 10–15 minutes. Arrange the potatoes on a serving platter. Top each with a dollop of the remaining sour cream. Top with the caviar or fish roe. Garnish the platter with watercress. Serve immediately.

Serves 10–12 as an appetizer

Endive Boats with Smoked Salmon Stuffing

Devotees of smoked salmon say you need little more than lemon and chives to highlight its flavor. True to that spirit, this recipe serves the lightly seasoned salmon nestled in Belgian endive (chicory/witloof) spears.

In a bowl, combine the smoked salmon, oil, lemon juice, chives, and salt and pepper to taste. Stir until well blended. Cover and refrigerate for 1 hour.

Remove the outer leaves of the endives (reserve for another use). Separate from the heart the tender leaves that are large enough for stuffing. You should have 6–8 leaves from each endive. Chill in the refrigerator.

At serving time, gently stir the salmon roe into the smoked salmon mixture. Spoon some of the salmon mixture into the wide end of each endive leaf. Arrange on a platter. Serve immediately.

Serves 8–10

6 oz (185 g) smoked salmon, roughly chopped

2 tablespoons extra-virgin olive oil

1 tablespoon fresh lemon juice

2 tablespoons finely chopped fresh chives

Salt and freshly ground pepper

4 large heads Belgian endive (chicory/witloof)

1 oz (30 g) salmon roe

Seafood Tempura

Lacy, crisp tempura batter coats fresh scallops and shrimp in this classic and surprisingly light Japanese preparation. In addition to the lemon wedges, you can serve the tempura with soy sauce.

12 large shrimp (prawns) peeled and deveined (page 328)

12 sea scallops

3/4 cup (6 fl oz/180 ml) very cold water

1 egg yolk

3/4 cup (4 oz/125 g) all-purpose (plain) flour, plus extra for dusting

Salt

Peanut oil or vegetable oil for deep-frying

Lemon wedges

Make shallow parallel cuts along the inside curve of each shrimp so they will not curl during cooking.

Slice each scallop in half horizontally to form 2 rounds. Set aside.

Pour the cold water into a bowl. Add the egg yolk and whisk rapidly with a fork. Quickly whisk in the 3/4 cup (4 oz/125 g) flour. Add salt to taste. Be careful not to overbeat the batter.

In a deep fryer or heavy saucepan over medium heat, pour oil to a depth of at least 2 inches (5 cm). Heat to 350°F (180°C) on a deep-frying thermometer, or until a small bit of bread tossed into the oil surfaces immediately. When the oil is ready, in batches, lightly flour 5 or 6 pieces of the shrimp and scallops, dip them into the batter, and then carefully slip them into the oil. Do not crowd the pan. Cook, turning with a slotted utensil, until lightly golden, 2 minutes for the scallops and 3 minutes for the shrimp. Remove with a slotted utensil to paper towels to drain briefly.

Arrange the shrimp and scallops on a large serving platter. Serve immediately with the lemon wedges.

Serves 6–8

Crab Fritters with Red Pepper Mayonnaise

Try serving these fritters with Rémoulade (page 319), Herb Vinaigrette (page 108), or Fresh Mexican Salsa (page 319) in place of the mayonnaise. If you like, garnish with lemon wedges or fresh parsley sprigs.

Preheat the broiler (grill).

In a large bowl, sift together the flour and salt. Make a well in the center and add the egg yolks, oil, and beer. Whisk together thoroughly. Let the batter rest for 1 hour at room temperature.

To make the Red Pepper Mayonnaise, cut the bell pepper in half lengthwise and remove the stem, seeds, and ribs. Place cut sides down on a baking sheet. Broil (grill) until blackened, 6–10 minutes. Transfer the pepper to a plastic or paper bag. Close tightly and let cool for 10 minutes. Using your fingers, peel off the skin. Chop the pepper coarsely and place in a blender or in a mortar. Blend or crush with a pestle until smooth. In a small bowl, stir together the 1 cup mayonnaise, roasted bell pepper purée, chives, cayenne, garlic, lemon juice, and salt and black pepper to taste. Cover and refrigerate until serving.

In a deep saucepan, pour in corn oil or peanut oil to a depth of 2 inches (5 cm). Heat to 375°F (190°C) on a deep-frying thermometer, or until a little batter sizzles on contact. Meanwhile, in a bowl, beat the egg whites until stiff. Gently fold the egg whites and crabmeat into the batter.

Drop the crab mixture by heaping tablespoonfuls into the hot oil. Do not crowd the pan. Fry, turning often, until golden brown, about 2 minutes. Using a slotted spoon, transfer to paper towels to drain.

Arrange the hot fritters on a platter. Serve the red pepper mayonnaise on the side.

Serves 6

1 cup (5 oz/155 g) all-purpose (plain) flour

1 teaspoon salt

2 eggs, separated

2 tablespoons olive oil

3/4 cup (6 fl oz/180 ml) beer, at room temperature

RED PEPPER MAYONNAISE:

1 red bell pepper (capsicum)

1 cup (8 fl oz/250 ml) homemade Mayonnaise (page 318) or store-bought

3 tablespoons chopped fresh chives

Pinch of cayenne pepper

2 cloves garlic, minced

2 tablespoons fresh lemon juice

Salt and freshly ground pepper

Corn oil for deep-frying

3/4 lb (375 g) fresh cooked crabmeat, picked over for shell fragments

Sizzling Scallops

This variation on the classic French Coquilles St. Jacques uses a reduced cream sauce instead of béchamel. Serve in 6 small (³/₄ cup/6 fl oz/180 ml) heatproof ramekins or scallop-shaped dishes.

1 lb (500 g) sea or bay scallops

3 tablespoons unsalted butter

¹/₂ small yellow onion, minced

1 cup (3 oz/90 g) thinly sliced fresh white mushrooms

¹/₂ cup (4 fl oz/125 ml) dry white wine

1 cup (8 fl oz/250 ml) heavy (double) cream

¹/₂ cup (2 oz/60 g) grated Parmesan cheese

2–3 tablespoons fresh lemon juice, or to taste

Salt and freshly ground pepper

1 tablespoon chopped fresh flat-leaf (Italian) parsley

If using sea scallops, cut them horizontally into slices ¹/₄ inch (6 mm) thick. If using bay scallops, leave them whole.

Preheat the broiler (grill).

In a frying pan over medium heat, melt 1 tablespoon of the butter. Add the scallops and sauté, turning as needed, until just firm to the touch, about 2 minutes. Using a slotted spoon, transfer the scallops to a plate. Set aside.

Add the remaining 2 tablespoons butter to the same pan over medium heat. Add the onion and sauté, stirring, until soft, about 5 minutes. Raise the heat to high and add the mushrooms. Sauté, stirring occasionally, until the liquid evaporates, about 5 minutes. Add the wine and cook until the liquid is reduced by half. Reduce the heat to medium-low. Add the cream and simmer until thickened, 2–3 minutes. Add the Parmesan, scallops, and lemon juice and salt and pepper to taste. Stir until well combined.

Divide the hot scallop mixture among 6 heatproof dishes (see note) arranged in a shallow heatproof pan. Slip under the broiler. Broil (grill) until the tops are golden and bubbling at the edges, 1–2 minutes.

Sprinkle with the parsley. Serve immediately.

Serves 6

Parchment-Baked Oysters

Cut into these parchment packets in the kitchen, or place them on individual plates for guests to open at the table. Be careful; the escaping steam will be quite hot.

If using oysters in the shell, shuck them as directed in the recipe on page 257. Set aside. Preheat the broiler (grill). Cut the bell pepper in half lengthwise and remove the stem, seeds, and ribs. Place cut side down on a baking sheet. Broil (grill) until blackened, 6–10 minutes. Transfer the pepper to a plastic or paper bag, close tightly, and let cool for 10 minutes. Using your fingers, peel off the skin. Cut the pepper into 1/4-inch (6-mm) dice. Set aside.

Meanwhile, in a small bowl, combine the onion with water to cover. Let stand for 5 minutes, then drain. In another bowl, combine the drained onion, roasted bell pepper, radishes, chives, parsley, and salt and pepper to taste. Set aside. In another small bowl, mash together the orange juice and zest, saffron and water, the 1/4 cup (2 oz/60 g) butter, and salt and pepper to taste.

Preheat the oven to 400°F (200°C). Cut out 6 heart shapes from parchment (baking) paper, each 12 inches (30 cm) tall and 12 inches (30 cm) wide at its widest point. Brush the hearts on one side with the melted butter. Place 4 oysters on the right half of each heart. Top the oysters with equal amounts of the vegetable mixture. Season with salt and pepper. Dot each portion with the saffron-orange butter. Fold the other half of each heart over the filling and crease the edges together securely so the juices will not escape. Wrap each packet in aluminum foil and place on ungreased baking sheets. Bake until the packets have puffed considerably, 6–10 minutes. Remove from the oven and cut open the top of each packet (see note). Serve immediately.

Serves 6

24 oysters in the shell or bottled shucked oysters, drained

1 red bell pepper (capsicum)

1/2 small red onion, cut into 1/4-in (6-mm) dice

10 large radishes, thinly sliced

1/4 cup (1/3 oz/10 g) finely chopped fresh chives

1/4 cup (1/3 oz/10 g) chopped fresh flat-leaf (Italian) parsley

Salt and freshly ground pepper

1 teaspoon fresh orange juice

1/2 teaspoon grated orange zest

1/4 teaspoon saffron threads, steeped in 1 teaspoon hot water

1/4 cup (2 oz/60 g) unsalted butter, at room temperature, plus 2 tablespoons unsalted butter, melted

Mini Potato Pancakes with Smoked Salmon

These make a lovely hors d'oeuvre or first course. Smoked trout or caviar is also an option here. Cook the pancakes just before serving time — they lose their crispness quickly. They are excellent with your favorite sparkling wine.

Place the onion in a sieve and use a wooden spoon to press out all excess liquid. Transfer the onion to a bowl. Press the excess liquid from the potatoes in the same way and add them to the onion. Add the eggs, salt, pepper, and flour. Using the wooden spoon, beat until the mixture is the consistency of a thick batter.

Preheat the oven to 300°F (150°C). Line a large baking sheet with a double layer of paper towels.

Pour oil to a depth of $^1/_2$ inch (12 mm) into a large nonstick frying pan over medium-high heat. Spoon a rounded $^1/_2$ tablespoon of batter into the pan to test the oil; the batter should hold together and begin to brown. When the oil is hot, working in batches, spoon 2 rounded tablespoons of the batter for each pancake into the pan; make sure the pancakes do not touch. Flatten the pancakes with the back of a spoon; they should be about 1 $^1/_2$ inches (4 cm) in diameter. Use a spatula to round and smooth the sides, if necessary. Fry until golden brown on the first side, about 2–3 minutes. Flip and fry on the second side until golden brown, 2 minutes longer.

Transfer the pancakes to the lined baking sheet to drain and place in the oven until all are cooked. Arrange the pancakes on a warmed serving platter. Garnish each with sour cream, smoked salmon, and a dill sprig. Serve immediately.

Makes 30–36 pancakes; serves 8–12 as an appetizer

1 small yellow onion, grated

2 baking potatoes, about $^1/_2$ lb (250 g) each, peeled and shredded

2 eggs

$^1/_2$ teaspoon salt

Pinch of freshly ground pepper

2 tablespoons all-purpose (plain) flour

Vegetable oil for frying

$^1/_3$ cup (3 oz/80 g) sour cream

$^1/_4$ cup (1$^1/_2$ oz/35 g) chopped smoked salmon

Fresh dill sprigs

Gravlax with Mustard-Dill Sauce

It is easier to cut gravlax into thin slices if you start with a good-sized piece of salmon. Aquavit, the Scandinavian caraway-flavored spirit, is the traditional curing liquor. Offer the gravlax as a first course with dark rye or pumpernickel bread.

1 whole salmon fillet with skin intact, about 2 lb (1 kg)

3 tablespoons sugar

3 tablespoons kosher salt

1/2 teaspoon freshly ground pepper

1/2 teaspoon ground allspice (optional)

24 dill sprigs

3–4 tablespoons aquavit, gin, or vodka, or to taste

FOR THE MUSTARD-DILL SAUCE:

1/4 cup (2 fl oz/60 ml) Dijon mustard

1 teaspoon dry mustard

2 tablespoons sugar

2 tablespoons distilled white vinegar

1/2 cup (4 fl oz/125 ml) peanut oil

2–3 tablespoons chopped fresh dill

Three or four days before you plan to serve the gravlax, place the salmon, skin side down, in a shallow nonaluminum container. In a small bowl, stir together the 3 tablespoons sugar, salt, pepper, and allspice, if using. Rub the mixture over the top surface of the salmon. Place the dill sprigs on top. Sprinkle with the aquavit. Cover with plastic wrap and set a heavy weight (3–4 lb/1.5–2 kg) on top. Refrigerate for 3–4 days, basting daily with the juices that accumulate.

At serving time, make the mustard-dill sauce. In a food processor or a blender, add the Dijon mustard, dry mustard, 2 tablespoons sugar, and vinegar. Pulse to combine. With the motor running, slowly add the oil and continue to process until the sauce thickens. Transfer to a bowl and fold in the chopped dill.

To serve, remove and discard the dill sprigs from the salmon. Slice the salmon thinly across the grain. Serve the sauce on the side.

Serves 8–12

Crab Omelet with Sweet-and-Sour Sauce

Cooked crab meat is widely available in fish markets. For best flavor and texture, use fresh crab meat. It is best to purchase a whole, cracked crab and remove the meat yourself (page 322).

3 tablespoons extra-virgin olive oil

1 lb (500 g) red bell peppers (capsicums), stemmed, seeded, deribbed, and cut into 3/8-inch (1-cm) squares

3 tablespoons water

2 tablespoons plus 1/2 teaspoon superfine (caster) sugar

Salt

9 eggs

Freshly ground pepper

1 clove garlic, cut into tiny matchsticks

13 oz (410 g) fresh cooked crabmeat

1 teaspoon sweet paprika

4 pinches of hot paprika

3/4 cup (6 fl oz/180 ml) plus 3 tablespoons tomato sauce

1/2 cup (4 fl oz/ 100 ml) rice vinegar

In a nonstick frying pan over medium heat, warm 2 tablespoons of the oil. Add the peppers, water, 1/2 teaspoon sugar, and salt to taste. Bring to a boil. Stir well. Cover partially and cook, turning often, until the peppers begin to brown, 10 minutes. While the peppers brown, break the eggs into a large bowl. Add salt and pepper to taste and the remaining 1 tablespoon oil. Beat with a fork until blended. Set aside.

Add the garlic to the frying pan and stir for 1 minute. Add the crabmeat and cook, stirring, for 3 minutes. Add the sweet and hot paprikas and stir again. Stir in the 3/4 cup (6 fl oz/180 ml) tomato sauce, followed by the beaten eggs. When the eggs begin to set, smooth the surface with the back of a spoon and cover the pan. Reduce the heat to low and cook for 8 minutes.

Lightly oil a plate. When the outer edges of the omelet are firm, invert it onto the plate. Slide it back into the pan, browned side up. Cover and cook over low heat until firm and golden brown, about 8 minutes longer. Transfer to the plate and let cool to room temperature.

To make the sauce, combine the vinegar and the remaining 2 tablespoons sugar in a small, heavy saucepan. Bring to a boil over low heat. Cook until the mixture is syrupy, about 2–3 minutes. Add the 3 tablespoons tomato sauce and boil for 1 minute, then remove the pan from the heat and cool to room temperature.

Just before serving, cut the omelet into cubes. Spoon the sauce into a small serving bowl. Spear the omelet cubes with toothpicks and dip into the sauce.

Serves 8

Fish Tartare

Use very fresh, sashimi-quality, firm, white-fleshed fish and salmon for this dish. Serve with garlic-rubbed toasted bread, and garnish with capers, sliced green (spring) onion, olives, and lemon wedges.

Cut the white fish and salmon into long, thin strips. Place the strips in a bowl nested in a larger bowl filled with ice cubes. Add a generous amount of salt and pepper. Mix thoroughly. Sprinkle with the olive oil and mix again.

Transfer the fish to a deep plate. Cover and refrigerate until serving time, no more than 2–3 hours.

Arrange the fish on a serving platter. Serve at once.

Serves 4

6 oz (185 g) white fish fillets such as sea bream, sea bass, cod, sole, halibut, or flounder

6 oz (185 g) salmon fillets

Salt and freshly ground pepper

3 tablespoons extra-virgin olive oil

Crab Cakes with Rémoulade Sauce

Crab cakes are perfect for an elegant first course. As an alternative to the rémoulade, you can also serve with Red Pepper Mayonnaise (page 265) or Aïoli (page 286). Garnish with lemon or lime wedges and the leafy tops of celery stalks.

2 tablespoons unsalted butter

6 green (spring) onions, including 2 inches (5 cm) of tender green tops, thinly sliced

2 small celery stalks, chopped

1 cup (4 oz/125 g) finely crushed saltine crackers

1 tablespoon dry mustard

1 teaspoon hot-pepper sauce

2 teaspoons Worcestershire sauce

2 eggs, well beaten

1/4 cup (2 fl oz/60 ml) homemade Mayonnaise (page 318), or store-bought

3 tablespoons finely chopped fresh flat-leaf (Italian) parsley

1 lb (500 g) cooked crabmeat, shell fragments removed

Salt and freshly ground pepper

About 2 cups (4 oz/120 g) Toasted Bread Crumbs (page 320)

4 tablespoons (2 fl oz/60 ml) vegetable oil or 4 tablespoons (2 oz/60 g) unsalted butter

Rémoulade (page 319)

To make the crab cakes, in a large frying pan over low heat, melt the butter. Add the green onions and celery. Cover and cook, stirring occasionally, until soft, about 10 minutes. Using a slotted spoon, transfer the onions and celery to a bowl and let cool. Discard the butter.

To the cooled onion-celery mixture, add the crushed saltines, mustard, hot-pepper sauce, Worcestershire sauce, eggs, mayonnaise, parsley, crabmeat, and salt and pepper to taste. Mix well. If the mixture seems too wet to hold its shape, add enough of the bread crumbs, about 1/2 cup (1 oz/30 g) or as needed, to absorb the moisture. Shape the mixture into 6 cakes, each 3 inches (7.5 cm) in diameter and 1/2 inch (12 mm) thick. Place the remaining bread crumbs in a large shallow bowl. Dredge the cakes lightly in the crumbs.

In a frying pan over medium heat, warm 2 tablespoons of the vegetable oil. Add half of the crab cakes and sauté, turning once, until golden brown, about 3 minutes on each side. Using a slotted spatula, transfer to paper towels to drain. Keep warm. Sauté the remaining crab cakes in the same way, using the remaining oil.

Serve the crab cakes immediately, with the rémoulade sauce.

Makes 6 cakes; serves 6

Pan-Fried Croutons Topped with Spiced Crab

These hors d'oeurves are also delicious as an accompaniment to a bowl of vegetable soup or served alongside a garden salad. The chunky topping can be made with other shellfish such as cooked and chopped shrimp (prawns), lobster, or scallops.

Crush the garlic with a pestle in a mortar or pass it through a garlic press to form a smooth paste. Transfer to a small bowl. Add the mayonnaise, lemon juice, paprika, chives, green onions, cayenne, and salt and black pepper to taste. Stir well. Add the crabmeat and mix to combine.

In a large frying pan over medium heat, melt 1 tablespoon of the butter with 1 tablespoon of the oil. Place about one-third of the bread slices in a single layer in the pan and sauté, turning once, until golden on both sides, 2–3 minutes. Using a slotted spatula, transfer the bread slices to a plate. Repeat with the remaining butter, oil, and bread slices in two more batches.

Spread the spiced crab mixture on the pan-fried bread slices, dividing it equally. Arrange on a platter and garnish with lemon wedges. Serve immediately.

Serves 6

1 clove garlic

1/3 cup (3 fl oz/80 ml) home-made Mayonnaise (page 318), or store-bought

1 teaspoon fresh lemon juice

1/2 teaspoon sweet paprika

1/4 cup (1/3 oz/10 g) finely chopped fresh chives

3 green (spring) onions, including 2 inches (5 cm) of tender green tops, thinly sliced

1/8–1/4 teaspoon cayenne pepper, or to taste

Salt and freshly ground pepper

6 oz (185 g) fresh cooked crabmeat, shell fragments removed

3 tablespoons unsalted butter

3 tablespoons olive oil

1/2 baguette, cut on a sharp diagonal into slices 1/4 inch (6 mm) thick

Lemon wedges

Sesame Shrimp

Fried butterflied shrimp (prawns) get a crisp, rich coating from sesame seeds. If you like, serve the shrimp with the Sweet-and-Sour dipping sauce on page 272. You can also coat and cook thin strips of boned and skinned chicken breast in the same way.

Butterfly the shrimp: deepen the slit that was made to remove the vein, but do not cut all the way through. Open the shrimp so that it lies flat.

In a small bowl, beat the egg whites with a fork until frothy. Put the sesame seeds in another small bowl.

In a deep fryer or heavy saucepan over medium heat, pour oil to a depth of at least 2 inches (5 cm). Heat to 350°F (180°C) on a deep-frying thermometer, or until a small piece of bread tossed into the oil surfaces immediately. When the oil is ready, dip the shrimp in the egg whites, and then roll them in the sesame seeds. Being careful not to crowd the pan, drop 5 or 6 shrimp into the hot oil and cook, turning them with a slotted spoon, until golden brown, 2–3 minutes.

Using the slotted spoon, transfer the shrimp to paper towels to drain. Repeat with the remaining shrimp. Serve hot, warm, or at room temperature.

Serves 6

24 large shrimp (prawns), peeled and deveined (page 328)

2 egg whites

3 tablespoons sesame seeds

Peanut oil or vegetable oil for deep-frying

Baked Filo Triangles with Moroccan-Spiced Shellfish

The combination of assertive herbs and spices here lends a distinctive North African flavor. Just before serving, squeeze a fresh lemon wedge over the tops of these feather-light triangles for a refreshing hint of citrus.

2 tablespoons olive oil

1/4 lb (125 g) bay scallops

1/4 lb (125 g) shrimp (prawns), peeled and deveined (page 328)

2 cloves garlic, minced

1/4 cup (1 1/2 oz/45 g) finely chopped yellow onion

1 large tomato, chopped

4 tablespoons chopped fresh cilantro (fresh coriander)

3/4 teaspoon ground cumin

Pinch of cayenne pepper

Pinch of saffron threads, crumbled

1/4 cup (1/2 oz/15 g) Toasted Bread Crumbs (page 320)

Salt and freshly ground black pepper

1/2 cup (4 oz/125 g) unsalted butter, melted

1/2 lb (250 g) filo dough, thawed in the refrigerator if frozen

In a frying pan over low heat, warm 1 tablespoon of the oil. Add the scallops, shrimp, and half of the garlic. Sauté, stirring, until the shellfish are almost firm, about 2 minutes. Transfer to a cutting board and chop coarsely. Set aside.

Add the remaining 1 tablespoon oil to the same pan and raise the heat to medium. Add the onion and tomato. Sauté, stirring occasionally, until the onion is tender, 10 minutes. Add the remaining garlic, the cilantro, cumin, cayenne, and saffron. Simmer gently until the moisture evaporates, about 10 minutes. Remove from the heat. Mix in the shellfish mixture and bread crumbs. Season with salt and black pepper.

Preheat the oven to 375°F (190°C). Lightly brush 2 baking sheets with some of the melted butter. Cut the stack of filo sheets lengthwise into strips about 3 inches (7.5 cm) wide. Keep the strips covered with plastic wrap and a damp kitchen towel to prevent them from drying out. Remove 2 strips from the stack of filo sheets, then re-cover the sheets. Brush 1 strip lightly with melted butter. Lay the second strip directly on top of the first and brush with butter. Place 1 teaspoon of the shellfish mixture on the top strip about 2 inches (5 cm) from one end. Fold the end at an angle over the filling to form a triangle. Continue to fold the dough, preserving the triangle shape, until you have folded the entire strip. Place the triangular pastry on a prepared baking sheet. Repeat until all of the dough strips and filling have been used.

Bake until golden, about 15 minutes. Transfer to a platter and serve immediately.

Makes about 30 pastries; serves 6

Butterflied Shrimp

The shrimp (prawns) can also be cut into pieces, mixed with the remaining ingredients, and then mounded in peeled avocado halves. Accompany with crusty bread or salted crackers.

1/4 onion plus 1 onion, finely chopped

1 bay leaf

Salt

30 large shrimp (prawns)

3 fresh jalapeño or serrano chiles, finely chopped

1 cup (8 fl oz/250 ml) fresh lime juice

6 tablespoons (3 fl oz/90 ml) olive oil

6 tablespoons (3 fl oz/90 ml) soy sauce

6 tablespoons (3 fl oz/90 ml) Worcestershire sauce

Freshly ground pepper

Bring a large saucepan three-fourths full of water to a boil. Add the $1/4$ onion, bay leaf, salt, and shrimp. Boil the shrimp until they turn pink and curl loosely, about 3–5 minutes. Drain well. Immerse in cold water to halt the cooking and drain.

Peel each shrimp, then devein by making a lengthwise slit along the outside curve and removing the dark intestinal vein. To butterfly the shrimp, deepen the slit, but do not cut all the way through, and open the shrimp so that it lies flat.

Arrange 5 butterflied shrimp on each of 6 individual plates. Sprinkle each serving with an equal amount of the chopped onion, chiles, lime juice, oil, soy sauce, and Worcestershire sauce. Season to taste with pepper and serve.

Serves 6

Spanish Clams with Tomatoes and Herbs

Spanish cooks have paired clams with fresh tomatoes for centuries. Mussels can be substituted for the clams; be sure to remove their beards and scrub the shells well before adding them to the pan (page 327).

In a frying pan over medium heat, warm 2 tablespoons of the oil. Add the onion and sauté, stirring, until it begins to turn golden, 12–15 minutes. Add the tomatoes and tomato paste. Sauté, stirring occasionally, until thickened, 5–6 minutes. Add the wine and cook uncovered until reduced by half, about 5 minutes. Add the fish stock, raise the heat to high, and cook until thickened, about 5 minutes. Remove from the heat and let cool slightly.

In a food processor or blender, purée the tomato mixture until smooth. Season to taste with salt and pepper. Set aside.

In a frying pan large enough to hold the clams in a single layer, warm the remaining 2 tablespoons oil over high heat. Add the garlic, parsley, and clams, discarding any clams that do not close to the touch. Cover and cook, shaking the pan periodically, until the clams open, 3–5 minutes, depending on their size. Discard any clams that failed to open.

Using a slotted spoon, transfer the clams to a plate and keep warm. Add the puréed tomato mixture to the same pan and boil uncovered until reduced by one-fourth. Add the clams and mix well.

Transfer to a platter and serve immediately.

Serves 6

4 tablespoons (2 fl oz/60 ml) olive oil

1 yellow onion, chopped

3/4 cup (4 1/2 oz/140 g) peeled, halved, seeded, and chopped tomatoes, fresh (page 329) or canned

1 tablespoon tomato paste

1/2 cup (4 fl oz/125 ml) dry white wine

1 cup (8 fl oz/250 ml) Fish Stock (page 317) or bottled clam juice

Salt and freshly ground pepper

1 large clove garlic, minced

2 tablespoons chopped fresh flat-leaf (Italian) parsley

2 lb (1 kg) clams, well scrubbed

Shrimp and Garlic Omelet

In Spain, this simple omelet, known as *tortilla de gambas y ajo*, is served as part of an assortment of tapas. Garlic chives, flat-bladed chives also called Chinese chives, have a distinctive taste that goes nicely with shrimp (prawns).

3/4 lb (375 g) small shrimp (prawns), peeled and deveined (page 328)

1/2 lb (250 g) pencil-thin asparagus, tough stem ends removed, cut into 1-inch (2.5-cm) lengths

6 tablespoons (3 fl oz/90 ml) olive oil

1 small yellow onion, finely chopped, or 8 green (spring) onions, including tender green tops, finely chopped

12 garlic chives or regular chives, chopped

2 cloves garlic, minced

6 extra-large or 7 large eggs

Salt and freshly ground pepper

Bring a saucepan three-fourths full of water to a boil over high heat. Cook the shrimp in the boiling water until they turn pink and begin to curl, about 4 minutes. Drain and set aside to cool.

Refill the saucepan three-fourths full of water, salt it lightly, and bring to a boil over high heat. Add the asparagus and cook until tender-crisp, 3–5 minutes. Drain and immerse in cold water to halt the cooking. Drain again.

In a sauté pan over medium heat, warm 3 tablespoons of the oil. Add the onion. Sauté, stirring occasionally, until tender, about 8 minutes. Reduce the heat to low and add the chives, garlic, shrimp, and asparagus. Cook, stirring, for 2 minutes. Remove from the heat.

In a bowl, lightly beat the eggs. Add the shrimp mixture, stir well, and season to taste with salt and pepper. In a 10-inch (25-cm) omelet pan or sauté pan, warm the remaining 3 tablespoons oil over hight heat. When the oil is very hot, pour in the egg mixture and reduce the heat to medium. Cook until the underside of the omelet is golden and the top is slightly set, 5–6 minutes, running a spatula around the edges of the pan a few times during cooking to prevent sticking. Invert a plate over the pan and carefully flip the pan and plate together so the omelet is golden side up. Slide the omelet back into the pan and cook briefly on the second side until pale gold, 2–3 minutes longer. Do not overcook, or the omelet will be dry.

Slide the omelet onto a serving plate. Let cool briefly. Cut into wedges to serve.

Serves 6

Pizza with Shrimp and Aïoli

For a crispy crust, use a pizza stone or unglazed terra-cotta tiles. Transfer the pizza to the hot stone using a baker's peel. If you do not have a pizza stone, bake the pizzas on a baking sheet or pizza pan.

3/4 lb (375 g) Basic Pizza Dough (page 320)

FOR THE AÏOLI:

1/3 cup (3 fl oz/80 ml) homemade Mayonnaise, (page 318), or store-bought

1 clove garlic, minced

2–3 teaspoons warm water

FOR THE TOPPING:

1/4 lb (125 g) fontina cheese, coarsely shredded

1/4 lb (125 g) mozzarella cheese, coarsely shredded

2 tablespoons olive oil

1/2 small red onion, thinly sliced

1/2 teaspoon red pepper flakes

6 oz (185 g) small shrimp (prawns), peeled and deveined (page 328)

2 teaspoons chopped fresh flat-leaf (Italian) parsley

Place a pizza stone or unglazed terra-cotta tiles on the lowest rack of the oven and preheat the oven to 500°F (260°C).

Divide the pizza dough in half and, on a floured work surface, roll out half into a 9-inch (23-cm) round, then transfer it to a peel or baking sheet.

To make the aïoli, in a small bowl, stir together the mayonnaise and garlic. Add enough of the warm water to make the mixture barely fluid. Set aside.

To make the topping, in another small bowl, combine the cheeses. Brush 1 tablespoon of the oil on the pizza round to within 1/2 inch (12 mm) of the edge. Sprinkle half of the cheeses over the oil. Spread half of the onion slices over the cheese, then sprinkle with 1/4 teaspoon of the red pepper flakes.

Slide the pizza directly onto the pizza stone or tiles and bake for 5 minutes. Using the peel or baking sheet, remove the pizza from the oven and arrange half of the shrimp on top. Continue to bake until the shrimp are cooked and the dough is crisp and golden, 4–5 minutes longer.

Using the peel or baking sheet, remove the pizza from the oven. Drizzle with half of the aïoli and sprinkle with half of the parsley. Cut into wedges and serve immediately. Repeat with the remaining ingredients to make a second pizza.

Makes two 9-inch (23-cm) pizzas; serves 6

Greek-Style Caviar Spread

Tarama, or salted cod roe, can be found in well-stocked supermarkets or Greek and Middle Eastern markets. Use tarama to make this rich purée to spread on vegetable slices or scoop up with oven-crisped pita bread.

In a food processor or blender, combine the tarama, yogurt, lemon zest and juice, bread crumbs, oil, paprika, and cayenne to taste. Process to a smooth purée.

Transfer to a serving bowl. Serve at room temperature or cover tightly, refrigerate, and serve chilled.

Serves 8

13 oz (410 g) tarama

3/4 cup (6 fl oz/185 ml) plain yogurt

Grated zest of 1 lemon

2 tablespoons fresh lemon juice

1/3 cup (1 1/3 oz/41 g) Toasted Bread Crumbs (page 320)

3 tablespoons extra-virgin olive oil

1/4 teaspoon paprika

4–6 pinches of cayenne pepper

Broiled Oysters with Herbed Bread Crumbs

This is a popular dish wherever fresh oysters are found. The topping can be varied with the addition of 3 tablespoons chopped wilted spinach, green (spring) onion, fennel bulb, or fresh mushrooms. Serve these oysters with lemon wedges.

Shuck the oysters as directed in the recipe on page 257, reserving their liquor in a bowl. Place the oysters in their bottom shells on a baking sheet. Cover and refrigerate the oysters and the bowl of liquor.

Preheat the oven to 450°F (230°C).

In a frying pan over medium heat, melt 4 tablespoons (2 oz/60 g) of the butter. Add the shallots and sauté, stirring, until soft, about 8 minutes. Add the garlic and continue to sauté for 1 minute. Add the bread crumbs, parsley, chives, oregano, and thyme. Sauté, stirring occasionally, until the bread crumbs are lightly golden, about 10 minutes. Add the reserved oyster liquor, the fish stock, lemon juice, and salt and pepper to taste. Mix well and remove from the heat. The mixture should be slightly moist.

Spoon the topping on the oysters, dividing it evenly. In a small saucepan or frying pan, melt the remaining 2 tablespoons butter. Drizzle the butter evenly over the topping. Bake the oysters until very hot, about 6 minutes. Remove from the oven.

Preheat the broiler (grill). Broil (grill) the oysters until the topping is a light golden brown, 1–2 minutes. Serve hot.

Serves 6

36 oysters in the shell, well scrubbed

6 tablespoons (3 oz/90 g) unsalted butter

4 large shallots, minced

1 clove garlic, minced

2 1/2 cups (5 oz/155 g) fresh bread crumbs

2 tablespoons chopped fresh flat-leaf (Italian) parsley

1 tablespoon chopped fresh chives

1/2 teaspoon chopped fresh oregano

1/2 teaspoon chopped fresh thyme

2 tablespoons Fish Stock (page 317) or bottled clam juice

2–3 teaspoons fresh lemon juice, or to taste

Salt and freshly ground pepper

Salt Cod Purée

This classic Provençal dish made from salt cod filets is called *brandade de morue*. The word *brandade* means "something that is stirred." Here a food processor is used to make the purée, without a sacrifice in taste.

1¹/₂ lb (750 g) boneless
salt cod

2 cloves garlic

Salt

1¹/₂–3 cups (12–24 fl oz/
375–750 ml) olive oil

1¹/₄ cups (10 fl oz/310 ml) milk

Juice of 1 lemon

Freshly grated nutmeg

Freshly ground pepper

1 loaf coarse country bread,
1¹/₂ lb (750 g), sliced ¹/₃ inch
(9 mm) thick and toasted
or grilled

A day or two before you serve the dish, place the salt cod in a bowl with water to cover. Refrigerate for 24–48 hours, changing the water at least 4 times. (Very thick or very salty pieces of cod will require longer soaking.) Drain the cod and place in a large saucepan. Add water to cover generously, cover the pan, and place over low heat. Bring to a simmer very slowly; do not allow to boil, or the cod will become tough. Poach gently until the cod is just tender, about 10 minutes. Drain and let cool slightly. Remove all traces of skin and any remaining bones. Flake the cod with your fingers or a fork. Place in a food processor.

Using the flat side of a chef's knife, crush the garlic. Transfer to a small bowl and use a fork to blend in salt to taste until a fine paste forms. (Alternatively, place the garlic in a mortar and use a pestle to crush the garlic and blend in the salt.) Add to the food processor and pulse once to combine with the cod. In a small saucepan over low heat, warm 1¹/₂ cups (12 fl oz/375 ml) of the oil. In another saucepan over low heat, warm the milk. With the food processor's motor running, add half of the warm oil, a bit at a time, then add half of the warm milk. Continue adding in the warm oil and warm milk alternately. Add as much of the remaining 1¹/₂ cups (12 fl oz/375 ml) oil, a little at a time, as needed to achieve a pale, thick, and smooth mixture. Add the lemon juice. Season to taste with nutmeg and pepper.

Serve the purée at once or transfer to the top pan of a double boiler and keep warm over hot water. Serve with the toasted bread.

Serves 6–8

Shrimp Quesadillas with Tomatillo Salsa

These quesadillas may also be filled with cooked crabmeat, scallops, or a combination of different shellfish. If fresh tomatillos are unavailable, use drained canned ones.

½ cup (4 fl oz/125 ml) Fish Stock (page 317) or bottled clam juice

1 lb (500 g) shrimp (prawns), peeled and deveined

1 cup (4 oz/125 g) coarsely shredded Monterey jack cheese

1 cup (4 oz/125 g) coarsely shredded mozzarella cheese

1 cup (4 oz/125 g) coarsely shredded white Cheddar cheese

4 green (spring) onions, including 2 inches (5 cm) of tender green tops, thinly sliced

6 large flour tortillas

Tomatillo Salsa (page 319)

In a frying pan, bring the fish stock to a boil. Add the shrimp. Reduce the heat to low. Cover and simmer until the shrimp curl and are almost firm, about 1 minute. Using a slotted spoon, transfer the shrimp to a cutting board and chop coarsely.

In a bowl, combine the shrimp, cheeses, and green onions. Stir to mix. Distribute the mixture evenly among 3 of the tortillas. Top with the remaining tortillas to form the quesadillas.

Place a large frying pan over medium heat. When the pan is hot, slip 1 quesadilla into the pan and cook until the cheese begins to melt, 2–3 minutes. Turn the quesadilla over and cook on the other side until the cheese is melted and the tortilla is slightly golden, 1–2 minutes. Remove from the pan and keep warm. Repeat with the remaining quesadillas.

Cut each quesadilla into 6 wedges. Serve immediately, with the salsa.

Serves 6

Ceviche

If you want more spice, add a small chile—stemmed, seeded, and chopped. You can refrigerate the ceviche for up to 12 hours in advance. Serve alone or with toast.

Cut the fish fillets into 3-inch (7.5-cm) dice and place in a large nonreactive bowl. Pour the lime juice over the fish, making sure all the pieces are covered. Refrigerate for 3–4 hours.

Drain the fish cubes and pat dry on paper towels. Put the fish cubes into a large bowl. Add the tomatoes, pimiento, green onion, cilantro, and salt and pepper to taste. Stir to blend and refrigerate for at least 2 hours.

At serving time, pit the avocado (page 324) and dice it. Stir into the fish mixture, along with the olives and oregano. Serve at once.

Serves 6

1¼ lb (625 g) white fish fillets such as sea bream, halibut, or flounder

Juice of 5–6 limes

2 tomatoes, peeled, seeded and diced (page 329)

1 small fresh pimiento or other sweet pepper, stemmed, seeded, deribbed, and chopped

1 green (spring) onion, chopped, including the green portion

⅓ cup (½ oz/15 g) finely chopped fresh cilantro (fresh coriander)

Salt and freshly ground pepper

1 avocado

10 black olives, pitted

1 teaspoon dried oregano

Eggs Mimosa with Tuna Filling

The name for this traditional stuffed-egg preparation derives from the mimosa tree's frothy yellow flowers, which the egg yolks — pressed through a sieve — resemble. If you like, add a few drained anchovy fillets to the filling mixture.

8 hard-boiled eggs, peeled

5 oz (155 g) canned tuna in water, well drained

2 tablespoons cream cheese, at room temperature

2 tablespoons extra-virgin olive oil

1 tablespoon dark rum (optional)

1 teaspoon curry powder

Salt and freshly ground pepper

1 lemon or lime

1 tablespoon tiny capers in brine, rinsed and well drained

Carefully cut the eggs in half lengthwise. Remove the yolks and reserve 3 of them for the "mimosa." Put the remaining yolks in a food processor or a blender. Set the egg whites aside.

Add the tuna, cream cheese, oil, rum (if using), curry powder, and salt and pepper to taste to the food processor or blender.

Grate the zest of the lemon, then halve it. Squeeze it and measure 1 tablespoon juice. Add the zest and 1 tablespoon juice to the food processor along with the capers. Process at medium speed to a thick creamy consistency, about 1 minute (the mixture should not be too liquidy).

Fill the egg white halves with the tuna mixture, using enough of the mixture to round the top so that it looks like the original egg shape. Arrange the stuffed eggs on a large, flat plate. Put the reserved yolks in a stainless-steel fine-mesh sieve held over the stuffed eggs and crush the yolks with the back of a spoon, forcing them through the mesh so that the stuffed eggs are evenly covered with the sieved yolks, or mimosa. Keep in a cool place until ready to serve.

Serves 8

Mussels in Spicy Vinaigrette

Try this simple first course when mussels are in the market. The blend of sweet and hot paprikas in the vinaigrette complements the sea-fresh flavor of the shellfish. Serve with crusty bread for dipping in the cooking juices.

Pour the oil and vinegar into a large stockpot. Add the sweet and hot paprikas, lemon pieces, garlic, parsley, and salt to taste. Bring to a boil and simmer for 1 minute. Add the mussels, discarding any that do not close to the touch. Cover and cook until the mussels open, 3–4 minutes.

Transfer the mussels and their cooking liquid to a deep serving platter. Discard any mussels that failed to open. Let cool to room temperature and then refrigerate for 2–4 hours before serving.

Serves 4–6

¼ cup (2 fl oz/60 ml) extra-virgin olive oil

¼ cup (2 fl oz/60 ml) red wine vinegar

1 teaspoon sweet paprika

1 teaspoon hot paprika

1 large lemon, cut into slices ⅛ inch (3 mm) thick, seeded and each cut into six sections

2 cloves garlic, finely chopped

2 tablespoons finely chopped fresh flat-leaf (Italian) parsley

Salt

6 lb (3 kg) mussels, debearded and well scrubbed (page 327)

Cornmeal Boats with Pork Filling

This recipe calls for masa harina, which is commercial flour ground from treated field corn, for use in making tortillas, tamales, and other corn-based specialties. Try this dish with chicken substituted for the pork, and the results will be equally delicious.

Place the masa harina in a bowl. Add the salt, the $1/3$ cup oil, and the water. Using your fingers, mix to form a soft dough that is not sticky. Divide into 12 equal balls. Roll each ball into a strip $5^{1}/2$ inches (14 cm) by $^{1}/2$ inch (12 mm).

Cover the lower surface of an opened tortilla press with a sheet of plastic wrap that extends beyond its edges and place a dough strip in the center. Cover with a sheet of plastic wrap. Lower the top and push down gently.

Heat a heavy frying pan or griddle over medium-high heat. Open the tortilla press and peel off the top sheet of plastic wrap. The chalupa should be an oval $1/8$ inch (3 mm) thick. Using the bottom sheet of plastic wrap, lift the chalupa from the press and turn it over onto your hand. Peel off the bottom sheet. Gently place the chalupa on the preheated surface of the pan or griddle. Cook until the edges begin to dry out, about 45 seconds. Turn and cook the second side until lightly browned, about 45 seconds, at the same time pinching up the edges of the cooked side to form a rim. Turn again and cook the first side until the edges begin to brown, 45–60 seconds. Transfer to a plate and cover with a kitchen towel. Repeat until all the chalupas are cooked. (At this point, you can set them aside for up to 3 hours.)

Just before serving, heat the pan over medium-high heat. Place the chalupas, a few at a time and rim sides up, on the hot surface and drizzle evenly with the 2 tablespoons oil. The chalupas are warmed through when the oil begins to sizzle. Transfer to individual plates and top with the meat, onion, cheese, and salsa.

Serves 6

3 cups (15 oz/470 g) masa harina (see note)

$1/2$ teaspoon salt

$1/3$ cup (3 fl oz/80 ml) plus 2 tablespoons corn oil, other vegetable oil, or melted vegetable shortening

$1^{1}/2$ cups (12 fl oz/375 ml) lukewarm water

1 cup (5 oz/155 g) shredded cooked pork or chicken

$1/2$ yellow onion, finely chopped

1 cup (5 oz/155 g) crumbled queso fresco or feta cheese

Fresh Mexican Salsa or Tomatillo Salsa (page 319)

Tandoori-Style Chicken

In this recipe, tandoori-style spices flavor oven-baked chicken. Serve with slices of tomato, cucumber, and radish and a selection of chutneys. If you like, wrap the chicken in Indian breads such as nan or paratha.

1 chicken, about 3¹/₂ lb (1.75 kg), or assorted pieces

¹/₄ cup (2 fl oz/60 ml) fresh lemon juice

1 clove garlic

³/₄ cup (6 fl oz/185 ml) plain yogurt

1 tablespoon sweet paprika

1 teaspoon ground cumin

1 teaspoon ground ginger

¹/₂ teaspoon ground cinnamon

¹/₂ teaspoon ground cloves

¹/₂ teaspoon freshly grated nutmeg

¹/₂ teaspoon ground cardamom

¹/₂ teaspoon freshly ground pepper

1 teaspoon fine sea salt

Cut the chicken into 8 serving pieces and remove the skin. With a sharp knife make several deep parallel cuts about ³/₄ inch (2 cm) apart in each piece of meat, cutting against the grain.

Put the chicken pieces into a deep plate or a bowl. Sprinkle with the lemon juice. Let stand for 15 minutes, turning each piece 2 or 3 times.

Meanwhile, pass the garlic through a garlic press held over a small bowl. Add the yogurt, paprika, cumin, ginger, cinnamon, cloves, nutmeg, cardamom, pepper, and salt. Stir together. Pour this mixture over the chicken and mix well. Cover and refrigerate for 8 hours, turning 2 or 3 times.

About 1 hour before serving time, remove the chicken from the refrigerator. Remove a rack from the oven. Transfer the chicken pieces from the marinade to the rack. Reserve the marinade. Line a baking sheet with aluminum foil and position it in the oven under where the rack will be, to catch any drips. Alternatively, place a small rack in a roasting pan and arrange the chicken pieces on the rack.

About 15 minutes before you wish to cook the chicken, preheat the oven to 500°F (260°C). When the oven is hot, bake the chicken until tender, about 35 minutes, turning the pieces after 15 minutes and basting them with the reserved marinade 3 or 4 times (do not baste during last 5 minutes of cooking). Serve hot.

Serves 8

Fried Tortilla Puffs with Chicken

Frying puffs up the thick tortillas that form the base for this appetizer from Mérida, a city in the Yucatán. Make the red-onion relish the day before so that its flavors can develop fully.

The day before serving, combine the red onion with the vinegar in a glass bowl. Cover and refrigerate.

Place the chicken in a saucepan and add water to cover. Bring to a boil, then reduce the heat to medium-low. Cover and cook until tender, about 25 minutes. Drain and let cool completely. Bone and skin the chicken. Using your fingers or two forks, shred the chicken. Set aside.

Place the masa harina and flour in a large bowl. Add the water, using your fingers to work it into the flours to form a soft but not sticky dough. Form into 12 balls, each about 2 inches (5 cm) in diameter.

Following the directions for forming tortillas on page 320, roll the balls into tortillas about 4 inches (10 cm) in diameter and $1/8$ inch (3 mm) thick.

In a frying pan over high heat, pour in oil to a depth of $1/2$ inch (12 mm). When the oil is hot, fry the tortillas, one at a time, until a very light gold, about 25 seconds on each side. Transfer to paper towels to drain. Keep warm.

To serve, place 2 tortillas on each plate. Top with the shredded chicken. Using a slotted spoon to drain off some of the vinegar, top with the red onion relish. Garnish with the tomato and avocado slices.

Serves 6

1 1/2 red onions, finely chopped

1 cup (8 fl oz/250 ml) apple cider vinegar

1 whole chicken breast or 2 breast halves

1 cup (5 oz/155 g) masa harina

1 cup (5 oz/155 g) all-purpose (plain) flour

1 1/3 cups (11 fl oz/330 ml) lukewarm water

Vegetable oil for frying

1 tomato, thinly sliced

1 avocado, halved, pitted, cut into lengthwise slices, and peeled

Beef Meatballs with Parmesan

Why do Italian meatballs have so much flavor? One of the secrets is the addition of Parmesan cheese. For a different presentation, thread the cooked meatballs on tiny skewers and serve with tomato sauce.

1½ lb (750 g) lean ground (minced) beef

Salt and freshly ground pepper

4 pinches of freshly grated nutmeg

½ cup (2 oz/60 g) grated Parmesan cheese

¼ cup (⅓ oz/10 g) finely chopped fresh flat-leaf (Italian) parsley

4 tablespoons (2 fl oz/ 60 ml) extra-virgin olive oil

Put the beef into a bowl and season with a little salt and plenty of pepper. Add the nutmeg, Parmesan, and parsley. Knead the ingredients together with your hands until thoroughly mixed.

Dampen your hands with cold water. Shape the mixture into walnut-sized balls by rolling a small amount between your palms.

In a large nonstick frying pan over medium heat, heat 2 tablespoons of the oil. Add half of the meatballs to the pan. Cook until golden brown, about 5 minutes, occasionally moving the pan in a smooth, circular motion so that the balls cook on all sides without breaking. Transfer the meatballs to a serving platter.

Add the remaining 2 tablespoons oil to the pan. Cook the remaining meatballs in the same manner and transfer to the platter.

Serve the meatballs hot, warm, or at room temperature.

Serves 6–8

Pork Meatballs with Peanuts

This mixture also works well with lamb or beef. Accompany with match-sticks of cucumber or wedges of fresh fruit. If you'd like a dipping sauce, mix soy sauce with a squeeze of lemon.

1¼ lb (625 g) pork loin, cut into ¾-inch (2-cm) dice

½ cup (3 oz/90 g) shelled unsalted raw peanuts

6 fresh mint sprigs, stemmed

6 fresh cilantro (fresh coriander) sprigs, stemmed

2 egg whites

2 teaspoons five-spice powder

Salt

4 tablespoons (2 fl oz/60 ml) peanut oil or vegetable oil

In a food processor, combine the pork, peanuts, mint, cilantro, egg whites, five-spice powder, and salt to taste. Process just until the mixture forms a medium-fine texture.

Dampen your hands with cold water. Shape the mixture into walnut-sized balls by rolling a small amount between your palms.

In a large nonstick frying pan over medium heat, heat 2 tablespoons of the oil . Add half of the meatballs to the pan. Cook until golden brown, about 10 minutes, occasionally moving the pan in a smooth, circular motion so that the balls cook on all sides without breaking. Transfer the meatballs to a serving platter.

Add the remaining 2 tablespoons oil to the pan. Cook the remaining meatballs in the same manner. Transfer to the platter.

Serve the meatballs hot, warm, or at room temperature.

Serves 6–8

Crisp Tortilla Packets with Pork

The colloquial Mexican name for this popular Yucatán appetizer, *chilindrinas*, means "trifle," or "a bit of fun." Serve on a bed of salad greens or shredded lettuce and top with shredded Cheddar cheese.

Heat a dry, heavy frying pan or griddle over medium heat. Roast the garlic head and half of the onion, turning often, until evenly charred, 4–5 minutes. Transfer the charred garlic and onion half to a saucepan and add 5 cups (40 fl oz/1.25 l) water, the oregano, the $^1/_2$ teaspoon salt, and the pork. Bring to a boil. Reduce the heat to medium-low. Cover and simmer until the pork is tender, 45–50 minutes. Remove the pork and let cool. Using your fingers or two forks, shred the meat. Set aside.

In a food processor or blender, combine the tomatoes, the remaining onion half, and the 2 tablespoons salt. Purée until smooth. In a saucepan over medium heat, warm the 1 tablespoon oil. Add the tomato purée and cook, uncovered, stirring often, to form a medium-thick consistency, about 10 minutes. In a bowl, stir together 2 cups (16 fl oz/500 ml) of the tomato sauce, the capers, olives, and shredded pork. Set aside. Keep the remaining sauce warm.

Following the directions for forming tortillas on page 320, divide the dough into 24 balls, each about 1 $^1/_2$ inches (4 cm) in diameter. Roll the balls into tortillas about 5 inches (13 cm) in diameter. Spoon 2 tablespoons of the pork mixture onto the center of each tortilla. Fold in the sides, then fold over the ends, and press closed. In a small frying pan over high heat, pour in oil to a depth of $^1/_2$ inch (12 mm). When the oil is hot, fry the filled tortillas, a few at a time and turning once, until golden, 2 minutes on each side. Transfer to paper towels to drain briefly.

Top the tortilla packets with warm tomato sauce and serve.

Serves 6

1 head garlic, loose outer peel removed

1 onion, cut in half

1 teaspoon dried oregano, crumbled

$^1/_2$ teaspoon plus 2 tablespoons salt

1 lb (500 g) pork tenderloin, cut into 2-inch (5-cm) chunks

2 lb (1 kg) tomatoes, coarsely chopped

1 tablespoon corn oil or other vegetable oil, plus oil for frying

5 tablespoons (2$^1/_2$ oz/75 g) well-drained capers, finely chopped

$^1/_3$ cup (2 oz/60 g) finely chopped green olives

2 lb (1 kg) dough for Flour Tortillas (page 320)

Lamb Tikka

Tikka-style foods are cut into bite-sized chunks for marinating and cooking quickly. Lamb, used here, is a favorite; chunks of skinless, boneless chicken breast are also good. Serve with crisp vegetables such as cucumbers, radishes, or hearts of lettuce.

Place the lamb cubes in a bowl. In a blender or food processor, combine the garlic, onion, ginger, yogurt, lemon juice, garam masala, cumin, turmeric, mint, cilantro, and salt. Blend to a smooth mixture. Pour the yogurt mixture over the lamb. Mix thoroughly to coat evenly. Cover and refrigerate for 6–8 hours.

If using bamboo skewers, cover 6 skewers with water and soak for 30 minutes before cooking time.

Preheat the broiler (grill). Line a baking sheet with aluminum foil and lightly oil it.

Thread 3 lamb cubes onto each of 6 metal or bamboo skewers and lay the skewers on the baking sheet. Place about 2 inches (5 cm) from the heat and broil (grill) the lamb, turning once, until tender but still pink in the center, about 5 minutes on each side. Serve hot.

Serves 6

1½–2 lb (750 g–1 kg) boneless lamb from the leg, cut into 1-inch (2.5-cm) cubes

1 clove garlic, cut into quarters

1 onion, cut into quarters

1 tablespoon grated peeled fresh ginger

½ cup (4 oz/125 g) plain yogurt

3 tablespoons fresh lemon juice

1 tablespoon garam masala

1 teaspoon ground cumin

1 teaspoon ground turmeric

1 tablespoon chopped fresh mint

1 tablespoon chopped fresh cilantro (fresh coriander)

1 teaspoon salt

Mini Quiches Lorraines

The classic French quiche filling used in these bite-sized pastries may be dressed up with the addition of a little shredded Gruyère cheese. You can make the quiches in advance and reheat them in a preheated 425°F (220°C) oven just as guests arrive.

Prepare the pastry dough and refrigerate for at least 3 hours. Remove the pastry dough from the refrigerator about 30 minutes before you are ready to roll it out.

Preheat the oven to 425°F (220°C). On a lightly floured work surface, roll out the dough as thinly as possible. With a fluted pastry cutter about 1 1/2 inches (4 cm) in diameter, cut out 18 rounds. Use the rounds to line 18 individual tartlet pans or the cups in tartlet trays or miniature muffin pans. If using individual pans, arrange them on a large baking sheet.

In a small nonstick frying pan over medium heat, fry the bacon, stirring often, until crisp, about 5 minutes. With a slotted spoon, remove the crisp bacon pieces to paper towels to drain.

Break the eggs into a bowl. Add the nutmeg and salt and pepper to taste. Beat with a fork until completely blended. Continuing to beat, add the cream in a thin, steady stream.

Distribute the bacon pieces evenly among the pastry-lined pans, then pour in the egg mixture. Bake until the filling sets and the crusts are golden, about 15 minutes. Serve hot or warm.

Makes 18 mini quiches; serves 6

8 oz (250 g) Tart Pastry dough (page 321)

7 oz (220 g) lean smoked bacon, very thinly sliced and cut into 1/4-inch (6-mm) pieces

3 eggs

4 pinches of freshly grated nutmeg

Salt and freshly ground pepper

3/4 cup (6 fl oz/180 ml) heavy (double) cream

Melted Cheese with Mushrooms and Chorizo

This appetizer is traditionally cooked on top of the stove in *cazuelitas*—little clay casseroles. The melted cheese mixture is folded into warm flour tortillas with salsa and eaten out of hand.

1 small Mexican chorizo sausage, about ¼ lb (125 g), removed from casing and crumbled

1 tablespoon unsalted butter

3 oz (90 g) fresh white mushrooms, cut into slices ¼ inch (6 mm) thick (about 1 cup)

Salt and freshly ground pepper

2 cups (8 oz/250 g) shredded mild Cheddar or Monterey jack cheese

12 flour tortillas, heated

Fresh Mexican Salsa or Tomatillo Salsa (pages 319)

Preheat the oven to 400°F (200°C).

In a frying pan over medium-high heat, fry the chorizo until the fat is released and the sausage is slightly crisp, about 6–8 minutes. Remove from the heat. Cover and keep warm. Set aside.

In a sautè pan over medium heat, melt the butter. Add the mushrooms and sauté until just tender, 2–3 minutes. Season to taste with salt and pepper. Remove from the heat. Cover and keep warm. Set aside.

Lightly grease 2 small baking dishes. Divide the cheese evenly between the dishes. Add half of the mushrooms to one dish and half of the chorizo to the other dish. Bake until the cheese is melted and bubbling, 8–10 minutes.

Add the remaining mushrooms to the dish with the mushrooms and the chorizo to the dish with the chorizo. Serve hot with tortillas and salsa.

Serves 6

Beef and Currant Triangles

Crisp filo dough encases a savory-sweet mixture of lean ground beef, currants, pine nuts, and almonds. The filo sheets can be folded into triangles instead of rolls by following the instructions on page 280.

Preheat the oven to 425°F (220°C).

In a nonstick frying pan, heat 1 tablespoon of the oil over medium heat. Add the onion and sauté, stirring, until golden, about 5 minutes. Add the beef and 1 tablespoon of the remaining oil to the pan. Cook, breaking up the meat, until lightly browned, 3–4 minutes. Season to taste with salt and pepper.

Transfer the beef mixture to a bowl. Add the almonds, pine nuts, currants, and parsley. Mix thoroughly.

Cut the filo sheets in half crosswise. Place a half sheet on a work surface, keeping the remaining sheets covered with plastic wrap and a damp kitchen towel to prevent them from drying out. Spread one-twelfth of the beef mixture on the filo in a rectangle about 3 inches (7.5 cm) long and ³/₄ inch (2 cm) wide, leaving the bottom edge and sides uncovered. Fold the bottom edge over the mixture, then fold in the sides and roll up the pastry. Repeat with the remaining half sheets and the beef mixture.

Using a pastry brush, lightly brush a large baking sheet with some of the remaining 1 tablespoon oil. Arrange the rolls on the baking sheet at least ¹/₂ inch (12 mm) apart. Lightly brush the pastries with the remaining oil. Bake until golden and crisp, 18–20 minutes. Serve while still crisp, either hot or warm.

Makes 12 rolls; serves 6

3 tablespoons peanut oil or vegetable oil

1¹/₂ cups (7¹/₂ oz/235 g) finely chopped onion

13 oz (410 g) lean ground (minced) beef

Salt and freshly ground pepper

¹/₄ cup (1 oz/30 g) sliced (flaked) almonds, lightly toasted (page 328)

¹/₃ cup (¹/₂ oz/45 g) pine nuts, lightly toasted (page 328)

¹/₃ cup (2 oz/60 g) dried currants

2 tablespoons chopped fresh flat-leaf (Italian) parsley

6 sheets filo dough

Chinese Spareribs

Ask your butcher to cut the spareribs into bite-sized pieces. These aromatic
ribs are frequently served as part of the Chinese array of dishes known as dim sum.
Accompany with fresh, crisp vegetables such as green (spring) onions or radishes.

2¹/₂ lb (1.25 kg) pork spareribs,
cut into pieces 1¹/₄ inches
(3 cm) long

¹/₄ cup (3 oz/90 g) honey

2 tablespoons soy sauce

2 tablespoons dry sherry

1 teaspoon five-spice powder

1 teaspoon ground Sichuan
pepper

Place the spareribs in a shallow dish. In a small bowl, stir together the honey, soy sauce, sherry, five-spice powder, and Sichuan pepper. Add the honey mixture to the spareribs. Mix until the ribs are well coated. Let stand for 1 hour.

Preheat the oven to 300°F (150°C). Arrange the spareribs in a single layer on a nonstick baking sheet. Bake until tender, about 1 hour, turning them over halfway through the cooking time.

Serve hot, warm, or at room temperature.

Serves 8

Pork and Celery Root Terrine

A terrine is a classic French dish that is made from a mixture of meats, vegetables, and seasonings. Here, celery root, apple, and dried porcino mushrooms complement pork loin and ham.

1¼ lb (625 g) pork loin

5 oz (155 g) cooked ham, coarsely chopped

3 oz (90 g) white bread, crusts removed, coarsely chopped (about 1½ cups)

1 oz (30 g) dried porcino mushrooms, soaked in hot water to cover until soft, then drained

1 tablespoon finely chopped fresh flat-leaf (Italian) parsley

2 eggs

3 cloves garlic

1 teaspoon crushed peppercorns

¼ teaspoon grated nutmeg

Salt

1 celery root (celeriac)

1 apple

1 tablespoon peanut oil or vegetable oil

1 teaspoon sugar

Preheat the oven to 300°F (150°C). Lightly oil a terrine or loaf pan. Set aside.

Coarsely chop half of the pork and put it in a food processor. Add the ham, bread, and drained porcini. Process for 2 minutes. Add the parsley and eggs. Pass the garlic through a garlic press held over the food processor. Process for 2 minutes. Transfer the mixture to a large bowl.

Cut the remaining pork into ³/8-inch (1-cm) dice and add it to the large bowl. Add the peppercorns, nutmeg, and salt to taste. Mix thoroughly.

Peel the celery root. Cut the apple in half lengthwise, core, and peel one half. In the food processor, grate the celery root and the peeled apple half using the matchstick-cut grating disk. Add the grated mixture to the large bowl with the pork and mix until well blended.

Pack the pork mixture into the prepared pan and press down well. Lightly brush the oil over the surface. Slice the remaining apple half into thin semicircles and lay them on top, slightly overlapping. Sprinkle evenly with the sugar. Bake for 1 hour, then reduce the oven temperature to 250°F (120°C) and bake for 45 minutes longer.

Remove from the oven and let cool to room temperature. To serve, cut into slices.

Serves 8

Baby Artichokes in Prosciutto

Artichokes are the immature flowers of an edible thistle. Baby artichokes are the buds that have not yet developed a fuzzy choke; they need only a light trimming of their outer leaves before they can be eaten whole.

Squeeze the juice from the lemon wedges into a large bowl of water and discard the lemon.

Remove and discard the tough outer leaves of each artichoke. Using a sharp knife, cut off the top third of each artichoke, then cut off the stem flush with the base. Trim away the fibrous green layer around the base. Cut any larger artichokes in half lengthwise. As you work, drop the trimmed artichokes into the lemon water.

In a saucepan over medium heat, bring the stock to a boil. Drain the artichokes, and add them to the stock. Return to a boil. Reduce the heat to low and simmer until tender when pierced with a knife, about 7 minutes.

While the artichokes are cooking, in a shallow bowl, combine the vinegar and a pinch of salt. Stir to dissolve. Add pepper to taste. Whisk in the oil until a thick emulsion forms. Stir in the green onions.

Drain the artichokes and add them to the bowl. Toss to coat well. When cool, wrap each artichoke in a short strip of prosciutto and secure with a toothpick. Arrange on a platter or individual plates, garnish with lemon slices and parsley if desired, and serve.

Serves 4

1 lemon, cut into wedges, plus slices for optional garnish

1 lb (500 g) baby artichokes

2 cups (16 fl oz/500 ml) Chicken Stock (page 317)

2 teaspoons white wine vinegar

Salt and freshly ground pepper

3 tablespoons olive oil

2 green (spring) onions, white part only, finely chopped

1/4 lb (125 g) very thinly sliced prosciutto

Flat-leaf (Italian) parsley for garnish (optional)

Basic Recipes & Techniques

These basic recipes and techniques are used throughout *Soups, Salads & Starters*. Once you master them, you'll find that you turn to them again and again to create delicious meals.

Court Bouillon

French for *short broth,* court bouillon is a quickly prepared cooking liquid of aromatic vegetables and herbs simmered in water for a short amount of time and used for poaching or moistening seafood recipes. Cooking crabs, lobsters, and other shellfish in this liquid enhances their individual flavors and imparts the subtle taste of the broth.

8 cups (64 fl oz/2 l) water

1 bottle (3 cups/24 fl oz/750 ml) dry white wine, such as Pinot Grigio or Sauvignon Blanc

2 carrots, peeled and coarsely chopped

6 fresh parsley stems

Pinch of fresh or dried thyme

4 bay leaves

10 peppercorns

1 tablespoon salt

In a large stockpot, combine all the ingredients and bring to a boil. Reduce the heat to low and simmer, uncovered, for about 40 minutes. Remove from the heat and strain through a fine-mesh sieve. Use immediately, or cover and refrigerate for up to 1 week or freeze for up to 2 months.

Makes about 8 cups (64 fl oz/2 l)

Vegetable Stock

Many of the soup recipes in this book can become vegetarian dishes by using this flavorful vegetable stock instead of chicken or meat stock. This recipe can easily be doubled.

2 large leeks, trimmed and carefully washed

2 large carrots, sliced

2 large celery stalks, sliced

2 large yellow onions, sliced

3 cloves garlic, unpeeled

3 fresh parsley sprigs

2 fresh thyme sprigs

1 bay leaf

8 cups (64 fl oz/2 l) water

1 teaspoon white peppercorns

Salt

Slice the white portion of the leeks and place in a large stockpot. Reserve the green tops. Add the carrots, celery, onions, and garlic to the pot. Place the parsley, thyme, and bay leaf between the reserved leek tops and tie securely with kitchen string. Add to the pot along with the water.

Over medium-low heat, slowly bring the liquid to a simmer, skimming off the foam that rises to the surface until no more forms. Add the white peppercorns, reduce the heat to low, cover partially, and simmer gently for about 1–1 1/2 hours.

Line a strainer with a double layer of dampened cheesecloth (muslin) and set it inside a large bowl. Pour the contents of the pot into the strainer. Discard the solids. Season to taste with salt and let cool to room temperature. Cover tightly and refrigerate. The stock may be stored in the refrigerator for up to 3 days or in the freezer for up to 6 months.

Makes about 6 cups (48 fl oz/1.5 l)

Quick Fish Stock

If you get into a bind and don't have access to the necessary ingredients for making fish stock, this simple recipe is the next best thing.

1 cup (8 fl oz/250 ml) dry white wine

2 cups (16 fl oz/500 ml) bottled clam juice

2 cups (16 fl oz/500 ml) water

1/2 yellow onion, chopped

1/2 carrot, peeled and chopped

6 fresh parsley stems

Pinch of fresh or dried thyme

1 bay leaf

In a large saucepan, combine all the ingredients and bring to a boil. Reduce the heat to low and simmer, uncovered, for 20 minutes. Remove from the heat and strain through a sieve. Use at once, or cover and refrigerate for up to 3 days or freeze for up to 2 months.

Makes about 4 cups (32 fl oz/1 l)

Fish Stock

Most fish markets will sell you trimmings for making stock. Use those from any mild white fish; avoid oily, strong flavored fish such as mackerel, mullet, bluefish, or salmon. If you are short on time, make Quick Fish Stock (page 316).

2 leeks, trimmed and carefully washed

4 lb (2 kg) fish heads (gills removed), bones, and trimmings

2 yellow onions, sliced

2 carrots, sliced

2 celery stalks with leaves, sliced

6 fresh parsley sprigs

3 fresh thyme sprigs

1 bay leaf

4 qt (4 l) water

Salt

Slice the white portion of the leeks and place in a large stockpot. Reserve the green tops. Add the fish parts, onions, carrots, and celery to the pot. Place the parsley, thyme, and bay leaf between the reserved leek tops and tie securely with kitchen string. Add to the pot along with the water.

Over medium-low heat, slowly bring the liquid to a simmer, skimming off the foam that rises to the surface until no more forms. Reduce the heat to low, cover partially, and simmer gently for 30–40 minutes, skimming occasionally.

Line a strainer with a double layer of dampened cheesecloth (muslin) and set it inside a large bowl. Pour the contents of the pot into the strainer. Discard the solids. Season to taste with salt and let cool to room temperature. Cover tightly and refrigerate. The stock may be refrigerated for up to 3 days or frozen for up to 6 months.

Makes about 3 qt (3 l)

Chicken Stock

This is one of the most versatile stocks you can make. If you're not using all of it right away, freeze the unused portion in small containers.

1 leek, trimmed and carefully washed

6 lb (3 kg) stewing chicken parts

1 large yellow onion, unpeeled, root trimmed

1 large carrot, cut into 1-inch (2.5-cm) pieces

1 celery stalk with leaves, cut into 1-inch (2.5-cm) pieces

6 fresh parsley sprigs

3 fresh thyme sprigs

1 bay leaf

5 qt (5 l) water

1/2 teaspoon peppercorns

Salt

Cut the white portion of the leek into 1-inch (2.5-cm) pieces and place in a large stockpot. Reserve the green tops. Add the chicken, onion, carrot, and celery to the pot. Place the parsley, thyme, and bay leaf between the reserved leek tops and tie securely with kitchen string. Add to the pot along with the water.

Over medium-low heat, slowly bring the liquid to a simmer, regularly skimming off the foam that rises to the surface until no more forms. Add the peppercorns, reduce the heat to low, cover partially, and simmer gently for about 2 hours, skimming occasionally.

Line a strainer with a double layer of dampened cheesecloth (muslin) and set it inside a large bowl. Pour the contents of the pot into the strainer. Discard the solids. Season to taste with salt and let cool to room temperature, then refrigerate. A layer of fat will solidify on the surface of the stock; lift or spoon it off and discard. The stock may be stored in a tightly covered container in the refrigerator for up to 3 days or in the freezer for up to 6 months.

Makes about 4 qt (4 l)

Quick Full-Bodied Stock

Just 30 minutes or so of simmering with aromatic vegetables will help canned broth taste almost like homemade. You can use this stock whenever you are short on time and the recipe calls for meat or chicken stock.

3–4 cups (750 ml–1 l) canned beef or chicken broth

1 carrot, sliced

1 celery stalk, sliced

1 yellow onion, sliced

1 leek, white portion only, trimmed, carefully washed, and sliced

1 bay leaf

Put all the ingredients in a saucepan and bring to a boil over low to medium heat, regularly skimming off the foam that rises to the surface until no more forms. Partially cover and simmer for about 30 minutes.

Line a strainer with a double layer of dampened cheesecloth (muslin) and set it inside a large bowl. Pour the contents of the pot into the strainer. Discard the solids. The stock may be stored in the refrigerator for several days or frozen for up to 6 months.

Makes 3–4 cups (24–32 fl oz/750 ml–1 l)

Meat Stock

2 leeks, trimmed

4 lb (2 kg) meaty beef bones

2 lb (1 kg) stewing chicken parts or wings, backs, or necks

6 cloves garlic, unpeeled

4 large carrots, cut into 1-inch (2.5-cm) pieces

2 celery stalks with leaves, cut into 1-inch (2.5-cm) pieces

3 whole cloves

2 large yellow onions

6 fresh parsley sprigs

3 fresh thyme sprigs

1 bay leaf

5 qt (5 l) water

1 teaspoon peppercorns

Salt

Slice the white portion of the leeks, rinse carefully, and place in a large stockpot. Reserve the green tops. Add the beef bones, chicken, garlic, carrots, and celery to the pot. Stick the cloves into one of the onions and add both onions to the pot. Place the parsley, thyme, and bay leaf between the reserved leek tops and tie securely with kitchen string. Add to the pot along with the water.

Over medium-low heat, bring the liquid to a simmer, regularly skimming off the foam that rises to the surface until no more forms. Add the peppercorns, reduce the heat to low, cover partially, and simmer gently for $3^{1}/_{2}$–4 hours, skimming occasionally.

Line a colander with a double layer of dampened cheesecloth (muslin) and set it inside a large bowl. Pour the contents of the pot into the strainer. Discard the solids. Season to taste with salt and let cool to room temperature, then refrigerate. A layer of fat will solidify on the surface of the stock; lift or spoon it off and discard. The stock may be stored in a tightly covered container in the refrigerator for up to 3 days or in the freezer for up to 6 months.

Makes about 4 qt (4 l)

Mayonnaise

Mayonnaise is an excellent addition to salads because it is so flexible. If you need to stretch it or make the flavor lighter, add a bit of light (single) cream. Or mix in finely chopped anchovy fillets, capers, and a little garlic to create a robust mayonnaise capable of turning the simplest potato salad into a heavenly dish.

1 egg yolk

1 tablespoon fresh lemon juice

1 teaspoon Dijon mustard

Salt and freshly ground pepper

$^{2}/_{3}$ cup (5 fl oz/160 ml) extra-virgin olive oil

In a food processor or blender, combine the egg yolk, lemon juice, mustard,

and salt and pepper to taste. Process briefly to combine. With the motor running, add the oil in a thin, steady stream and continue to blend until the mixture has a thick, smooth consistency.

Makes about $^{3}/_{4}$ cup (6 fl oz/180 ml)

Pesto

This fragrant green sauce originated in Liguria, a region on Italy's northwest coastline. In addition to its many uses in this book, it is also excellent as a pasta sauce, or as a condiment to accompany prepared fish or meat.

2 cups (2 oz/60 g) firmly packed basil leaves

2 teaspoons finely chopped garlic

2 tablespoons pine nuts

$^{1}/_{2}$ teaspoon ground pepper

About 1 cup (8 fl oz/250 ml) pure olive oil, plus extra for topping pesto

$^{1}/_{2}$ cup (2 oz/60 g) freshly grated Parmesan cheese

About 1 teaspoon salt

In a food processor fitted with the metal blade or in a blender, combine the basil, garlic, nuts, pepper, and $^{1}/_{2}$ cup (4 fl oz/125 ml) of the olive oil. Pulse or blend briefly to form a coarse paste. With the motor running, gradually add as much of the remaining oil as needed to form a thick purée. Do not overmix; the purée should contain tiny pieces of basil leaf.

Add the Parmesan cheese and process briefly to mix. Taste and add salt; you may need less than 1 teaspoon if the cheese is salty.

Transfer the pesto to a jar and pour a film of olive oil onto the surface, to preserve the bright green color. Cover and refrigerate for up to 1 month.

Makes about 2 1/2 cups (20 fl oz/625 ml)

Rémoulade

Rémoulade, is a classic French sauce that, when chilled, is an excellent accompaniment to fish or shellfish. If fresh horseradish is unavailable, buy it prepared at a well-stocked market.

1 cup (8 fl oz/250 ml) store-bought or homemade Mayonnaise (page 318)

3 tablespoons Dijon mustard

2–3 tablespoons white wine vinegar

1 tablespoon paprika

2 tablespoons grated prepared horseradish

1 clove garlic, finely chopped

1/3 cup (1 oz/30 g) finely chopped green (spring) onions

1/3 cup (2 oz/60 g) finely chopped celery

2 tablespoons finely chopped fresh parsley

2 tablespoons tomato sauce

Salt and freshly ground pepper

To make the rémoulade, in a large bowl, stir together the mayonnaise, mustard, vinegar, paprika, horseradish, garlic, green onions, celery, parsley, and tomato sauce. Add salt and pepper to taste. Mix well. Cover tightly and refrigerate until ready to serve.

Makes about 2 cups (16 fl oz/500 ml)

Fresh Mexican Salsa

The bright flavors of fresh salsa make it far superior to bottled versions. This versatile condiment is used throughout this book, and it is also excellent with grilled meat, chicken, or seafood. For a milder version, simply reduce the amount of fresh chiles.

3 tomatoes, finely chopped

1/2 cup (2 1/2 oz/75 g) finely chopped red onion

4–6 serrano chiles, seeded and finely chopped

1 tablespoon finely chopped fresh cilantro (fresh coriander)

2 teaspoons salt

2 teaspoons fresh lime juice

In a bowl, stir together the tomatoes, onion, chiles, cilantro, salt, and lime juice. Let stand for 1 hour to blend the flavors before serving. The salsa can be stored in a tightly covered container in the refrigerator for up to 1 week.

Makes about 1 1/2 cups (12 fl oz/375 ml)

Tomatillo Salsa

Found on most tables in Mexican homes and restaurants, this versatile condiment enhances many savory dishes. It is made with tomatillos, known in Mexico as *tomates verdes*. Although they are not in fact related to tomatoes, their size, shape, and texture are similar. Find them fresh, covered in their brown papery husks, in Latin American markets, well-stocked markets, or in fruit and vegetable shops; they are also sold canned.

3 cups (24 fl oz/750 ml) water

2 1/2 teaspoons salt

2 cloves garlic

4 serrano chiles

1 lb (500 g) tomatillos, husks removed

1/2 cup (2 oz/20 g) loosely packed fresh cilantro (fresh coriander) leaves

1/4 cup (1 1/4 oz/37 g) finely chopped red onion

In a saucepan over high heat, combine the water and 1 teaspoon of the salt. Bring to a boil. Add the garlic, chiles, and tomatillos. Cook, uncovered, until the tomatillos are soft, 8–10 minutes. Drain, reserving 1/2 cup (4 fl oz/125 ml) of the cooking liquid. When cool enough to handle, stem the chiles and tomatillos. If a milder sauce is desired, seed the chiles (page 325).

In a food processor or a blender, combine the garlic, chiles, tomatillos, reserved cooking liquid, cilantro, and the remaining salt. Process to form a smooth purée. Transfer to a bowl. Stir in the onion.

Let the salsa cool to room temperature. The salsa can be stored tightly covered in the refrigerator for up to 1 week.

Makes about 2 cups (16 fl oz/500 ml)

Flour Tortillas

Flour tortillas are a specialty of northern Mexico, the principal wheat-growing region of the country. To store cooked tortillas, let cool, seal in plastic wrap, and refrigerate for 2–3 days or freeze for several weeks. Reheat in a nonstick frying pan, on a griddle over medium-high heat, or in a microwave oven for about 30 seconds.

2–2¼ cups (8–9 oz/250–280 g) all-purpose (plain) flour, sifted before measuring, plus flour for rolling

¼ cup (2 oz/60 g) vegetable shortening or lard

1 teaspoon salt

1 cup (8 fl oz/250 ml) warm water

In a bowl, combine 2 cups of the flour, the shortening, and salt. Using your fingers, rub the ingredients together until the mixture resembles fine crumbs. Gradually add the warm water, stirring with a fork. Continue to mix until a soft dough forms. Add the remaining ¼ cup (1 oz/30 g) flour if the mixture is sticking to your fingers. (Alternatively, combine the flour, shortening, and salt in a food processor. Process to form fine crumbs. Gradually add the warm water, ¼ cup/2 fl oz/60 ml at a time. Process until a soft mass forms.)

Gather up the dough and pat it into a ball. Place in a large bowl. Knead the dough inside the bowl until elastic, about 2 minutes. Cover with a clean kitchen towel and let stand at room temperature for 2 hours.

Break off small pieces of the dough. Rolling each piece between your palms,

form into balls 1½ inches (4 cm) in diameter. On a floured work surface, using a rolling pin, roll out each ball into a thin round, 6–7 inches (15–18 cm) in diameter. As you roll out each tortilla, turn it over from time to time and add flour to the surface as needed to prevent sticking.

Heat a dry, heavy frying pan or griddle over medium heat. Place a tortilla on the pan or griddle and cook until it looks dry and the underside begins to brown, about 30 seconds. Turn the tortilla over and cook the second side until browned, about 30 seconds. Transfer the tortilla to one end of a kitchen towel. As the tortillas are cooked, stack them and completely cover them with the other half of the towel to keep them warm and moist until serving.

Makes about 24 tortillas

Toasted Bread Crumbs

In Mediterranean cuisines, these crunchy crumbs are sprinkled liberally on cooked vegetables, stirred into pasta, or used as a topping for soups. You can add dried herbs, such as oregano or thyme, to the crumb mixture, but be sure that the seasoned bread crumbs will not interfere with other flavors when you use them in a recipe.

1 loaf coarse country bread, 1½ lb (750 g), crusts removed

1 teaspoon salt

1 teaspoon freshly ground pepper

½ cup (4 oz/125 g) unsalted butter, melted, or ½ cup (4 fl oz/125 ml) pure olive oil

Preheat the oven to 350°F (180°C).

Break up the bread into chunks and place in a food processor fitted with the metal blade. Using on-off pulses, process until the bread is broken into coarse or fine crumbs, as needed. Spread the crumbs onto a baking sheet. In a small bowl, stir the salt and pepper into the butter or oil. Drizzle the mixture over the bread crumbs.

Bake, stirring occasionally for even browning, until golden, about 20 minutes. Remove from the oven, let cool, and transfer to a container with a tight-fitting lid. Store at room temperature for up to 2 days.

Makes about 1½ cups (6 oz/185 g)

Basic Pizza Dough

Here is an all-purpose dough that complements both traditional and modern pizzas. If short on time, you may also puchase a good-quality frozen pizza dough from a well-stocked market.

1 tablespoon active dry yeast

¾ cup (6 fl oz/180 ml) plus 2 tablespoons warm water (105°F/40°C)

2¾ cups (14 oz/440 g) all-purpose (plain) flour, plus flour for kneading

1 teaspoon salt

1 tablespoon extra-virgin olive oil

In a small bowl, dissolve the yeast in the warm water and let the mixture stand until slightly foamy on top, about 10 minutes.

In a large bowl, stir together the 2¾ cups flour and the salt. Form into a mound. Make a well in the center and add the yeast mixture to the well. Using a fork and stirring in a circular motion, gradually pull the flour into the yeast mixture. Continue stirring until a dough forms.

Lightly dust a work surface with flour and transfer the dough to it. Using the heel of your hand, knead the dough until it is smooth and elastic, about 10 minutes. Form the dough into a ball.

Brush a large bowl with the oil and place the dough in it. Cover with plastic wrap and let rise at room temperature until doubled in bulk, 1–2 hours.

Turn the dough out onto a lightly floured work surface. Punch the dough down. Using your hands, begin to press it out gently into the desired shape. Then, place one hand on the center of the dough. With the other hand, pull, lift, and stretch the dough, gradually working your way all around the edge, until it is the desired thickness, about $1/4$ inch (6 mm) thick for a crusty pizza base and $1/2$ inch (12 mm) thick for a softer one. Flip the dough over from time to time as you work with it. (Alternatively, roll out the dough with a rolling pin.) The dough should be slightly thinner in the middle than at the edge. Lift the edge of the dough round to form a slight rim.

Transfer the dough to a baker's peel or baking sheet. Cover with a cotton towel and let rise again until almost doubled, about 20 minutes. Top and bake as directed in individual recipes.
Makes about $1^1/4$ lb (625 g) dough, enough for one 12-inch (30-cm) thin-crust pizza or one 9-inch (23-cm) thick-crust pizza

Tart Pastry

Tender, flaky, and buttery, this classic pastry dough forms the foundation for both sweet and savory tarts. The dough should be made at least 3 hours ahead, or preferably the night before, so that it has time to chill. It may be wrapped tighty or stored in a plastic bag for up to 4 days in the refrigerator or for up to 2 months in the freezer.

$1^1/2$ cups ($7^1/2$ oz/235 g) all-purpose (plain) flour

2 pinches of salt

6 tablespoons (3 oz/90 g) unsalted butter, at room temperature, cut into rough chunks

1 egg

To make the dough in a food processor, put the flour and salt in the work bowl and pulse a few times to mix. Add the butter and egg and pulse briefly just until the mixture comes together to form a ball.

To make the dough by hand, combine the flour and salt in a large bowl. Add the butter and, with your finger-tips, mix and smear the ingredients together until the butter is broken into large flakes coated with flour. Add the egg and continue to mix until the ingredients are the consistency of coarse crumbs. Gather the dough together to form a ball.

Put the ball of dough into a plastic bag and let it rest in the refrigerator for at least 3 hours before using. Remove the dough from the refrigerator about 30 minutes before rolling it out.
Makes 11 oz (345 g) dough

Puff Shell Pastry

With its high proportion of eggs, butter, and water, this pastry dough puffs up into light, airy, well-rounded shapes. The dough may be stored in a plastic bag for 2 days in the refrigerator or for up to 2 months in the freezer.

6 tablespoons (3 oz/90 g) unsalted butter, cut into small dice

1 cup (8 fl oz/250 ml) water

1 teaspoon salt

$1^1/4$ cups ($6^1/2$ oz/200 g) all-purpose (plain) flour

5 eggs

In a saucepan, combine the butter, water, and salt. Bring to a boil over medium heat, stirring often. Remove from the heat. Immediately pour in the flour all at once and stir vigorously with a wooden spoon until the mixture is smooth. Return the pan to low heat, and continue to stir until there are no lumps and the mixture pulls away from the pan sides, 1 minute.

Remove from the heat and add the eggs, one at a time, making sure each egg is thoroughly mixed in before adding the next. Work the dough as little as possible after adding the first egg. The dough should be shiny and stiff enough to hold a shape.

The dough is now ready to be used. It can be formed by spoonfuls or with a pastry bag fitted with a plain or decorative tip. The dough should be spooned or piped onto baking sheets lined with parchment (baking) paper or onto non-stick baking sheets.
Makes about 1 lb (500 g) dough

Cleaning and Cracking Cooked Crab

Several species of hard-shell crabs are commonly available. Blue crabs are popular on the Atlantic and Gulf Coasts. Closer to the Pacific, large Dungeness crabs are more common.

To cook a crab, bring a large pot of water to a full boil. Drop live crabs in headfirst, taking care to avoid splashing. Once the water returns to a boil, reduce the heat to medium to maintain a gentle simmer. Cook small crabs, such as blue crabs, for 20 minutes. Dungeness crabs and other larger varieties can require up to 30 minutes of simmering. Remove cooked crabs with tongs and let them cool before handling.

1. Removing the apron
Using your hands, twist off the crab's legs and claws and set them aside. Turn the crab upside down. Using your thumb or the tip of a short, sturdy knife, pry off the small, triangular apron-shaped shell flap.

2. Removing the top shell
Insert your thumbs in the small crevice between the underside of the crab's body and its top shell. Pull them apart, lifting the top shell away from the body.

3. Cleaning the crab
Pull or scrape out the dark gray intestines from the center of the body, along with any orange roe you might find. Scrape and rinse out the top shell if it is to be used for serving the crabmeat.

4. Removing the gills
Using a spoon or your fingers, scrape or pull off and discard the spongy, feather-shaped white gills on either side of the crab's body.

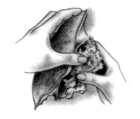

5. Removing the meat
Using your hands, break the crab's body in half to reveal the meat. Using your fingers, a knife, or a lobster pick, carefully remove the meat from all the body cavities. Set aside.

6. Cracking the claws and legs
Using a mallet or lobster cracker, crack the shells of the claws in several places, as well as any legs large enough to contain a good amount of meat. Break away the shell pieces and remove the meat with your fingers or a lobster pick.

Depending on the species, a crab will yield 15 to 25 percent of its weight as crab meat. A 1 lb (500 g) crab will yield about 3 oz (90 g) of meat.

Cleaning and Cracking Cooked Lobster

When buying live lobsters, be sure to select ones that are lively and have been stored in a clean tank. To cook, bring a large pot of water to a full boil. Use about 4 qt (4 l) of water for 1 lobster; add 1 qt (1 l) for each additional lobster. Drop a live lobster in headfirst, taking care to avoid splashing. Once the water returns to a boil, reduce the heat to medium to maintain a gentle simmer. Cook lobster for 8 minutes for the first pound, plus 2 minutes for each additional $^1/_4$ lb (125 g).

1. Draining the excess water
Drain any residual water from boiled or steamed lobsters by making a small cut between the eyes on the lobster head. Hold the lobster by its tail over a sink to drain the excess cooking liquid.

2. Halving the lobster
Insert the tip of a large, sharp, sturdy knife into the point where the tail and body sections meet. Carefully cut through the tail. Turn the lobster around and continue to cut from the center through the head, cutting the lobster into two equal halves.

3. Removing the tail meat
Firmly grasp the fins of a tail half, with one hand. With the other hand, firmly pull out the tail meat in a single piece, using a fork to pry it loose if needed. Repeat with the other tail half.

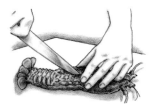

4. Removing the body meat
Pull out and discard the black vein that runs the length of the body meat, as well as the small sand sac at the base of the head. Remove the white meat from the shell.

5. Cleaning the body cavity
With a small spoon, scoop out the liver, known as the tomalley. It will be black if uncooked and green if cooked. Also remove any coral, or eggs, which will be black if uncooked and bright red if cooked. Both the tomalley and the coral can add flavor to sauces and soups.

6. Removing the claws and legs
Firmly twist off the claws from the body shells. You can also remove the small legs and crack them to extract the meat.

7. Cracking the claws
With a lobster cracker or mallet, break the hard shell of each claw in several places. Pull away the shell pieces, taking care not to damage the claw meat if a recipe calls for it to be left whole.

Lobsters generally yield 20 to 25 percent of their weight as lobster meat. A 1-lb lobster will yield about 4 ounces of meat.

Glossary

Anchovies Tiny saltwater fish, related to sardines, most commonly found as canned fillets that have been salted and preserved in oil. Imported anchovy fillets packed in olive oil are the most commonly available.

Arugula (Rocket) Green leaf vegetable, Mediterranean in origin, with slender, multi-lobed leaves that have a peppery, slightly bitter flavor. It is often used raw in salads.

Avocado The finest-flavored variety of this popular fruit is the Haas, which has a pearlike shape and a thick, bumpy, dark green skin. Ripe avocados will yield slightly to fingertip pressure.

TO REMOVE THE PIT NEATLY
First, using a sharp knife, cut down to the pit lengthwise all around the avocado. Gently twist the halves in opposite directions to separate. Lift away the half without the pit.

Cup the half with the pit in the palm of one hand, with your fingers and thumb safely clear. Hold a sturdy, sharp knife with the other hand and strike the pit with the blade of the knife, wedging the blade firmly into the pit. Then twist and lift the knife to remove the pit.

Beans All kinds of dried beans may be added to, or used as the main ingredient of robust and hearty dishes. Before use, they should be carefully picked over to remove any impurities such as small stones or fibers, or any discolored or misshapen beans. Next, to rehydrate whole beans, shorten their cooking time, and improve their digestibility, presoak them in cold water for at least 4 hours.

Many types of beans are used in cuisines worldwide. Some of the more common varieties that are used in this book include:

Cannellini Italian variety of small, white, thin-skinned, oval beans. Great Northern or white (navy) beans may be substituted.

Chickpea (Garbanzo) Round, tan-colored member of the pea family, with a slightly crunchy texture and nutlike flavor. These are also known as ceci beans.

Cranberry (Borlotti) Italian variety of medium-sized dried beans, kidney shaped with pink or beige skins speckled with burgundy. Available in Italian delicatessens and specialty food stores. Substitute pink kidney beans or pinto beans.

Fava (Broad) Italian variety containing a slightly bitter flavor. Resembling an oversized lima bean, fresh fava beans are sold in their long, plump, flattened pods. They are easily shelled. Unless the beans are very young and tender, remove the tough skin.

White (Navy) Small, white, thin-skinned, oval beans that are also known as Boston beans. Great Northern beans may be substituted.

Belgian Endive (Chicory/Witloof) Leaf vegetable with refreshing, slightly bitter spear-shaped leaves, white to pale yellow-green—or sometimes red—in color. Tightly packed in cylindrical heads 4–6 inches (10–15 cm) long.

Bell Peppers (Capsicums) Sweet-fleshed, bell-shaped member of the pepper family. It is most common in the unripe green form, although ripened red or yellow varieties are available. Creamy pale-yellow, orange, and purple types may also be found.

TO ROAST PEPPERS
Place the peppers, resting on their sides, directly on the grid of a stove-top gas burner with a medium-high flame. Using metal tongs, turn the peppers as they scorch, until blackened, 5–6 minutes. Transfer to a paper bag and let steam for about 10 minutes. Using your hands, rub off the loosened, blackened skin. It will come off easily. Cut in half lengthwise, and remove the core, seeds, and ribs.

Butter, Clarified Butter is often clarified—that is, its milk solids and water are removed—when it is to be used for cooking at higher temperatures or as a sauce. To clarify butter, melt it in a small, heavy saucepan over very low heat; watch carefully to avoid burning. Remove from the heat and let it sit briefly. Then, using a spoon, skim off and discard the foam from the surface. Finally, carefully pour off the clear yellow oil and reserve, discarding the milky solids and water left behind in the pan. Clarified butter can be refrigerated for up to 1 month or frozen for 2 months.

Capers Small, pickled buds of a bush native to the Mediterranean. Used whole as a savory flavoring or garnish.

Celery Root (Celeriac) Large, knobby root of a species of celery plant, with a crisp texture and flavor closely resembling that of the stalks. Choose smaller, younger roots, to be peeled and eaten raw or cooked and added to soups and stews.

Chicory (Curly Endive) This relative of Belgian endive has loosely packed, curly leaves characterized by a bitter flavor. The paler center leaves, or heart, of a head of chicory are milder than the green outer leaves.

Crème Fraîche Lightly soured and thickened fresh cream, generally used as a topping or garnish for savory or sweet dishes. This French specialty is available in supermarkets, although a similar cream may be prepared at home by stirring 2 teaspoons well-drained sour cream into 1 cup

Chile

Any of a wide variety of peppers prized for their mild-to-hot spiciness. Some of the most common varieties include:

Anaheim Slender chile measuring 6–8 inches (15–20 cm) long, with a sharp, astringent, mild to medium-hot flavor. Sold fresh in its green state, it is sometimes labeled *chile verde.*

Jalapeño Small, thick-fleshed, fiery chile, usually sold green, although red, ripened specimens may sometimes be found.

Poblano Mild to hot dark green chile that resembles a tapered, triangular bell pepper.

Serrano Small, slender, very hot green chile also sold in its ripened red form and pickled in brine.

TO SEED A FRESH CHILE

The seeds and white ribs found inside a chile are intensely hot and are often removed before use. To prepare a chile that will be stuffed, simply cut a slit along its length with a small, sharp knife. Carefully use the knife tip to scrape out the seeds and ribs.

To prepare a chile that will be chopped up, cut the chili in half lengthwise. With your fingers or using the knife blade, remove and discard the tough

stem. Use the tip of the knife to scrape out the seeds and cut out the ribs, cutting into the flesh of the chile to remove all the pale parts.

The heat of chiles can linger for hours on your skin, so be sure to wash your hands, the cutting board, and the knife with hot soapy water as soon as you have finished with them.

TO ROAST CHILES

Chiles may be roasted to develop their flavor, soften their flesh, and loosen their skins. You can roast them in a broiler or directly over a gas flame.

1. Set the flame to medium. Grasp a chile with a pair of metal kitchen tongs. Turn the chile over the flame until its skin is completely blistered, 5–10 minutes depending upon the pepper's size.

2. Place the chile in a paper bag. Let it steam until it is cool enough to handle, about 10 minutes.

3. Peel off all the blistered skin and discard it. Carefully cut open the chile and remove the stem, seeds, and ribs.

If the chile is very spicy, reduce its fieriness by then soaking for at least 40 minutes in a mixture of 1 cup (8 floz/250 ml) water, 1 tablespoon distilled white vinegar, and 2 teaspoons salt.

(8 fl oz/250 ml) lightly whipped heavy (double) cream.

Croutons   To make croutons, cut slightly stale bread into slices $^1/_2$–$^3/_4$ inch (12 mm–2 cm) thick. Brush with olive oil, melted butter, or a mixture of both. Cut into $^1/_2$–$^3/_4$ inch (12 mm–2 cm) cubes and spread on a baking sheet in a single layer. Bake in a 350°F (180°C) oven, turning occasionally, until crisp and golden brown, about 30 minutes. You can also make smaller croutons, but watch that they do not burn. Croutons may be stored in an airtight container for 2–3 weeks.

Dijon Mustard   Mustard made in Dijon, France, from dark brown mustard seeds (unless marked *blanc*) and white wine or wine vinegar. Pale in color, fairly hot, and sharp tasting, true Dijon mustard and non-French blends labeled *Dijon style* are widely available in supermarkets.

Egg, Raw   Some dressings in this book contain raw eggs, which may be infected with salmonella or other harmful bacteria. The risk of food poisoning is of most concern to small children, older people, pregnant women, or anyone with a compromised immune system. If you have health or safety concerns, do not consume raw egg. Instead, seek out a pasteurized egg product to replace it.

Fennel   Crisp, mildly anise-flavored bulb vegetable, valued for its feathery stems and leaves, which are used as a fresh or dried herb, and for its small, crescent-shaped seeds, which are dried and used as a spice.

Filo   Tissue-thin sheets of flour-and-water pastry used throughout the Middle East as crisp wrappers for savory or sweet fillings. May be found in the frozen-food section of well-stocked supermarkets, or purchased fresh in Middle Eastern delicatessens. Thoroughly defrost frozen filo before use. The sheets generally measure 10 by 14 inches (25 by 35 cm) and must be separated and handled carefully to avoid tearing. As you work with the filo, keep the unused sheets covered with plastic wrap and a lightly dampened towel to prevent them from drying out. The name *filo* comes from the Greek word for *leaf*.

Food Mill   A hand-cranked tool that purées ingredients by forcing them through a disk, which functions simultaneously as a sieve, removing fibers, skins, and seeds. Most models come with both medium and fine disks, offering a choice of coarser or smoother purées.

Gelatin   Unflavored commercial gelatin gives delicate body to molded dishes. It is sold in envelopes holding

Herbs

Many fresh and dried herbs can be used to embellish the flavors of recipes. Those called for in the book are:

Chervil   Herb with small leaves resembling flat-leaf (Italian) parsley. It has a subtle flavor reminiscent of both parsley and anise.

Cilantro (Fresh Coriander)   Green, leafy herb resembling flat-leaf (Italian) parsley. Cilantro has a sharp, aromatic, somewhat astringent flavor. It is often used in many Latin American and Asian cuisines.

Epazote   There is no substitute for this unusually flavored pungent herb. Although seldom available commercially outside of Mexico or India, it is easily grown from seed and is self-sowing. Purchase seeds and plants from specialty plant catalogs.

Lemongrass   Thick, stalklike grass with a sharp, lemony flavor. It is popular in Southeast Asian cooking and available fresh or dried in some Asian food stores. If fresh or dried lemongrass is unavailable, substitute long, thin strips of lemon peel.

Tarragon   Fragrant, distinctively sweet herb used fresh or dried as a seasoning for salads, seafood, chicken, light meats, eggs, and vegetables.

about 1 tablespoon ($^1/_4$ oz/7 g). One packet is sufficient to jell about 2 cups (16 fl oz/500 ml) of liquid.

TO UNMOLD A GELATIN SALAD
Once it has set, carefully run a knife tip around the edge of the salad inside the mold. Then dip the mold, almost to the top, into a bowl of hot water for a few seconds. Place the serving plate over the top of the mold, making sure it fits snugly against the mold. With both hands, firmly hold the plate and mold together. Swiftly invert and give them one sharp downward shake to help dislodge the salad. Carefully lift off the mold. If the salad does not unmold, repeat the procedure.

Grape Leaves In Greek and other Middle Eastern cuisines, grape leaves are commonly used as edible wrappers. They are most often found bottled in brine in ethnic delicatessens and the specialty-food section of well-stocked supermarkets. Rinse gently and remove tough stems before use. If fresh leaves are available, briefly blanch or steam to soften them before use.

Lentils Small, disk-shaped dried legumes, prized for their rich, earthy flavor when cooked.

Mango Tropical fruit with a very juicy, aromatic orange flesh. Ripe mangoes yield slightly to finger pressure. Ripen firm mangoes at room temperature in an open paper or plastic bag. The skin peels easily when slit with a knife. Slice the flesh from both sides of the large, flat pit, as well as from around its edges.

Mushrooms

Porcini (Cepes) Widely used Italian term for *Boletus edulis,* a popular wild mushroom with a rich, meaty flavor. Most commonly sold in its dried form in Italian delicatessens and specialty food stores. Dried porcini can be reconstituted in liquid as a flavoring for soups, stews, sauces, and stuffings.

Shiitake Meaty-flavored Asian mushroom variety with flat, dark brown caps usually 2–3 inches (5–7.5 cm) in diameter. Available fresh in well-stocked supermarkets, it is also sold dried. Soak dried shiitakes in warm water to cover for approximately 20 minutes before use.

Mussels Before cooking, the popular, bluish black–shelled bivalves require special cleaning to remove any dirt adhering to their shells and to remove any "beards," the fibrous threads by which the mussels connect to rocks or piers in coastal waters. Thoroughly rinse the mussels under cold running water. One at a time, hold them under the water and scrub with a firm-bristled brush to remove any stubborn dirt. Firmly grasp the fibrous beard attached to the side

Spices

Cardamom Intense spice that is the dried fruit of a plant in the ginger family. It is used ground in curries, fruit dishes, and baked goods.

Five-Spice Powder Popular Chinese seasoning for savory dishes that often combines ground star anise, fennel or aniseed, Sichuan peppercorns, cloves, or cinnamon.

Garam Masala A common Indian seasoning blend that differs from region to region, but which may include such dried ground spices as cloves, cardamom, cinnamon, cumin, coriander, fennel, fenugreek, ginger, and turmeric.

Paprika Powdered spice derived from the dried paprika pepper. It is popular in some European cuisines and available in sweet, mild, and hot forms. Hungarian paprika is the best, but Spanish paprika, which is mild, may also be used.

Saffron Intensely aromatic spice, golden orange in color, and made from the dried stigmas of a species of crocus. It is used to perfume and color many classic Mediterranean and East Indian dishes. Saffron is sold either as threads—the dried stigmas—or in powdered form.

Turmeric Pungent, earthy-flavored ground spice that adds a vibrant yellow color to any dish.

of each mussel and pull it off. Discard any mussels whose shells do not close to the touch.

Nuts   Rich in flavor and crunchy in texture, nuts complement both sweet and savory recipes. For the best selection, look in specialty food stores or the supermarket baking section.

Toasting brings out the full flavor and aroma of nuts. To toast nuts, preheat the oven to 325°F (165°C). Spread the nuts in a single layer on a baking sheet and bake until they are fragrant and just begin to change color, about 5–10 minutes. Remove from the oven, transfer immediately to a plate, and let cool to room temperature before using. Toasting loosens the skins of nuts such as hazelnuts and walnuts, which may be removed by wrapping the still-warm nuts in a clean kitchen towel and rubbing against them with your palms.

Olive Oil, Extra-Virgin   Extra-virgin olive oil, extracted from olives on the first pressing without use of heat or chemicals, is valued for its distinctive fruity flavor. Many brands, varying in color and strength of flavor, are now available. Choose one that suits your taste. Today, there are many inexpensive extra-virgin olive oils to choose from. Purchase one from a well-stocked food store. Be sure to store in an airtight container or cabinet away from heat and light.

Pine Nuts   Small, ivory-colored seeds extracted from the cones of a species of pine tree, with a rich, slightly resinous flavor. They are used whole as an ingredient or garnish, or are puréed as a thickener.

Potatoes   Although potato varieties and the names that they go by vary from region to region, some common ones include:

Baking Potatoes Large potatoes with thick brown skins that have a dry, mealy texture when cooked. Also known as russet or Idaho potatoes.

Boiling Potatoes, *White-Fleshed* Medium-sized potatoes with thin, tan skins. When cooked, this potato's texture is finer than that of a baking potato's, but coarser than that of the yellow-tinged waxy varieties.

New Potatoes Any variety of potato harvested in early summer when small and immature. Several heirloom varieties are also available at farmer's markets. Their flesh is sweeter and more tender than other varieties. Most are red-skinned, although yellow-skinned new potatoes can also be found.

Radicchio   Leaf vegetable related to Belgian endive. The most common variety has a spherical head, reddish purple leaves with creamy white ribs, and a mildly bitter flavor. Other varieties are slightly tapered and vary a bit in color. Served raw in salads or cooked, usually by grilling. Also called red chicory.

Scallops   Bivalve mollusks that come in two common varieties. The round flesh of sea scallops is usually 1 1/2 inches (4 cm) in diameter; the bay scallop is considerably smaller. It is usually sold shelled.

Sesame Oil   Rich, flavorful, and aromatic, sesame oil is pressed from sesame seeds. Sesame oils from China and Japan are made with toasted sesame seeds, resulting in a dark, strong oil used for flavor; their low smoke point makes them unsuitable to use alone in cooking. Cold-pressed sesame oil, made from untoasted seeds, is lighter in color and taste and is used for cooking.

Shrimp (Prawns)   Fresh, raw shrimp are usually sold with the heads already removed but the shells still intact. Before cooking, they are often peeled and their thin, veinlike intestinal tracts are removed.

TO PEEL AND DEVEIN SHRIMP
Using your thumbs, split open the thin shell along the concave side, between its two rows of legs. Peel away the shell, leaving the last segment with tail fin intact and attached to the meat. With a small, sharp knife, make a shallow slit along the peeled shrimp's back, just deep enough to expose the long, usually dark, veinlike intestinal tract. With the tip of the knife, lift up and pull out the vein, discarding it.

Smoked Salmon Purchase smoked salmon freshly sliced from a good-quality delicatessen or fish market. Lox, which is a brine-cured salmon, and Nova, which is a cold-smoked salmon both have oilier textures and in most cases are not acceptable substitutes for smoked salmon.

Soy Sauce Asian seasoning and condiment made from soybeans, wheat, salt, and water.

Tomatillo The small, green tomatillo resembles, but is not related to, the tomato. Fresh tomatillos, available in some Latin markets and well-stocked supermarkets, usually come encased in brown, papery husks, which are easily peeled off before the tomatillos are cut. Canned tomatillos may be found in specialty-food sections of markets.

Tomato During the summer, when tomatoes are in season, use the best red or yellow sun-ripened tomatoes you can find. At other times of year, plum (Roma) tomatoes, sometimes called egg tomatoes, are likely to have the best flavor and texture. For cooking, canned whole plum tomatoes are also good. Small cherry tomatoes, barely bigger than the fruit after which they are named, also have a pronounced flavor that makes them ideal candidates for quick pasta sauces.

TO PEEL FRESH TOMATOES
Bring a saucepan of water to a boil. Using a small, sharp knife, cut out the core from the stem end of the tomato. Then cut a shallow X in the skin at the tomato's base. Submerge for about 20 seconds in the boiling water, then remove and dip in a bowl of cold water. Starting at the X, peel the skin from the tomato, using your fingertips and, if necessary, the knife blade. Seed if directed. Then cut as directed.

TO SEED A TOMATO
Cut it in half crosswise (or, for plum tomatoes, lengthwise). Squeeze gently to force out the seeds.

Tuna, Canned Most domestic brands of tuna are packed in water or vegetable oil. Imported tunas are often packed in olive oil, which gives the fish a more complex yet delicate flavor that lends itself to Italian-style recipes.

Vinaigrette Translated as *little vinegar,* a classic French dressing or sauce for salad greens, vegetables, meats, poultry, or seafood. It combines vinegar or another acidic flavor such as lemon juice, with oil. Herbs and other seasonings are often added for flavor.

Vinegar Translated as *sour wine,* vinegar results when certain strains of yeast cause wine or some other alcoholic liquid, such as apple cider or Japanese rice wine, to ferment for a second time. The process makes vinegar acidic. The best-quality wine vinegars begin with good-quality wine. Red wine vinegar, like the wine from which it is made, has a more robust flavor than vinegar produced from white wine. Balsamic vinegar, a specialty of Modena, Italy, is an aged vinegar made from reduced grape juice. Sherry vinegar has a rich flavor and color reminiscent of the fortified, cask-aged aperitif wine. Cider vinegar has the sweet tang and golden color of the apple cider from which it is made. Rice wine vinegar, a specialty of Japan, has a delicacy that suits Asian dishes.

Zest Thin, brightly colored, outermost layer of a citrus fruit's peel, containing most of its aromatic essential oils—a lively source of flavor. Try to use organic citrus, if available. Zest may be removed with a simple tool known as a zester, drawing its sharp-edged holes across the fruit's skin to remove the zest in thin strips. Alternatively, use a fine handheld grater. For wide strips, use a vegetable peeler or a paring knife held away from you and almost parallel to the fruit's skin, taking care not to remove any of the bitter white pith with it. You can then slice or chop the strips.

Index

First published in the USA by Time-Life Custom Publishing.

Originally published as Williams-Sonoma Kitchen Library:
Hors d'Oeuvres (© 1992 Weldon Owen Inc.)
Fish (© 1993 Weldon Owen Inc.)
Mexican Favorites (© 1993 Weldon Owen Inc.)
Potatoes (© 1993 Weldon Owen Inc.)
Salads (© 1993 Weldon Owen Inc.)
Soups (© 1993 Weldon Owen Inc.)
Vegetables (© 1993 Weldon Owen Inc.)
Shellfish (© 1995 Weldon Owen Inc.)
Breakfasts & Brunches (© 1997 Weldon Owen Inc.)
Cooking Basics (© 1997 Weldon Owen Inc.)
Healthy Cooking (© 1997 Weldon Owen Inc.)
Mediterranean Cooking (© 1997 Weldon Owen Inc.)

In collaboration with Williams-Sonoma Inc.
3250 Van Ness Avenue, San Francisco, CA 94109

OXMOOR
HOUSE®

OXMOOR HOUSE INC.
Oxmoor House books are distributed by Sunset Books
80 Willow Road, Menlo Park, CA 94025
Telephone: 650-321-3600 Fax: 650-324-1532
Vice President/General Manager: Rich Smeby
National Accounts Manager/Special Sales: Brad Moses

Oxmoor House and Sunset Books are divisions of
Southern Progress Corporation

WILLIAMS-SONOMA
Founder and Vice-Chairman: Chuck Williams

WELDON OWEN INC.
Chief Executive Officer: John Owen
President and Chief Operating Officer: Terry Newell
Creative Director: Gaye Allen
Publisher: Hannah Rahill
Associate Creative Director: Leslie Harrington
Senior Designer: Charlene Charles
Assistant Editors: Donita Boles, Mitch Goldman
Editorial Assistant: Juli Vendzules
Production Director: Chris Hemesath
Production Coordinator: Libby Temple
Color Manager: Teri Bell

Williams-Sonoma Soups, Salads & Starters was conceived and
produced by Weldon Owen Inc.
814 Montgomery Street, San Francisco, CA 94133
Copyright © 2004 Weldon Owen Inc.
and Williams-Sonoma Inc.

First printed in 2004.
10 9 8 7 6 5 4 3 2

ISBN 0-8487-2806-8

Printed in China by SNP Leefung Printers Ltd.

CREDITS
Authors: Joyce Goldstein: Pages 37, 40, 70, 100, 122, 125, 141, 145, 164, 170, 177, 207, 233, 240, 270, 284, 290, 318 (Pesto), 320 (Toasted Bread Crumbs); Norman Kolpas: Pages 14, 18, 20, 21, 23, 24, 28, 31, 35, 39, 42, 45, 46, 47, 49, 50, 53, 54, 57, 58, 61, 68, 69, 73, 78, 80, 81, 84, 86, 87, 88, 91, 92, 93, 94, 97, 98, 99, 103, 104, 105, 114, 166, 185, 190, 316 (Vegetable Stock), 317, 318 (Meat Stock); Jacqueline Mallorca: Pages 17, 38, 108, 130, 245, 252, 315; Susanna Palazuelos: Pages 32, 209, 212, 214, 221, 231, 244, 247, 282, 299, 301, 305, 310, 319, 320 (Flour Tortillas); John Phillip Carroll: Pages 27, 29, 116, 120, 129, 135, 239; Dianne Rossen Worthington: Pages 146, 181, 200, 208, 234, 258, 269; The Scotto Sisters: Pages 204, 211, 217, 218, 220, 222, 225, 226, 227, 228, 235, 236, 242, 246, 249, 250, 261, 262, 272, 273, 279, 287, 293, 294, 297, 300, 302, 304, 307, 309, 311, 312, 314, 320 (Basic Pizza Dough), 321; Emanuela Stucchi Prinetti: Pages 111, 112, 113, 117, 119, 123, 127, 128, 133, 134, 136, 138, 142, 143, 148, 151, 152, 153, 155, 156, 163, 165, 169, 178, 183, 188, 189, 192, 194, 195, 197, 198, 318 (Mayonnaise); Joanne Weir: Pages 64, 67, 72, 74, 77, 79, 83, 160, 171, 173, 174, 176, 182, 186, 257, 265, 266, 267, 274, 277, 280, 283, 286, 289, 292, 316 (Court Bouillon, Quick Fish Stock), 319 (Rémoulade)

Photographers: Noel Barnhust (front cover), Allan Rosenberg (recipe photography), and Chris Shorten (recipe photography for pages 16, 51, 106, 109, 131, 245, 253, and 315).

ACKNOWLEDGMENTS
Weldon Owen would like to thank Desne Ahlers, Linda Bouchard, Carrie Bradley, Kimberly Chun, Ken DellaPenta, Arin Hailey, Karen Kemp, Melinda Levine, and Joan Olson for all their expertise, assistance, and hard work.